The Autobiography of
ROY COHN

The Autobiography of

ROY COHN

By Sidney Zion

LYLE STUART INC.
SECAUCUS, NEW JERSEY

Copyright © 1988 by Sidney Zion

Published by Lyle Stuart, Inc.
120 Enterprise Ave., Secaucus, N.J. 07094
In Canada: Musson Book Company
a division of General Publishing Co. Limited
Don Mills, Ontario

Queries regarding rights and permissions should be
addressed to: Lyle Stuart, 120 Enterprise Avenue,
Secaucus, N.J. 07094

Manufactured in the United States of America

Library of Congress Cataloging-in-Publication Data

Cohn, Roy M.
    The autobiography of Roy Cohn by Sidney Zion.

    Includes index.
    1. Cohn, Roy M. 2. Lawyer--United States--Biography.
I. Zion, Sidney. II. Title.
KF373.C62A3 1988   340'.092'4 [B]   88-2232
ISBN 0-8184-0471-X

For Roger Zissu
Our Blackstone Houdini

Introduction

The jury was out on Roy Cohn when I first met him. It will be out on him for as long as he is remembered, but on that spring afternoon in 1964, metaphor had nothing to do with it. A jury of twelve was trying him for perjury and obstruction of justice, and after three days of deliberation the word was out that they were going to put him away. Roy Cohn was about to be history. I thought it was a perfect time to go over to the Federal Courthouse and rag him a little.

I was a rookie reporter on the New York *Post*, then the most liberal paper in town. During the flush days of Joe McCarthy, the *Post* went after him fists flying. This attracted me to the tabloid in my college days when too many Establishment newspapers cowered before Tailgunner Joe and his banty little mouthpiece Cohn. But I had no assignment to work over Roy as he awaited his verdict. Not from editors, that is. Mine came from a higher authority: the Rosenbergs and all the victims of McCarthyism.

He was standing on the steps of the courthouse, talking to a few guys, none of them with notebooks out. The reporters had obviously exhausted every angle by now and had left him alone with his cronies. I introduced myself, flashing my press card. He didn't give the card a tumble, he shook my hand and said, "I've been reading your stuff, you're terrific."

"I can't say the same about you," I said, with a smirk in my heart and probably on my face. "How does it feel to get what you used to give so well. How do you like waiting for your own jury?"

"No problem, we've got this thing beat." He smiled when he said that.

I laughed. "You're probably down to one holdout, who do you think you're kidding."

He said, "Let's go for a drink."

We went to a corner saloon and I started in on him with the Rosenbergs. I don't remember his answers, except that he disappointed me. His stuff was too pat, too generalized. He was much better on the Army-McCarthy business, he had an interesting perspective that I hadn't heard before. But the only thing that really got me was my wristwatch. When I checked, we had clocked ninety minutes, with Roy Cohn talking about everything but the jury that we all knew was about to wipe him out.

At that moment, I decided to think twice about Roy Marcus Cohn.

I had been both criminal lawyer and prosecutor in New Jersey and so saw plenty of defendants waiting for their juries. I saw strong men weeping, weak men screaming profanities, Mafia dons praying, con men turning green, hit men banging their heads against walls—I saw everything except what I was seeing now. Nobody ever talked about *issues*. Even lawyers couldn't keep their minds on anything but the jury while the jury was out, and the lawyers weren't going to do the time.

It couldn't be clearer, and for my money it couldn't be better. I was in the presence of a new strain of sonofabitch. Then and there I promised myself that one day I would get to know all I could about Roy Cohn. I wasn't sure how, or where, or when. But oh yeh, oh yes.

The great lyricist, Sammy Cahn, when asked what comes first, the words or the music, invariably answers, "The phone call." Mine came on a hot, hazy afternoon in the late summer of 1985. Would I help Roy Cohn "fix up" his autobiography? The editorial director of a top publishing house was asking me this question. What means "fix up"? I said. I didn't know Roy had written an autobiography. The editor said, "He's done 700 manuscript pages, but it's not there. You know all about him, you've been around him for twenty years, all we want is for you to do a series of interviews with him, ask him the right questions and get him to give us some hot stories. The book needs color, it's flat now, and the whole thing will take you a month or two at best. And don't worry, the money's good. Will you come to lunch with us and talk about it? Roy wants you on this and we want you." I told him to send me over the 700 pages and I'd be back to him. "You don't have to read it," he said. "It's not very good, I don't think it's beneficial for you to read it." I said hand-deliver it or no dice.

I read it in one sitting and it was about the dopiest manuscript I ever came across. No wonder the editor didn't want me to see it. It wasn't simply a whitewash of his life, it wasn't even that. It was nothing at all, just words strung together. Joe McCarthy was a nice guy, Justice Douglas was a nice guy, Eisenhower was not a nice guy, the Rosenbergs were guilty, Alger Hiss was guilty, Roy Cohn was not guilty, and God Bless America. He had worked nearly three years to produce this zero.

I had been true to the promise I made to myself on that long ago day while he waited on his jury. I got to know him, I watched him over the years as if he were a potato bug, I saw him operate in all kinds of situations, I thought I understood him as well as anybody could understand him. He was unlike anyone else, he was one of the most fascinating characters imaginable, he was made for the novel, he was an invention that had self-created. I wanted that lunch to find out how a man who seemed to know everything about everybody could know so little about himself.

He showed up an hour late, which was par, and with his boyfriend, also par. He came on strong about his so-called book.

"I figure there are ten front-page stories," he announced, and started to tick them off, interrupting himself to say that he was sure *Parade* Magazine would make it a cover and *Penthouse* would serialize it. When he finished he turned to me. "The way I see it, Sid," he said, "with your way with words you can shape it up in two, three weeks and we're home. What do you think?"

I think I'll have a drink, I said. And waited for it to arrive. And gulped half of it down. And I said, "Roy Cohn wouldn't take a phone call from the schmuck who wrote that manuscript." Roy stared straight ahead for a few seconds. And then he laughed, threw his head back and laughed. "Well, I said you had a way with words," he said. "Now what'll we do about it?"

"When you were a young man," I said, "you went to Europe and burned a lot of books in American libraries. I suggest you put a match to this one, for starters."

"Nothing good?"

"One line."

"What?"

"Where you say Frank Costello made Irving Saypol the U.S. attorney. That's a good line. But then you drop it. What's the story, I never heard that one."

He told us the story in detail. It was great. I asked him about his back-door scenes with Judge Irving Kaufman during the Rosenberg case. He laid it out. Beautiful. I told him to give us the inside on how he faked out the judge and the United States attorney in the Fifth Avenue Coach case and suddenly became his own lawyer and did not have to take the stand and won the case. Marvelous!

It went on like that for an hour. Obviously, there was a helluva book here, only he hadn't told it. He had written the Roy Cohn story and left out Roy Cohn. I was hooked, I was going to do this thing. But I wanted to sound out a few people before signing on the dotted line.

I was surprised at the vehemence of a number of my friends. "Why would you want to help out that sonofabitch?" "How could you put your name next to his?" It was the same song and dance I heard twenty years earlier when I first invited Roy to a party. Time heals everything, right?

But this stuff didn't worry me; I liked it. It proved, if proof were needed, that the fire was still there, that this odd coupling might be just the thing. It was always hard for some folks to understand how a flaming civil libertarian like me could have truck with a guy whose name conjured up the trashing of the Bill of Rights; how a man so closely connected with *The New York Times* could stand, much less like, this rogue, this legal executioner, this notorious bastard who cared nothing for the conventions, who flouted the civil decencies.

To all of this I invoked H. L. Mencken: "What a dull world it would be for us honest men if it weren't for its sinners."

So it was Go, and go it did and great—for about three weeks. Then Roy's health went into a tailspin. The day I met him at lunch, with the publishing people, he looked terrible, but his mind was fine. Now it wandered, sometimes into hallucination. I assumed the AIDS virus had reached his brain. When he entered the hospital, in early November, I thought I'd never see him again.

He denied AIDS, of course. I say "of course" because he denied he was *gay*. He said it was liver cancer. I didn't push him on it, but one day I asked him, I guess you could say slyly, "When were you diagnosed?" And he said, "I was diagnosed on October 14, 1984."

Just before Thanksgiving, he called me. "Can you come up today with the tape recorder?" His voice was strong, he talked as if nothing had happened. I drove up to his place in Greenwich and it was truly amazing. His mind was sharp as ever, he even looked pretty good.

There was no great mystery, as I later discovered. The doctors simply took him off some drugs that were screwing up his mind. Alas, it didn't save his life. But it saved his book.

The result is what you are about to read. Roy Cohn's words, his life. Organized by my hand but in his voice.

There is more. We didn't have time, he knew he was dying fast and so, often, he'd wave me aside when I'd remind him of a terrific story, one of his power-broker moves, say, or one of his unknown acts of vengeance, even (occasionally) a nice thing he did without fanfare. He'd say, "Sure, but let's get to what you don't know."

I will include a baker's dozen of these stories here. They are

culled from my memory bank and the hours of tapes I did with
Roy, but they are first-hand Roy stories. My voice will appear
now and again, and maybe dominate once in a while. In that respect, this book is something of a hybrid. Which fits the subject
just so.

He wanted these stories published, he'd tell me so every time
I dropped in on him. Except for the gay business. He lived in a
closet that was the oddest in history—a closet with neon lights—
but he maintained it fiercely. And it paid off for him, the way he
looked at life. The public didn't know he was homosexual until
the end, when Jack Anderson broke the hospital records that
showed AIDS.

Anyway, old buddy, you don't have to worry about it no more.

The
Autobiography
of
ROY COHN

Chapter One

A question has been floating over me for 35 years, as in a cartoon-balloon. It asks: "Why would a nice Jewish boy from the Bronx, the son of a renowned liberal Democratic judge, choose to make his name by prosecuting the Rosenbergs and working for Joe McCarthy?"

For my enemies, the question answers itself. I was an opportunistic young bastard who grabbed the brass ring of Cold War anti-Communism and rode with it—in utter contempt of my family, my friends, and my party.

For my supporters, the question answers itself. I was a brave young man who recognized the danger of the Soviet Union and overcame my liberal upbringing to fight the good fight—despite my family, my friends, and my party.

I am constrained to say that the truth does not lie somewhere in between.

The truth is my family supported me, my friends supported me, and my party supported me.

Did I say the Democratic party supported me? The man who became chief counsel to Senator Joseph McCarthy? Not at a certain point in time, of course not. But until that time came, my anti-Communist activities represented mainstream Democratic party policies, from the ward-heeler to the White House.

I know this will shock most people, including many who were there when it all happened, when the Truman administration led the war against domestic and international Communism. In 1947, long before anyone heard of Joe McCarthy, Truman instituted by executive order the first loyalty-security program in United States history, opening every government employee to an FBI probe of his Americanism. The Truman Justice Department indicted and convicted the leading lights of the Communist party, U.S.A., in what was known as the Dennis Case. The Truman Justice Department indicted and convicted the Communist spy Judith Coplon. The Truman Justice Department indicted and convicted Alger Hiss, and then William Remington, and then Julius and Ethel Rosenberg. All of these cases were tried before Democratic judges by Democratic prosecutors and, except for Coplon, all were upheld on appeal by the United States Supreme Court, whose members included only one Republican—Harold Burton, a Truman appointee.

So why do I need to begin this memoir by even noting these historical facts, much less explaining them? Because a careful campaign of distortion has been successfully conducted across the years by a myriad of liberal historians and journalists out to "purge" the Democratic party and the Truman administration of the "taint" of its anti-Communist fervor. It amounts to nothing less than a massive sequence lie, where what happened last is said to have happened first.

All that was needed was the epithet "McCarthyism." Take that, shake it up and roll it backwards and what do you have? Presto! An America that was innocent, pristine in its civil libertarianism, a nation led by good old salt-of-the-earth Harry Truman who tried his damndest to save us from that evil sonofabitch red-baiting witch-hunting junior senator from Wisconsin, Joe McCarthy.

What Truman really wanted to do was to save the Democratic

party from the force of his own logic, and in the doing protect the bipartisan foreign policy that had long since turned the Republicans into "me too" losers. McCarthy, by taking Truman's policies—the prosecutions, the loyalty oath—to its logical conclusion (that under Democratic rule the tentacles of the Soviet Union had spread to the highest levels of the State Department) was turning treason and espionage back on the party that both produced it and exposed it.

Harry Truman understood the dangers immediately. His response was to red-bait McCarthy! On March 30, 1950, less than two months after McCarthy broke out on the front pages with his assault on Communists in the State Department, Truman called him "the Kremlin's greatest asset." Why? Because, as he explained in a letter to a friend the very next day, McCarthy, a "pathological liar from Wisconsin," was "going along with the Kremlin to break up our bipartisan foreign policy."

I was on the President's side. Hell, I was working for him; I was a 23-year old assistant United States attorney in Manhattan, busy prosecuting Communist spies. Why would I buy the "rantings" of an obscure Republican senator against a man who was totally dedicated to fighting the Communist menace?

Of course, I knew nothing of Truman's concerns and strategy, but had I been aware of everything I still would have been with the President. At the time I had only recently converted to anti-Communism; it had taken me long enough to think Truman was right, that he wasn't a red-baiter. Was I now to believe that he was soft on Communism?

The truth is, that while I voted for Truman in 1948—my first vote, and as it turned out, the only vote I ever cast for a Democratic presidential candidate—I held my nose in the booth. I thought he was too conservative, that he was trying to scare the public with his anti-Communist rhetoric and actions. In that sense I was indeed something of a renegade. My father had no such qualms, nor did my friends—and my friends included such latter-day left-wingers as Anthony Lewis and Allard Lowenstein. They loved Truman. I went for him against Dewey mainly because of his stand-up loyalty to his mentor, Boss Tom Pendergast of Missouri. When Harry Truman went to Pendergast's funeral, against the heaviest kind of pressure—Pendergast had just gotten out of jail and was nobody to be caught dead with—I knew HST was my kind of man. So my friends voted for Truman despite Boss Pendergast; I voted for Truman because of Boss Pendergast.

For me, the overriding value of loyalty has seemed as natural as snow falling. Because I didn't know it was being taught. Lessons that were never intended as lessons are the lessons you never forget. I got mine at my father's table. And what a table it was! Virtually every heavy hitter in politics, law, the judiciary made it to our apartment while I was growing up. Looking back on it now, I guess I always took it for granted that I'd be around powerful people; it was normal, which may help explain why in this way at least my life never changed. The address changed, from a nine-room apartment in the Bronx to a townhouse in the East Side of Manhattan, but otherwise I suppose I turned out to be my father's son more than I would have dreamed as a boy.

It will no doubt strike people funny to read that once upon a time in New York, shakers and movers would show up in the Bronx. And the South Bronx, no less—a couple of blocks from Yankee Stadium, an area which for years now has been a national symbol for urban decay. Remember Jimmy Carter's campaign promise in 1976? He'd fix up the South Bronx. It worked out the way Iran worked out.

In the 1930's, however, the South Bronx was a wonderful place, and our apartment house—975 Walton Avenue—was *the* building, where *everyone* lived. The district attorney, the most influential judges, the postmaster, the top businessmen. My father was a Bronx county court judge. Which describes his power about as accurately as calling Lou Gehrig a first baseman.

He was Ed Flynn's chief lieutenant, and had been since the Twenties when Flynn led an insurgency against the Bronx regular Democrats. To think of Ed Flynn as an insurgent, which implies "reformer," sounds ridiculous today, but it was real as rain then. My father, who was president of his regular Democratic Club and an assistant district attorney, took his political life in his hands when he backed Flynn—who became the ubiq-

uitous "Boss" Flynn, a confidant of Franklin Roosevelt and the
man who put Harry Truman across as vice-president in 1944.

Flynn and my father, whose name was Albert (but Al to everybody), were very tight, and it was through Flynn's intervention
that FDR, as Governor of New York, made my father his first
judicial appointment in 1929. The robes didn't change the
friendship or the nature of the political alliance. Judges didn't
drop politics in those days—many of them don't today, either,
but then it wasn't considered necessary to hide it. Ed Flynn and
Al Cohn were my definition of loyalty. Until I was ten years old,
that is.

In 1937, the year I hit double figures, an opening came up on
the appellate division for the first department, which covered
the Bronx and Manhattan. Next to the court of appeals, the
state's highest tribunal, this was the most prestigious, powerful
court in New York. Everyone assumed my father would get the
appointment from Governor Herbert H. Lehman, because of
his relationship with Ed Flynn, who was now not only the leading boss in the state; he was, next to James A. Farley, the biggest boss around President Roosevelt.

So if anyone was ever a lead-pipe cinch for a job, it was Al
Cohn for the appellate division. And then suddenly the word
slipped out that Flynn was dumping my father for Judge Joseph
M. Callahan. Flynn and Callahan had become buddies—
socially, on the golf course, and politically on the most important
course of all, the Irish course. Callahan was junior to my father
on the bench and junior by far in service and friendship. Nor
could he hold my father's Blackstone, which in the world of Ed
Flynn mattered least of all.

I remember my father coming home one night looking disturbed. This was a rare thing for him, since on the surface he
was the essence of calm. My mother said, "What's the matter?"
Mothers have said this forever, but, until then, not my mother
to my father, at least not in my presence.

"I saw Ed Flynn tonight," my father said. "I went up to him
and said, 'Ed, after an association of this many years, after I
broke with the club of which I was president, after I broke with

the party leadership, after what I did to make you county chairman—as you publicly and generously acknowledged at the time—how can you do this to me?' "

"What did Ed say?" my mother asked.

"He said he needed 'balance.' "

"What kind of balance?" my mother said.

"Exactly. I said those very words to him. 'What kind of balance?' I said, you've got a Bronx majority against Manhattan, and Callahan and I are both Bronx. But even if you needed balance, what would that mean next to our friendship?"

"What did Mr. Flynn say, Dad?" I chimed in.

"What could he say? He's already committed to Callahan."

I was crestfallen. My father shrugged. "You live and learn," he said. "But maybe Mr. Flynn will learn there are two playing in this ballgame." He smiled and I felt better. I had seen that smile before. It was the smile that could look a double-crosser in the face and cut his throat at the same time.

My father had two men in his corner for the seat on the appellate division: Francis Martin, presiding justice of the appellate division, and Irving Lehman, chief judge of the court of appeals, the brother of Governor Lehman. Both knew my father was a far superior jurist to Callahan, but so did everybody else. The difference was that they thought they could do something about it. Martin because he was a powerhouse figure, an arrogant man who wanted things his way and to hell with Boss Flynn; and Lehman because he was an idealist who understood his influence with his brother in judicial matters.

Martin had my father draft a letter requesting the governor to appoint him. He put this letter on his judicial stationery and got every member of the appellate division to sign it. It was hand-delivered to Irving Lehman, who laid it on the governor's desk—two hours before Ed Flynn showed up to present Callahan's name.

Herbert Lehman pushed the letter across the desk to Flynn. "This just came in," he said. "In light of it, I have no choice. Judge Callahan will just have to wait for the next opening."

Flynn was obviously pissed off, but he was middled and he did what all smart politicians do when they can't do anything else. He swallowed hard and made peace with my father. My father was anything but a sore winner, and although I'm sure he never felt the kind of warmth he once had for Ed Flynn, he and Flynn remained close political allies until the end.

Things took a different turn with Judge Martin. Two years after Martin engineered my father's appointment to the appellate division, Martin stopped talking to him. And ten years later went to the grave without having talked to him again. He thought my father had double-crossed him. My mother agreed. And so did I. It had to do with a case. I can't remember the name of the case or what it was about. But I remember, as if it were yesterday, the story that goes with it.

Martin took my father aside one day and asked him to vote his way in a case before the appellate division. It was a split court and my father would be the deciding vote. My father told Martin he felt strongly the other way. Martin asked him to do it as a personal favor, no matter how he felt. My father said he'd think it over.

The judge on the other side was Edward J. Glennan. He and my father were great pals, they'd have drinks together, they'd go out together, they were real buddies way beyond the collegiality of brothers on the court. Unlike Martin, who (pardon the pun) was a martinet—his welcoming speech to new members of the Bar was on disbarment—Glennan was a hail-fellow who hated nobody but his wife.

He couldn't divorce her, given his Catholicism and the politics of the time, but he could make his disdain for wedlock plain whenever a colleague asked him to perform a marriage ceremony. "You want to marry him?" he'd ask the bride. "Yes, your honor." "You want to marry her?" "Yes, your honor." "O.K. You're married. Now get out of here."

I didn't know this part as a kid, but I suspect that's one reason my mother didn't like Edward Glennan. All I remember is my mother saying to my father, as he and Glennan grew closer and closer, "Al, I don't like it."

It hit the fan when my father went with Glennan against Martin in the case. To this day, I don't know whether he did it as a matter of principle or just because he liked Glennan. It didn't matter to my mother and it didn't matter to me. We felt it was inconceivable that my father would support anybody or anything against Francis Martin, given the role Martin had played in getting him appointed to the appellate division.

The day after my father cast this vote, fatal to his friendship with Martin, my mother called the judge and his wife on the phone. She said, "Without being disloyal to Al, I want you to know I'm one hundred percent with you and I want to continue our social relationship." It worked with Mrs. Martin. At my barmitzvah, a year later, 1940, Mrs. Martin and her son, Frark Jr. sat with us at the reception at the Waldorf-Astoria. But not the judge.

So these were my first lessons in the lack of loyalty in politics: first on the part of Ed Flynn towards my father, and second on the part of my father towards Judge Martin.

Writing this today, I have to smile, because of course there was a difference in kind between what Flynn tried to do to my father and what my father refused to do for Martin. The point is, I saw no difference at the time and I think my father got a kick out of that because I was his creature when it came to standards of loyalty. My mother's as well, because she was every bit her own woman, and indeed my father never argued with us about the episode and never objected to our friendship with the Martin family.

What amuses me in looking back at this is how smug I must have been, how morally superior I must have felt to a father who had committed this terrible sin of saying no to his sponsor on a judicial decision.

Twenty years later, Edward Weisl, Sr., the Democratic power broker who was to become President Johnson's chief confidant, poured out an earful of venom against Supreme Court Justice William O. Douglas, who had voted against Paramount Pictures in a major anti-trust case. Weisl, a friend of Paramount's president Barney Balaban, had gone to Douglas to ask for his vote. He thought he had every right to do this because he was one of Douglas's closest pals. As Weisl put it to me: "We got him in as head of the Security Exchange Commission, we put him over the rim for the Supreme Court nomination with FDR when there were five other people ahead of him, we *made* the bastard. And now we ask him for something like this, something perfectly proper, and he tells us to drop dead. You can't trust any of these intellectuals, they're all the same, all sonsof-bitches."

I agreed a hundred percent with Ed Weisl. Until a few months later, when I ran into Justice Douglas in the Drake Room, a great Manhattan bistro on the ground floor of the Drake Hotel. We could not have been more distant politically: I was working for McCarthy and Douglas was one of the leading liber-tarians on the Court. But Bill Douglas was a man of the world and a good drinker, which is probably a redundancy. Anyway, he didn't give a damn that we were on opposite sides of the spec-trum. We had a couple of shooters together and I got up the nerve to tell him what Ed Weisl had told me about the Para-mount case.

Douglas shrugged. The way my father had shrugged way back when. He said, "If I had to worry about that personal stuff, I'd resign. Ed Weisl's not the only guy I owe. When you go on the bench, any bench, from magistrate's court to the Supreme Court, you'd better call 'em as you see 'em. Or get out."

How argue with that? Maybe if my father had put it to me that way, I'd have understood. On the other hand, he may not have been acting out of principle, he may have been doing it for Ed Glennan. Whatever, he didn't think he had to explain to me or my mother. And he didn't owe us explanations, particularly not to me.

I close my eyes and I hear it now. A phone call in 1938. Francis Martin, Jr., runs over a girl and kills her. My father gets a call from Justice Martin. I hear him say, "I'll take care of it, Frank. Be calm, Frank. It's going to be all right."

It was the middle of the night. Within ten minutes, my father is dressed and out of the apartment. I stay up until he comes home.

"Is Frank in trouble, Dad?"

"I straightened it out."

"How?"

"I talked to the detective. There won't be any trouble."

And there wasn't. So my father settled all markers with Justice Martin that night, and I can only plead youth for not understanding it.

Even so, and having said all the above, I still can't accept that he didn't give Martin that one vote. I'd have done it. As my father's son, I'd have done it, and certainly as my mother's son.

Maybe that's why I never wanted to be a judge. I like to think it was Providence. Had I been a judge, with that attitude, I'd have likely wound up in jail. As it is, I made a lot of judges. And no jail—although I practically started life in prison. I went to kindergarten during the week and Sing Sing on Saturday. It was fun, like a picnic. Unusual grounds for a picnic, but then I was there to see my favorite uncle and one of my favorite people of all time—Bernard K. Marcus, Uncle Bernie, my mother's brother, who was scapegoated for the failure of the Bank of the United States.

The bank was founded by my grandfather, Joseph Solomon Marcus, who died in late 1927, nine months after I was born. Uncle Bernie took it over and he brought it to sensational new heights. Too good to last in the high-toned Gentile world of banking where Jews were supposed to be the suckers with the money. The WASP establishment went after the Bank of the United States with a vengeance that was pure in its anti-Semitism.

In the "great" tradition of anti-Semitism, a Jew was put to catch a Jew. The establishment hired Max D. Steuer, the legendary trial lawyer, to be counsel to the Legislative Committee on Banking Practices. Maybe Steuer didn't know he was being used by the WASPs. In the event, it didn't matter. Because Uncle Bernie hired as his counsellor Isador Kresel. Steuer hated Kresel, and vice-versa. In the battle between these two gigantic egotists, Uncle Bernie was fodder. Steuer was more ruthless, more devious, and probably more brilliant than Kresel. The result: Uncle Bernie was railroaded for an alleged technical violation of the banking laws, and the Bank of the United States was thrown into bankruptcy.

I'm aware that this will look to some like the sentimental

claptrapping of a wide-eyed kid out to clean up his favorite uncle. I refer all skeptics to the Nobel Prize-winning economist Milton Friedman, who just a few years ago confirmed what I've said in his *Newsweek* column.

More important, the depositors recovered nearly all of their funds. And this was before there was a Federal Deposit Insurance Corporation. The government settled with stockholders for fifteen cents on the dollar. My father, to show you what kind of man he was, paid 100 cents on the dollar on every share he owned.

The only real loser was Uncle Bernie, the kindest, most unpretentious man I ever knew. His lovely, easygoing style, his lack of bitterness, made those visits to the Big House on the Hudson seem like a picnic to a little boy. It was hardly a picnic to my mother and to his wife, my Aunt Libby, who's still going strong today, in her late eighties. But I remember those Saturdays, which lasted almost two years, with almost as much fondness as I remember Uncle Bernie.

He didn't let it destroy his life. He became a business broker after prison and he did fine. When I began showing some stuff as a lawyer, he'd say to me, "Roy, if only I could have had you then. . . . " One of my few regrets in life is that I was too young to help him. I'd have put Max D. Steuer away, into the vault with his WASP anti-Semites. Not because I was better than Steuer—I'm not sure *anybody* was ever better than Max Steuer—but only that for Uncle Bernie I'd have had the edge of a *kamikaze*. If you're willing to go all the way, and you have a decent level of skill, it throws a psychic wave over the greatest opponent. Certainly enough to beat a frame-up.

Uncle Bernie died of a heart attack at age 63, while riding a horse. A day after I resigned as chief counsel to the McCarthy Committee. My resignation made front-page headlines, and many people told me not to go to the funeral because my presence would attract too much attention, it would embarrass my family. In my heart I knew this was ridiculous. Nobody in my family was embarrassed by my work for McCarthy. But I had to think about it; maybe it was wrong to have all kinds of press showing up at my uncle's funeral. So I called my parents and my Aunt Libby. I said, "If it's going to be a problem, I won't come. But you know I want to be there."

My family. Me asking my family *that*. Just get here, they said. What's taking you so long, they said.

My father said, "Don't become a victim of McCarthyism."

Chapter Two

It didn't seem like a unique childhood when I was living it, but I'd be hard-pressed now to give it any other kind of call. There was no running out after dinner to play ringaleevio, I didn't hang around arguing with my buddies about whether DiMaggio was better than Mel Ott, and I picked up such zero knowledge of sex from the streets that the first time I whacked off I couldn't wait to tell my parents about it because I was sure I had some kind of fatal disease. On the other hand, I learned more about the way the world works at my father's side than the savviest kids on the street, and although I was pretty much a loner I was never lonely. Whatever I missed by not having a "normal" childhood was anyway more than made up for by the unquestioned and unquestioning love I got from my parents.

I was an only child. Writing these words I can hear the response, a chorus of "of course," the one that says, "That explains everything." The oldest established permanent floating class libel in history is the libel directed at the only child. We are, "of course," self-centered, egotistical, vain, and that good old wraparound, spoiled.

I wonder what Abel would have thought. I always believed that Planned Parenthood would do much better in its generally losing fight against the population explosion if it took as its standard the mark of Cain. But don't get me wrong, I love big families. It's just that I never felt deprived by missing out on sibling rivalry, and I never met an only child who thought luck had bested him by not giving him the opportunity of enjoying an estate battle. And I know an awful lot of spoiled brats in families of five, and three, and seven.

Which is not to say it wouldn't have been different for me had I had a bunch of brothers and sisters. It would, however, have been far more different for me had I been born black, or in Australia, or in my father's father's hometown somewhere in the Russian-Polish pale.

Anyhow, what I did as a kid after dinner was to go over my father's cases with him. He was on the appellate division and he'd bring home the briefs and the trial records, and he'd tell me which were the interesting cases and then I'd read the briefs and the records. And he'd ask me for my thoughts. I was eight years old when this process began, and before I was ten I had a dramatic impact on his thinking about eyewitnesses in criminal cases.

I don't recall the details of the case, only that we argued for hours, my father and I, and that I was adamant, because having read the trial record I was convinced that the "eyewitness" whose testimony cooked the defendant was unreliable. We got beyond the case itself, into a philosophical discussion regarding eyewitnesses, and I wouldn't be moved because it seemed crazy and unfair to convict a person based on a flash sighting, generally in extreme circumstances.

In the event, I brought him around. Then he brought the court around. And never again did he vote to uphold a conviction based primarily on eyewitness testimony.

Obviously, it was remarkable for a young kid to have this kind of influence on a father—but the point is, it didn't seem remarkable to me at the time. In retrospect, I can see why. My father took my mind seriously; he didn't treat me like a little boy, he discussed things with me as if I were his colleague. And he didn't make a fuss over it, he didn't lunch on how bright a kid he had, he never turned me into a performing seal. In that way, he made sure it didn't go to my head. At the same time, it couldn't help but give me confidence in my ability to think and reason things out. I don't know what more a father could do for a son.

He was forty when my mother, after several years of courtship, finally agreed to marry him. By then she was 31, which in the Twenties was hopeless Old Maidsville. The main reason she held him off was she didn't want to leave her father. And if that's not enough to convene a psychiatrists' convention, consider this: I was a tough birth; they had to blow air up my mother's tubes to alleviate her labor pains. I wasn't your ordinary only child, I was an only child by default. Maybe that's why my parents were so good to me; they knew from the outset there'd be no second acts.

My education was not approached casually, to say the least. My father, a prominent alumnus of the College of the City of New York—CCNY—consulted his good friend Dr. Frederick B. Robinson, the long-time president of City, as to where to start me off. Robinson was an arch-conservative presiding over one of the most radical campuses in the country, an anti-Communist who counted among his students in the Thirties one Julius Rosenberg. Well, City College was tuition-free and he couldn't choose his students, but he had no problems with his educational priorities. Frederick Robinson believed in the three Rs, and none of them spelled Rosenberg. He picked the Community School for me, and I never had a better experience in learning. I was taught to spell, to read—to *speed* read—and believe it or not, to add, subtract and multiply. The three Rs.

But it was not to last. My mother's family had a life-long friend, Dr. S. Philip Goodhart, a neurologist of great distinction. He came to our Bronx apartment one night for dinner, and examined my homework. His verdict: the Community School was too far advanced and onerous for little Roy. Send him to the Fieldston Lower School, the Riverdale branch of the Ethical Culture Society, he said. My parents nodded—until this day I don't understand why, any more than I can explain why I never asked them why—and the next thing I knew I was learning how to knit and sew. Basics were outrageous in that place at that time, and if they didn't have Parents' Day, who knows how I might have turned out?

Of course, such a modern school *did* believe in involving parents, and the first chance my father had to make one of those Days, he caught me doing knit-one, pearl-two. I was out of there in no time flat and into the Horace Mann School for Boys. Where I learned Latin (and loved Latin) and English Lit and poetry and, most memorably, American history, from a cantankerous elderly gent named Harry Martin, who relished dirty jokes and Thomas Jefferson, in that order.

I spent five years at Horace Mann, and they rank with the best years of my life. I made good friendships there—not many, I wasn't gregarious, I wasn't a mingler—but quality friendships, two of which have stood the test of time: Si Newhouse and Gene Pope. Both happened to be heirs to empires, and both more than filled their fathers' shoes. Si added to the Newhouse newspaper chain *The New Yorker* and Random House. Gene left his father's businesses—Colonial Sand & Stone and the Italian-language paper *Il Progresso*—for the New York *Enquirer* (now the *National Enquirer*), a shell he purchased for forty thousand dollars and wouldn't sell today for a hundred million. I lent him ten grand on that forty, and if I'd taken a piece, which he offered, I certainly wouldn't have had twenty years of trouble with the Internal Revenue Service. No regrets. I wasn't brought up to take pieces of favors, and I've been more than recompensed by Gene's unswerving loyalty to me.

Politics would eventually curdle our friendship into cordiality, but at Horace Mann I had no closer buddy than Tony Lewis. Yes, the very Anthony Lewis who won two Pulitzers, who covered the United States Supreme Court and ran the London Bureau for *The New York Times*, and during the last fifteen years has conducted a column in the *Times*.

Is there anybody out there who can believe that once upon a time Tony Lewis spent his nights baiting Roy Cohn as an "obsessive liberal"? Anthony Lewis, who rode the Ho Chi Minh Trail into Palestine and became known as Anthony of Arabia? Wow, did I know him when!

He was the son of Kassel Lewis, originally Kassel Oshinsky, who with his brothers owned Crown Fabrics, one of the leading firms in the garment center.

Ours was a happy friendship that went beyond the classrooms of Horace Mann. With my father on the appellate division, which covered Manhattan as well as the Bronx, we had moved to a spacious apartment on Park Avenue and 92d Street. Tony lived four blocks away on 88th and Park. The Lewis's also had a weekend home in Norwalk, Connecticut, where I was a frequent guest. His mother, Sylvia, was a warm, joyous woman who always made me feel like a member of the family. And indeed, we had a family tie. Kassel's sister Frankie married my Aunt Libby's older brother, Arthur Phillips, who went to an early grave.

Anyway it was always Tony and Roy, Roy and Tony. Those all-night conversations obviously weren't limited to politics. We talked about everything from sex to geometry. Tony's mom got such a kick out of it, she turned it into the Passover liturgy. At every Seder during those years, Sylvia Lewis would interrupt the service after the reference to Rabbi Akeeba, who, as it is said, stayed up all night before the Passover talking with his disciples until the morning prayer. "Rabbi Akeeba," Sylvia said, "had nothing on Tony and Roy."

Tony's conversion to the left was 20 years later than mine to the right. His began in the late Sixties, with his disillusionment with the war in Vietnam. It might have started earlier had he not come under the successive conservative spells of Justice Felix Frankfurter, Attorney General Robert F. Kennedy, and the London upper crust.

In the mid-fifties, Felix Frankfurter got Arthur Hays Sulzberger, publisher of *The New York Times*, to hire Tony from the Washington *News* and assign him to cover the Supreme Court. For years, Justice Frankfurter was properly upset with the way the press covered the High Court—ordinary beat reporters with no legal knowledge were regularly assigned, even by *The New York Times*. Frankfurter proposed to Sulzberger that he'd get Tony Lewis a Nieman Fellowship at the Harvard Law School, and then the *Times* would really have something: a brilliant reporter with a year of the best legal education Harvard Law could offer. It was an offer Sulzberger couldn't refuse and they were off to the races. Lewis had a new career, Frankfurter had his man on the *Times*, and Sulzberger was a pioneer in the creation of serious legal reportage.

Felix Frankfurter was a great source of strength to those of us who were trying to wake the American people to the danger of the Soviet Union. He voted our way on nearly all the great anti-Communist cases of the 1950s, and because of his reputation as a liberal, he provided a vital intellectual underpinning to our efforts, at a time when many intellectuals were painting our crusade as a gross, anti-civil libertarian attack on the Bill of Rights. Justice Frankfurter was actually one of the most conservative men on the Court, but his old connections with Woodrow Wilson, his defense of Sacco and Vanzetti, his insider role with FDR, his fidelity to Zionism were so imbedded in the mass-mind and mass-media that he was often bitterly attacked by the right he was so effectively helping. This irony ironed out well for us in the long run, as did Tony Lewis's adulatory coverage of Frankfurter, which, because it appeared in the "hated" *Times*, drew the same attacks from the right—and the tacit support of the influential liberal intelligentsia we otherwise would have lost.

Similarly, though not so happily for the country, Tony's wide-eyed backing of Attorney General Robert F. Kennedy provided Bobby a kosher label for his massive assaults on privacy and the Bill of Rights. Tony covered the Justice Department as part of his duties for the *Times*, and in my opinion we wouldn't have had legalized wiretapping and bugging in this country without his support. Bobby Kennedy was a holy terror on civil liberties, and it's not too much to say that every mistake Richard Nixon made in Watergate could be directly traced to what Bobby did as attorney general. The difference was that the liberals loved Bobby and hated Dick; none more than Tony, who by then had "seen the light."

Long before that time, Tony had left Washington to head the London Bureau of *The New York Times*. Where he conducted a journalistic version of the Court of St. James's. On Fleet Street, the reporters said that while it took most Yank reporters years to become High Tory, Tony Lewis was converted on the plane coming over.

What they didn't know was that he was that way from the start, that Crown Fabrics was for him a block away from Bond Street where in the mid-Sixties he had his suits constructed.

A far cry, obviously, from the Anthony Lewis of today. But before I leave Tony with Yasir Arafat and the rest of his latter-day pals, an anecdote remains to be told.

During the Republican National Convention of 1972 in Miami, I was invited on a dinner-cruise aboard William F. Buckley, Jr.'s boat. Bill called me, in something of a panic, just before I left the hotel. "Roy," he said, "I've got Anthony Lewis coming tonight. Now please, Roy, don't get into a fracas with him. Say nothing about Vietnam, this is a purely social evening."

By then I'd known Bill, we'd been good friends, for twenty years. But he didn't know a thing about Tony and me. So when I got aboard, he nearly fainted when he saw Tony run over and embrace me.

Now I see Tony only by chance. We're always cordial. Nothing less. But nothing more.

My parents were forever trying to provide me with a "normal" childhood, and never succeeding. The big push would come in the summers, when they'd concentrate on getting me into one or another "terrific" camp, which they would work at with the diligence and delicacy others today associate with getting the perfect table at the "21" Club.

I'll limit this to Camp Menatoma, in Maine, my first camp, and a preview of all the rest of them. It was owned by a Dr. Friedenwald, whose son Johnny was my counselor. Johnny Friedenwald was the kind of creep whose idea of democracy was to beat the asses off everybody in the cabin when anything went wrong. It could be crystal clear that the "infraction" was caused by one kid only, but Johnny would make us all "assume the position" across his knee. It bugged him that I'd never cry. Not that he hurt me, he wasn't Captain Bligh, but he liked it when the other kids cried. I couldn't figure out why anybody would cry from a few whacks on the rear end.

In truth, I deserved the banging around more than the other kids, from the camp's point of view. I hated all the group activities, and the only thing I liked was swimming (they did teach me to swim). But bother me with arts and crafts and all the other crap, and it was no dice.

After the summer, the great Dr. Friedenwald—what was he a doctor of?—paid visits to all the campers' homes in order to set everybody up for the next season. He told my parents, in front of me, that I was a "good egg," that I excelled as a camper, I was a "natural," and he was sure I'd get even more out of the "experience" next summer.

My parents looked happy, and why not? Their boy was being praised and I hadn't said a bad word about the camp to them. But I hadn't figured on Friedenwald making this full-court press.

I think this was my first argument to a jury, though hardly to a jury of my peers. I lit into Friedenwald. I said I hated every minute at Menatoma, I said I was the worst camper in the history of Menatoma, I said that if I was a "good egg" there was no such thing as a bad egg; in fact, I said I was the worst egg ever hatched at Camp Menatoma.

Dr. Friedenwald hauled ass right out of our Park Avenue apartment. But nobody laughed. My father turned to my mother and said, "What do we do with him now?" She said, "We find another camp." And I kept going to camps, hating every summer, but turning into a good swimmer. So I can waterski without fear of drowning. It cost my mother and father a fortune for this great result, and the only thing that surprises me, in retrospect, is that I was so docile. Was that me, going quietly to all those dopey camps, doing clay and war games? If it were just that I wanted to please them, my parents, I could understand it. But I never told them I liked it—forget about loving it. The only way I can figure it out is that I didn't know there was any alternative. You went to camp in the summer the way you went to school in the fall. Roy Cohn, iconoclast. Big Deal.

Well, it all ended, no more camp, after my junior year at

Horace Mann. In the spring of that year, 1943, I decided I had gotten all there was for me to get out of Horace Mann. I was antsy to get my life moving quicker towards the real world, I wanted to go to college as soon as possible, and when I told this to my father he expressed no opinion but advised me to consult with the headmaster at Horace Mann, Dr. Charles C. Tillinghast.

Dr. Tillinghast looked over my record and listened to my pitch and with no hesitation said he'd let me skip senior year if I'd take private tutoring during the summer in chemistry, math and Spanish. I was delighted, but not at all surprised, which today surprises me plenty. What could have made me believe I could get a high school diploma after three years? Nobody I knew had done it and none of my friends were even dreaming of it. And there I was, just assuming that because I wanted it, and because it made sense to me, it would be done. Ah, the arrogance of youth!

But a bit too arrogant, as it turned out, when it came to my first-choice college, Columbia. I was so sure I'd get in I didn't bother to use a great connection, Judge Bernard L. Sheintag, one of my father's colleagues on the state supreme court, who was on the board of Columbia College. What I hadn't realized was that because of the student shortage caused by World War II, classes had been cut to the bone, and it was murder to get in. I was accepted by New York University and several other schools, but I wanted Columbia.

As it happened, this worked out better for me. Columbia told me they'd take me in January. So I spent the fall taking courses in Gregg shorthand and touch-typing, which I never would have done, and these skills have served me well ever since.

I was not quite seventeen when I entered Columbia College. I was not quite twenty when I graduated Columbia Law School. A modesty that has not exactly been my hallmark, somehow emerged and flourished around this particular issue across the years.

I mean, even my worst enemies have said, "Well, we have to admit, he's a brilliant little bastard. He got through college and law school before he was twenty." And I've invariably replied,

"It was no big deal, it was during and right after the war and a lot of people did it."

The truth is, I don't know anybody who did it. I don't know anybody who was Class of '46, Columbia College, Class of '47, Columbia Law School. That's what it says under my name, and under no other name.

There was no magic involved, I plain worked my butt off in college. In those days, merit was everything. If you did well in your courses, nothing else counted. For every six points of "A" you got credit for an extra six-point course—assuming that you had no other mark below "B." I never went below a "B" and hardly ever below "A." This, plus summer classes each year, plus what they called the "professional option," wherein the first year of law school was counted as the last year of college, enabled me to get it done fast.

The undergraduate school at Columbia in that time is best explained by its faculty. Mark Van Doren taught us Shakespeare; Jacques Barzun, history; Lionel Trilling, English Lit; Irwin Edman, philosophy. If it were baseball, it'd be Murderer's Row. And if that wasn't enough to spark a kid's mind, we had as lagniappe Dean Harry Carman, one of the kindest, most understanding men I ever knew. Harry Carman, who got me a waiver from math and gym, both compulsory courses. But what's compulsory if you have friends?

Fraternities appeared to be compulsary to a freshman on the Columbia campus. Everybody who was anybody was a fraternity man, and the "best" Jewish house was Zeta Beta Tau. I was "rushed" hard by ZBT, I suppose because my father was a famous judge. They wanted me so badly they tried to help me out in class. I prepared carefully for classes, and when the professor would ask a question I was generally the first to volunteer the answer. During the "rush" period, when the fraternities were out to get favored freshmen, one of the ZBT potentates took me aside and said, "My boy, it's not the thing to do." I said, "What are you talking about?" He said, "One doesn't push, one doesn't answer too many questions."

I was properly cowed—for a couple of days. Until I decided that it was all just a pile of crap, this fraternity business. They called me to a private meeting and regally offered me a pin, for which I was supposed to fall down and kiss their collective asses. I said thank you, but no thanks. I said I appreciated their support but I was too busy. They were pissed, I think they'd have run me out of school if they could. Well, I wonder who's kissing them now. All I know is, I got the A's and they got the Gentleman's C's. And if ever I was right, it was in rejecting the whole notion of snobbery and pretense that spell, ironically, *fraternity*. From that time on, I've had nothing but contempt for people who get their kicks by the power of the black-ball. And though I've often been in places where the proletariat weren't welcomed, that's never been why I've been there. The proof is, I'm not a member of any club. Any club, anywhere.

If Columbia College was my intellectual Eden, Columbia Law School was the Sinai. I was bored silly by law school, and not because the faculty was lousy, the faculty was first-rate. What I didn't like was the method of teaching, known as the "case book" method. I could see no sense to it then, and none now. The way it works is, you buy a casebook for each course, and this casebook contains a series of individual court opinions rendered by different courts and judges on the subject matter of the course—contracts, torts, negotiable instruments, criminal law, and the rest. I don't know what you're supposed to get out of this mish-mash; I wouldn't have been able to advise a client on a simple back-end auto accident if all I knew was what I gleaned out of the "case method."

It is not the only way to teach the law, thanks be to God. The one I prefer is the textbook method, which gives students the bottom line answers to what the law is, with cases used to illustrate the application of the general principles.

But at Columbia we had no choice, except to cut classes, which is what I did. As you can imagine, I didn't burn up the academic lights at Columbia Law. Half the time I was down at Tammany Hall helping manage political campaigns for friends running for judgeships. One was Henry Clay Greenberg, who ran successfully for the state supreme court. Another was the great Stanley H. Fuld, who won a seat on the court of appeals, the state's highest tribunal, in 1946. Judge Fuld was so talented that he went right to the court of appeals from the district attorney's office. Governor Thomas E. Dewey appointed him, and then he ran for election, as was the law at the time. I was with him on election night at his West End Avenue apartment, and I remember calling the papers to find out how we were doing. There was no such thing as a prognostication in those days, nobody told you who'd win based on exit polls or one percent of the vote. It was more fun waiting, though in Judge Fuld's case we were out front from the start and never looked back.

Of course, I didn't just walk in and work for Stanley Fuld. He was a good friend of my father's, which is where a lot of my connections began. But he didn't have to like me, and he didn't have to invite me to Saturday lunches with other judges. The point is, it's never simply family ties or contracts, that's just what gets you in the door. In any case, it sure beat the case method and I learned more from hanging around judges than sitting in classes.

But it was said best in a lyric written by Judge James Garret Wallace for a bar association show, way back when. I extract a few lines;

> *The man who burns the midnight oil is really quite a dud,*
> *He'd better spend his evenings at the Democratic Club;*
> *So if you'd be a lawyer, son, to these words give heed,*
> *The things you learn at law school, son, are not the*
>   *things you need.*

I remember the song as if I wrote it. Because I lived it.

Chapter Three

My youth caught up with me the day I walked into John F.X. McGohey's office on Foley Square. Mr. McGohey was the United States Attorney for the Southern District of New York, which meant he was the most powerful federal prosecutor in the country, after the attorney general. Why? Because his jurisdiction covered Manhattan, then and now the organized crime capital of the nation. Maybe a few mobsters younger than I was had been in McGohey's office before, but no budding lawyers. I was 20, a year away from eligibility to take the bar exam. But there I was, looking for a job, hungry as a billy-goat. My father was a good friend of Mr. McGohey, so I don't have to say any more about how I got in the door.

John McGohey was a tall man whose silver-streaked black hair lent a distinguished air to a face that had a pushed-in look more likely seen at Stillman's Gym than behind an imposing desk in the U.S. Courthouse. He came right to the point. "I'd like to help you, young fellow," he said, "but you aren't old enough to take the bar."

39

I was all ready for that one. I said, "Well, sir, I've read the U.S. Attorneys' Manual, and I found a provision that covers this very situation. As a non-lawyer, I could be a special assistant to the United States attorney."

Mr. McGohey cleaned off his spectacles, maybe because he didn't want me to miss the twinkle in his eyes. He said, "So you could. Yes indeed, so you could. And you could also be a photostat operator, which is the job I'm prepared to offer you."

I was almost as good at photostating as going for coffee.

In due course, I was promoted from go-fering to the law library, where I discovered that I didn't know the first thing about legal research. They hadn't bothered to teach it at Columbia, it was too declassé obviously for all us future philosophers of the law. So now I had to pick it up under game conditions and it was no big deal. Soon enough I was drafting briefs for the second circuit court of appeals.

In the meantime, like everybody else I took a cram course for the bar exam, and for the first time I liked studying law. The cram course gave you the law as it was, not as it "should be." More than anything, this course exposed the deficiencies of the Ivy League law school training. I passed the bar despite Columbia Law, which is hardly the way it's supposed to go. I think now it would have been a good idea to have sued Columbia for breach of contract. They promised to make me a lawyer, but all they did was give me the right to take the cram course.

A few days after I passed the bar, and just after my twenty-first birthday, my father invited me to lunch at the appellate division, a world-class landmark building on Madison Square.

A court officer met me in the lobby. "Mr. Cohn, come with me," he said. I smiled and politely noted that I knew where my father kept his chambers. He said, sternly, "Just do as I say." The next thing I knew I was in the chambers of the presiding justice, David W. Peck. So was my father. So were all the judges of the first department. So was my boss, McGohey.

Before I could get my bearings, my right hand was up and I was a member of the bar. A second later, Mr. McGohey moved in and swore me as an assistant United States attorney. Then everybody shook my hand while my father kissed me.

Mr. McGohey set me to work for Bruno Schachner, chief of the appeals division. The Viennese-born Bruno was brilliant—and to a neophite lawyer, more amused than amusing. Behind a continental air, Schachner was as tough a taskmaster as any marine drill instructor in Parris Island. The first time I brought him a draft of my brief I sat beaming, waiting for the compliment. Bruno smiled brightly and my heart took off. And then he tore my genius work in two and threw it in the trashcan. And said, "Try again!" I tried again, and he did it again. And again and again and again. A regular FDR. Or, in retrospect, a regular Don Shula. But when he was finished finishing me off, I knew how to write a brief.

And I knew how to argue it, too. By pushing me to write clearly, Schachner made me think clearly, which is the secret to success in oral argument before an appellate bench, if not in life itself. Of course, you need the ability to think quickly on your feet, which I either got through my father's genes or my father's table. If not harnessed, however, this talent can be destructive, because it can make you believe you can do anything off-the-cuff. It's called arrogance and it makes you lazy and it makes you lose. And while I was too nervous to be arrogant in my first few cases in the circuit court of appeals, the intellectual discipline Bruno Schachner imposed on me kept me honest throughout my career—kept me from being impressed by my boxscore and thus from trying to "wing it" by the men and women in black robes.

I argued a dozen cases in the second circuit court of appeals during my brief tenure in Bruno's appeals division, and I won them all. Having noted this, and despite all I said above about Bruno's leadership, I must quickly add that I very likely would have won every one of those cases had I been a dolt or a severe stutterer. The reason was—and remains—that the government does not lose many cases on appeal—or on trial, for that matter.

During the heyday of the Warren Court, in the Sixties, when the so-called "revolution" in criminal justice was taking place, this wasn't the rule. But otherwise, it's a big-deal exception to see a case reversed on appeal. As all federal prosecutors know, the minute you say *"United States vs. Jones,"* you're rounding third. They may not admit it, but that's the way the game goes.

That it went that way in the second circuit during the Forties and Fifties may surprise young lawyers who are still taught that in that time this was the most liberal court in the country. In some ways it was, but not when it came to the criminal law—and this despite an array of great liberal jurists such as Jerome Frank, Charles Clark, Augustus Hand and Thomas Swann. Indeed, it was Judge Clark, the former dean of the ultra-liberal Yale Law School (where Swann had also been dean and where Frank lectured), who devised the "harmless error" rule that to this day is the best friend a prosecutor has.

It goes like this, the "harmless error" rule. An appellate court reads a trial record and finds that certain rules of evidence were breached by the prosecution or the judge. These could range from hearsay improperly admitted, to prejudicial statements by the prosecutor, to a wrongful charge by the judge. If in the opinion of the upper court, the error was "harmless," that the jury would have convicted if the tainted stuff had not been admitted into evidence, the verdict stands.

In principle, there is nothing wrong with the "harmless error" rule; by definition, if something is harmless it would exalt form over substance to make anything of it, much less to upset convictions because of it. The trouble is in the application. Too often, pro-government judges who simply want to uphold convictions find "harmless" what was very harmful indeed to a defendant's rights. In fact, in most cases the government wouldn't chance a reversal on anything "harmless"—if it were harmless they wouldn't try to get it before the jury. That little piece of hearsay is usually loaded with poison, and the prosecutor thinks he needs the poison or he would not bother.

The same goes for a trial judge, who can kill a defendant with harmless error, and wouldn't go near it if he thought the government didn't need the help, in an evidentiary ruling or in a charge to the jury.

Moreover, as every trial lawyer knows, nobody can tell what swings a jury. We are often surprised, more times than not, when jurors tell us what got them to go our way, or against us. Sometimes they'll ignore what we consider the most crucial evidence and go all the way with something we hardly thought about, maybe just tossed in as make-weight. So how can anybody, reading a cold trial record, say what's "harmless"? Sometimes they can, when it's obviously nothing but a technical mistake, or the evidence was otherwise so overwhelming. This is what I'm sure Judge Clark had in mind, for he was anything but a hanging judge. In other, less scrupulous hands, however, it hasn't worked out the way Charles Clark intended. Nor, in a far different area of the law, has Clark's revolutionary Federal Rules of Civil Discovery turned out to be anything like its founding father expected.

Clark had the estimable notion that clients shouldn't unduly suffer because they had lousy lawyers. So he came up with the idea of discovery, whereby before the trial began each side would find out what the other side had. That way, surprise and great lawyering wouldn't give much of an advantage to one side or the other, and the whole process would lead to settlements and presumably the fairest result. In the event, the result has been disastrous for the clients, and wonderful for rapacious lawyers.

In a Hall of Fame example of tail-wagging-dog, discovery has become the be-all-and-end-all of trial practice. Years are spent in "discovering" the other fellow's case, in the privacy of conference rooms in brilliantly decorated law offices paid for by clients who are supposed to be getting a fair shake for their money and instead are all too often getting a shake-down by lawyers who wouldn't know how to try a case before a jury if their lives depended upon it. Depositions, it's called, and all it finally does is support incompetents who are afraid to show up in court, assuming they know where the courthouse is. The giant Wall Street law firms are today paying kids who haven't passed the bar

$70,000 a year, courtesy of the Federal Rules of Civil Procedure, a.k.a. discovery. If we changed this garbage and made everybody turn over everything within thirty days, we'd get justice for clients. And we'd be free of all the yuppie lawyers who are quickly taking over the best parts of New York, Chicago and San Francisco, to mention only my favorite towns.

So much for good intentions. But how explain the intentions of successive presidents who refused to appoint Learned Hand to the Supreme Court of the United States? Hand was chief judge of the second circuit and had been for many years when I arrived to argue up there as a neophyte. He was in a class by himself, he was just about everybody's all-world judge and the fact that he never made it to the High Court was a national disgrace. He was one of those rare jurists you didn't have to agree with to agree that he was great. I was not brought up to be in awe of judges but I was in awe of Learned Hand. And who wasn't? I suspect all the presidents who wouldn't give him the Supreme Court gavel were in awe of this Renaissance Man, which come to think of it is probably the best answer to why they never appointed him.

It was inconceivable for a kid lawyer to get close to the patrician Learned Hand, at least in *this* kid's mind, but the same was not so, not hardly, in the case of Jerome Frank. Judge Frank endeared himself to me at my first oral argument before the second circuit. I was hung over, not from booze but from staying up all night rehearsing to the mirror. But it may as well have been from the sauce for all I can remember of the case. What I'll never forget is that after I sat down, Judge Frank leaned over from the bench and said, "Mr. Cohn, your argument was almost as good as you think it was." Frank was a pioneer in the area of psychiatry and the law, but he was light years away from Dr. Freud on this one. I was scared shitless and if I had any idea I was good it was down there in the collective unconscious. Well, maybe. Jerome Frank was so wise he could pick things up from the West Wind. Plus he had a great sense of humor and that could have been it, too.

He was a big man in the New Deal, very tight with FDR and eventually head of the Securities and Exchange Commission.

Bruno Schachner took me to lunch with him one day and we hit it off great. We lunched frequently after that and on occasional Thursday's he'd take me to Yale Law to hear his lectures, which were not formal, to say the least. He'd teach pure Jerome Frank, down to telling the students how he arbitrated a price between a sailor and a whore in a bistro in Italy. He was a warm, generous man, who loved young people, always had time for them, and he was a natural teacher. Of the many friends who cooled me after I joined Joe McCarthy, he was the one I regretted most.

The famous line attributed to Vince Lombardi, that winning isn't everything, it's the only thing, was never true for me. I mean, I started where that thought left off. For me, I didn't count it as winning if the world didn't know about it. And while this was the case more when I was young, it was only because I needed it more then. So to pursue the past tense would be a consumer fraud. I admit it. I love publicity. But I didn't really know how much until the third Saturday in February, 1949.

I was in my first year as a full-fledged assistant United States attorney and this one was my Saturday. Every assistant drew one Saturday per year to hold down the fort, like being the Officer of the Day. Any case that came in on Saturday was yours. On every other day the hot cases went to the seniors. Of course, not much ever happens on Saturdays in the federal system. In a county district attorney's office Saturday night's the busiest night in the week. But there are few federal crimes that fit the Saturday Night Special description—murders, muggings, robberies, rapes. With us, as in the song, it's the loneliest. But on my first Saturday, I hit the jackpot.

The secret service agents came into my little cubbyhole office and told me they had just locked up a man named Giacomo Lauriano, whom they caught leaving a Bronx movie house with a paper bag. The bag held ten grand in counterfeit money. My job was to arraign Lauriano before the United States Commissioner, who would fix bail and set a date for the preliminary hearing.

On the face of it, this was no big deal, people are picked up with counterfeit dough quite often. But after the arraignment, which lasted maybe three minutes, a short, seedy-looking guy in his middle age came over to me, or rather shuffled over, and said, "How do you spell your name, young man?" He had a steno-type notebook in hand, so I was interested. I asked him who he was. He said he was the Associated Press stringer who covered the Federal Building and City Hall on Saturdays when (as he put it) "nothing ever happens." After I spelled my name—no "e," leave out the "e," I said—I asked him if he was filing a story on my case. "I'm thinking about it," he said. "But I'll need a little more if it's going to travel."

He looked down at his pad and said nothing, and I said nothing because I didn't know what more there was to this case. Finally he said, "I suppose this counterfeit dough comes from some big national ring?"

I put on my best long face. "You got it," I said. "You're quite a reporter." I didn't know what the hell I was talking about, but the dough had to come from somewhere, didn't it? He nodded and shuffled off, and I grabbed a subway to the Plaza where I had a standing Saturday lunch with a group of my father's friends. I said nothing to these wiser faces, but my mind was on the reporter. As soon as I could comfortably take leave, I made a bee-line to the closest newstand and picked up the afternoon edition of the *World-Telegram*. I ran through the paper and my heart dropped with every page. Not a line on my case, not a word.

I folded the paper with the top of page one belly-up. And nearly had cardiac arrest. There it was, a streamer across the front: "Close In on Phony U.S. Mint." The lead read: "Assistant U.S. Attorney Roy M. Cohn stated in court today that his office was about to close in on a large national counterfeiting ring." Well, who said newsprint couldn't send a glow? I was flyin' high all weekend, I must have read that story two hundred times. I just couldn't believe it—me in the headlines!

My bosses couldn't believe it, either. The minute I stepped into the courthouse on Monday, the elevator guard greeted me. "Roy," he said, "the U.S. attorney wants to see you. So does the chief assistant. So does the chief of the criminal division." I never had elevator sickness before but my heart sank pretty good right then. You didn't have to be a genius to know what they wanted but at least I wasn't dumb enough to walk in straightaway. I called Al Whitaker, the special agent in charge of secret service, and a great cop. I told him, "Al, they put an elevator watch on me, I hope you have some bullets for this empty gun of mine."

He chuckled and said, "Roy, it's not an empty gun, not at all. Of course there's a nation-wide operation and it continues because your bosses drag their feet on prosecuting when we make a case. And when they occasionally proceed with an indictment, the judge hands out 15 days instead of 15 years. So don't worry about what you said, what you said was one hundred percent correct. Just try this case quickly, and keep going. You'll prove your statement—and I guarantee we'll help all the way."

With that in my bonnet I was easily able to handle the chiding of my superiors. When they finished lecturing me about my responsibilities as a public servant and "team member" I told them I thought it was appropriate to inform the people about this immense counterfeit ring, that I had spoken to the A.P. reporter after a full-scale briefing by the secret service, and that I had no doubt we'd all look good when the Lauriano case was over.

Very ballsy stuff, as I look back on it, but it backed them off and I got lucky. Lauriano was convicted—that part was easy—but the good fortune came when a visiting judge from Wisconsin, Patrick F. Stone, sentenced him to 15 years. I don't think a New York judge would have done anything like that, but I didn't have to care anymore. I had my first victory in my first trial and I was off and running—and so were the counterfeiters, who no longer felt so free to print and print because now they were not going to just walk and walk.

As a prosecutor, I had as much to do with the conviction of Alger Hiss as the janitor at the courthouse. But Alger Hiss had plenty to do with turning my skepticism about American Communism into a conviction that our nation faced a real and serious menace from the domestic branch of Joe Stalin & Co.

Until I was assigned to write a legal memo on the case in the spring of 1949, I thought Alger Hiss was the victim of a witch-

hunt that had its roots in the Republican-led House Un-American Activities Committee. The GOP had controlled the House
of Representatives from 1946–48 and during this time HUAC
was rampaging against everything American as apple pie, particularly the movie industry. Ten screenwriters, called The Hollywood Ten, had been cited for contempt and accused of fostering
Russian propaganda in movies during the Forties. President
Truman denounced this stuff as a "witch-hunt" and when HUAC
(led by Richard Nixon) went after Alger Hiss, Truman called it a
"red herring." I fully agreed with the President. I was the
founder of the Columbia Law School Democratic Club and no
two-bit Republicans were going to get away with stamping my
party, my *father's* party, as "soft on Communism." Dean
Acheson had proclaimed, "I won't turn my back on Alger Hiss,"
and I was as proud of Acheson's loyalty to a friend as I had been
when President Truman went to Boss Pendergast's funeral.

Somehow it didn't occur to me that Hiss could never have
been indicted without the O.K. of the White House and I managed to forget that it was Truman's loyalty oath, not Nixon's, that
started the whole business in 1947. My excuse was youth. Did
everybody else have selective amnesia? Maybe it was just hypocrisy. Alger Hiss had been a darling of the New Deal, he had
been with FDR at Yalta, he was WASP establishment if there
ever was one, he went back as clerk to Justice Holmes, and now
he was head of the Carnegie Endowment for World Peace. Such
an icon of the Democratic party could not be disloyal, less the
whole party be implicated.

But he was indicted, by my boss McGohey, who worked for
Truman. I wasn't so naive that I didn't know grand juries were
run by prosecutors. Yet I didn't put two and two together. How
could I believe that Harry Truman thought Hiss was innocent
while his own Justice Department had secured an indictment
against Hiss for perjury, in denying his activities as a Communist spy?

In retrospect, I think Truman was hedging his bet. Nixon and
HUAC had pumped up public opinion to the degree that an indictment was inevitable. So the President ordered the indictment while charging that the whole thing was a "red herring."

He probably thought, at first, that Hiss would be exonerated. But when, before the trial, he learned that the secret documents Hiss had turned over to Whittaker Chambers were actually typed on Hiss's old typewriter, he knew the game was up. At that point, in any event, Truman stopped the rhetoric, stopped defending Hiss. Only we didn't notice it, we Democratic liberals. All we remembered was that Hiss was the victim of a "witch-hunt."

In the spring of 1949, the Hiss trial began. I was assigned to write a few legal memos. Very minimal stuff, as would befit a rookie lawyer in a major case. But it brought me into contact with some of the FBI agents working on Hiss. And this turned out to be the start of my ideological turnaround. It began, innocently enough, during lunch at Gasner's, a terrific restaurant a couple of blocks from the Federal Courthouse. All the top judges and lawyers lunched at Gasner's, it was the 21 Club for bench and bar, and this day I was there courtesy of the FBI agents who were going to brief me on this minor memo I had to write.

Right off the bat, I told them what I thought of the case. "This whole thing is a HUAC witch-hunt," I said. "Hiss is the scapegoat and I think it stinks the way herrings stink."

There were three FBI agents there but only one of them smiled. He said, "How much do you know about Alger Hiss and Whittaker Chambers?"

I didn't know enough to get through half a Bloody Mary. I didn't even know what a good liberal was supposed to know, forget about facts and inside details.

Patiently, the FBI men took me on a tour of the Hiss case. Nothing more, really, than had been in the newspapers, but a revelation to me; I'd been so sure of the "right-wing conspiracy" to get Hiss, I hadn't bothered to look at the bare bones of the case. Now, hearing it from people I instinctively trusted, it had the ring of truth.

Whittaker Chambers, a brilliant writer and thinker who rose to a senior editorship at *Time* Magazine, had come to regret his past as a Communist spy. Testifying before HUAC, whose most famous member was Richard M. Nixon of California, Chambers accused Alger Hiss of having been a member of his ring during the 1930's—while Hiss was a rising star in the State Department.

At first, Hiss flatly denied he knew Chambers. Then, at a face-to-face confrontation before HUAC, he suddenly recognized him as a man he knew as "George Crosley" and attributed his previous failure to recognize his old friend "George" to dental work! Crosley-Chambers had had his teeth repaired, so that was why Alger didn't know who he was. Of course, Hiss denied any complicity in Communist activities, he was never a Commie, much less a spy.

Hiss challenged Chambers to repeat his accusations on television, where congressional immunity did not apply. Chambers repeated it on TV and Hiss sued him for slander. During pretrial examinations, Chambers was asked to produce documentary evidence for his charges that Hiss had turned over secret State Department papers to him for delivery to the Soviet Union. It was a dare, all right, and a dare that fired back.

Chambers, it turned out, had made photocopies of the documents Hiss had stolen and retyped and then given to Chambers. Afraid for the safety of the vital copies, which were the "smoking gun" of Hiss's treachery, Chambers concealed them inside pumpkins on the field of his Maryland farm. After the dare, Chambers accompanied investigators to his farm and there the "pumpkin papers" were found, intact.

As I say, none of the above was new, probably every schoolkid had knowledge of most of what the FBI men told me that afternoon. But there was one difference: the agents showed me reports that substantiated these events one by one. As I read them, my resolved conception began running out like a gambler's lucky streak.

Finally, I said, "O.K., I buy that Alger Hiss is guilty. But what does it mean? There are always a few rotten apples in the barrel. You're not claiming this is more than an isolated instance, are you?"

They all laughed. Like I was some kind of schmuck, that kind of laugh.

It turned into a long afternoon's journey into Communism.

The agents gave me chapter and verse about Kremlin cells strategically placed in the most sensitive federal departments. Documents were systematically stolen and photostated by American governmental employees for delivery to the Russians. For the first time I learned of the "Silvermaster Group," a spy network headed by Treasury Department economist Nathan Gregory Silvermaster; and another run by Victor Perlo, an official of the War Production Board. Both were supplying information to Soviet couriers from a variety of government agencies, including the Foreign Economic Administration, the War Production Board, the Justice Department, and the Board of Economic Warfare. These networks had been exposed in 1945 by Elizabeth Bentley, an ex-Communist spy who had been the common-law wife of Jacob Golos, a Soviet commissar who was the head of the spy network in America. He was also head of a front called World Tourists, which posed as a legitimate travel agency, but which actually handled secret missions to Russia and forged passports for Communist functionaries.

I learned about one J. Peters, a Hungarian who arrived illegally in the United States in the 1930's. He was Whittaker Chambers' control and he fled to the Soviet Union in 1948—when HUAC broke the Hiss-Chambers case. He had written a spy manual, the agents told me. An actual "manual" on spying? Yes, and I could read it, they'd give it to me.

In the ensuing days and weeks they gave me documents up to my eyebrows. I devoured everything, I was on a kick, like a college kid into Existentialism. Plus I read Marx, Lenin, I read Stalin's *Foundations of Leninism,* I read *The History of the Communist Party.* If J. Edgar Hoover had seen my reading list . . .

Because I was assigned to do these minor memos, I had an excuse to watch the Hiss trial and I did at every opportunity. The great trial lawyer Lloyd Paul Stryker represented Hiss and he achieved a hung jury. In the second trial, Hiss was convicted; maybe because Stryker was no longer his lawyer, maybe because Judge Samuel Kaufman was no longer the judge. But I noticed something during that first Hiss trial. I noticed that Stryker never challenged the government's contention that Soviet espionage was a reality in these United States. Indeed, Stryker tried to blacken Chambers as a worse agent of the Kremlin than perhaps he ever was.

This may seem a truism today, that there was major Soviet espionage going on here during (and after) our love affair with the Soviet Union in World War II. But my "liberalism" and disdain for HUAC was based on the opposite assumption. I thought, to put it crudely, that all of this was horseshit. Or, to put it in Trumantalk, a witch-hunt, a red herring. Yet here was Stryker saying that of course there was espionage, of course Chambers was guilty, but of course Hiss had nothing to do with it all.

In all the spy trials that followed, this was invariably the defense. Yes there was Soviet espionage, but only the government witnesses were guilty. All the defendants were framed. All these years later, this remains the *sine qua non* of the revisionist historians who never tire of retrying the post-war Communist cases. Chambers was guilty but Hiss wasn't; Harry Gold was guilty but not the Rosenbergs: And the earth is flat.

I like to think that I would have come around to reality without that lunch at Gasner's, but I thank those FBI men today for straightening me out early on. As the blues number goes, "It ain't what you do, it's the time that you do it."

The timing could not have been more fortuitous for me, because now when Mr. McGohey put me to work on the famous case of the Top Eleven American Communists, I had something in my brain other than the dopey liberal notions the professors at Columbia Law had helped fill it with. I was only on the fringes of this case, known as the Dennis case, but that was sufficient to confirm in living color what the Gasner's lunch began for me. The trial lasted nine months between 1949 and 1950 and, while I was working on other cases during this period, I managed to spend many hours listening to witnesses who were about to testify. Many were government informants who had infiltrated the party and I heard them spell out what they learned—that the Communists believed absolutely that the violent overthrow of the "bourgeois state" was necessary for "true revolution" in America. I probably would have laughed this off as paranoia earlier on, but no more. The Top Eleven were convicted of conspiracy to teach and advocate the violent overthrow of our government.

After the Hiss case and before the Rosenbergs, the big headline Communist trial was *U.S. v. Remington*. I was no mere gofer on that one. I not only helped to convict William Remington of perjury, after the court of appeals ordered a new trial, I devised a strategy that sank him.

William Walter Remington. A handsome, brilliant WASP with everything going for him. Born in New York City in 1917, he was raised in Ridgewood, N.J., a picture postcard of a town that could have been the home of Judge Hardy. At 16, Remington enrolled in Dartmouth and made Phi Beta Kappa. Later he got a masters in economics at Columbia. In 1939, he married his college sweetheart, Ann Moos, and moved into her banker father's home in Croton-on-Hudson, New York. Then to Washington with the Commerce Department, the War Productions Board, the Navy, and after the war back to Commerce.

Behind this All-American façade was a dedicated Communist who ultimately became a spy for the Kremlin. Beginning in early 1943, Remington regularly delivered secret War Production documents to Elizabeth Bentley, who turned them over to her lover, Jacob Golos, the top Soviet agent in the country. Among the secrets Remington handed over (which included airplane production schedules) was a vital, unique item: the formula to produce synthetic rubber out of garbage. The government had spent fortunes of time and money on this top-secret process and Remington was a proud man when he was able to deliver the whole kit-and-caboodle to Miss Bentley, whom he knew only as "Helen."

Elizabeth Bentley made a confession to the FBI in 1945, detailing Remington's traitorous activities (she told on many other spies as well) but for years nothing came of it. Why? The FBI notified Remington's boss, Thomas C. Blaisdell, the New Deal economist who had brought him into government and continued to guide his career. Blaisdell asked Remington if he were a spy and Remington said no. And that was that.

Until 1948, that was that. Then Miss Bentley publicly exposed

Remington before the Senate Subcommittee on Investigations run by Homer Ferguson (R.-Mich.). Summoned before the committee, Remington allowed as how he knew Miss Bentley and Mr. Golos (as "Helen" and "John") but denied espionage and denied knowing they were Soviet agents. He said that Helen had claimed to be a reporter for a New York newspaper and that whatever information he gave her was for her articles and anyway none of it was secret. He admitted giving her money but denied it was for his Communist party dues, insisting it was a contribution to the Joint Anti-Fascist Refugee Committee, a Communist front organization.

The Civil Service Commission's Loyalty Board held hearings on Remington and in September, 1948, relieved him of his government office. The following February, however, the President's Loyalty Review Board reversed their decision and he was reinstated with back pay.

This decision unleashed an enormous liberal attack, a virtual carpetbombing of the "witch-hunters" by editorial writers and pundits, particularly in the east. Most of these people had vigorously supported Harry Truman for president despite the fact that he was the one who set up the loyalty program for the first time in American history. Now that his review board had overturned what his lower creation had wrought, the Smugness Brigade was out in full cry. And none more vociferous than James A. Wechsler, then the Washington Bureau Chief of the New York *Post*. In an impassioned article, not in the *Post* but in *The New Republic*, Wechsler pronounced (in his lead), "The case of William Walter Remington is officially closed."

It sure did look that way, especially after Elizabeth Bentley repeated her accusations against Remington on *Meet the Press*, without congressional immunity. Remington sued for $100,000, and NBC and its sponsor General Foods Corporation settled out-of-court for $10,000. Dead and buried, right? Let's go to the videotape.

In the spring of 1950, the House Un-American Activities Committee, now under Democratic party control, reopened the case. When the extent of Remington's involvement with Communists began to emerge at the HUAC hearings, a federal grand jury was impaneled in New York. Because the statute of limitations had tolled, Remington, like Alger Hiss, could not be indicted for espionage. But he could be and was indicted for perjury in denying that he had been a member of the Communist party and had passed secrets to Elizabeth Bentley. The key witness before the grand jury was Ann Moos Remington, his ex-wife.

The trial opened in early January, 1951. By then, Mr. McGohey had ascended to the bench, as they say, and his successor as U.S. attorney was Irving H. Saypol.

Behind Saypol were a group of young prosecutors who came to be known as the "pony backfield"—John M. Foley, Albert A. Blinder, James Kilsheimer III (at 29, the "old man") and me. Since I was the kid who got Saypol his job (*much* more on this later) he looked to me first. I told him, "We'll be ready for trial in three weeks."

As we expected, the defense was set for the destruction of Miss Bentley's credibility. Indeed, Remington's lawyer, former New York City Corporation Counsel William C. Chanler, made this his opening to the jury. We countered by putting Ann Moos Remington up as our first witness. Chanler looked like he had been hit blind-side by a Mack truck. He had no idea she had been a grand jury witness, and here she was first up for the government. (This couldn't happen today, when the defense has a right to know just about everything, including the relevant grand jury minutes. It's a good reform, but it wasn't around in those glorious liberal New Deal-Truman days.)

Ann Moos Remington was a terrific witness. Quietly, tersely, she told of her early acquaintance with Remington in 1937 when he was at Dartmouth and she was at Radcliffe. One night, in a parked car on the Dartmouth campus, he told her he was a member of the Young Communist League and "abjured me to secrecy." He needn't have, since this banker's daughter was a Communist herself. A year later, he told her he was dropping out of party membership because "he could do more good outside." When he asked her to marry him, she made it a condition that he "continue to be a Communist." Remington said she'd have no problem "on that score."

We had other witnesses, including (of course) Elizabeth
Bentley, who supplied a wealth of detail concerning Remington's espionage activities. For his part, Remington conceded a
youthful flirtation with left-wing causes but denied joining the
Communist party or the Young Communist League and said he
had never passed any of his country's secrets to anybody.

The jury convicted him in short order. But the second circuit
reversed and ordered a new trial on the grounds that the trial
judge's charge to the jury on exactly what constituted party
"membership" was "vague and indefinite." At that point, I really
got into the act.

Night after night I pored over the trial record. Obviously,
Remington had lied on numerous critical points. What worried
me about a retrial on the original indictment was that there
might always be this issue of defining "membership" in the
party. After all, this was no pro-Communist court of appeals we
were dealing with. If they thought the charge vague before they
might find any charge vague again. The problem wasn't the
charge, it was the very notion of defining "membership" without
proving it by showing a card.

Well, I lit upon something. Remington had denied that he
even knew of the existence of a Young Communist League at
Dartmouth. One morning I asked Jack Foley and Al Blinder:
"Can someone be indicted for perjury committed while testifying at his own trial, even though his conviction was reversed
on appeal?"

They checked the precedents. The answer was yes. There was
a U.S. Supreme Court decision squarely on point. I went to
Saypol. I told him that it would be foolish to try Remington
again on the same indictment, particularly in light of the second
circuit's failure to define in their opinion what it would accept as
a definition of "membership." Why not simply indict him anew
based on the statements he made at the trial?

The grand jury indicted him on two counts. That he lied at
trial when he said he didn't know of the Young Communist
League at Dartmouth. And he lied at trial when he denied giving secret information to Elizabeth Bentley.

Remington's lawyers hit the ceiling. This new indictment,

they charged, was a "vicious device" to avoid a Supreme Court review of the original conviction. In the event, they were wrong on that point as well as on the evidence. In March, 1952, the High Court rejected Remington's appeal for an outright reversal, or for a verdict of acquittal. Anyway, we tried him again, though I was now on other business. He was convicted, sentenced to three years and, after all the appeals were rejected, he entered Lewisburg Penitentiary.

His supporters were finally silenced. Jimmy Wechsler never mentioned William Walter Remington in the two books he wrote about the period.

Remington was silenced too. Less than two years after he entered prison, he was murdered by another inmate. At first there was suspicion that the killing had political implications. It turned out to be a turgid sexually motivated murder.

Today, nobody remembers Remington. So death, like life, is unfair. The Rosenbergs gave the secret of the Bomb to the Russians. Remington gave them garbage. Maybe the game is called "Never steal anything small." Well, I helped convict him. And I *really* helped convict the Rosenbergs. It's called, "Never knock your own game."

Not that it was a game, the Rosenberg case.

Chapter Four

The Rosenberg case thrust me onto center stage for keeps—and for me it was a matter of "at long last." That I was only 23 when Julius and Ethel Rosenberg were indicted for conspiracy to turn over atomic bomb secrets to the Soviet Union was of no matter to me. Everybody else might have thought (or known) I was a kid, but I wasn't even a kid when I *was* a kid, let alone in the summer of 1950. By then I had been in courtrooms for two and a half years on an almost daily basis as an assistant United States attorney and had prosecuted more than 200 defendants. With no losers, not one acquittal marked up against me. If anything, I thought I was overripe to work on this Crime of the Century, as J. Edgar Hoover rightly tabbed the Rosenberg case. Plus, I knew plenty about certain principals in this unfolding drama, and this knowledge knocked out the Awe Factor that would otherwise have humbled even the cockiest 23-year-old. I had loyalty and respect, depending on whom we are discussing—but no awe, no awe at all. Let's start with Irving Saypol, United States attorney and chief prosecutor of Julius and Ethel Rosenberg.

I got Irving Saypol his job. Yes. Not alone, of course not alone. Not without the O.K. from Frank Costello. In those days, nobody became U.S. attorney in New York without the O.K. from the mob. But Saypol would not have gotten the nod from Costello without me.

The jockeying for the post of U.S. attorney began, as usual, the day the then U.S. attorney resigned. In this case it was John F.X. McGohey, who after the conviction of Alger Hiss moved up to the federal beach—an almost natural occurrence after a popular and successful prosecution. Invariably, the chief assistant U.S. attorney is appointed as acting U.S. attorney by the federal district court judges. I don't know of a case in which it didn't happen, you have got to be a certified lunatic for it not to happen. Saypol was no lunatic but it almost didn't happen for him. He was chief assistant, all right, and from an impeccable Tammany Hall background, but some of the judges disliked him so much—he was one of the easiest men in the world to dislike—that he came within a whisker of losing the interim appointment to Myles Lane, the executive assistant U.S. attorney. "What do you have to have against this district to put that monster in?" one federal judge said to me. But custom won out and Saypol got the slot.

There was no inevitability or custom about the permanent job. Just politics, and hardly what you'd call pure politics. It was a couple of years before I learned that the four-star generals on the ground during this war between Irving Saypol and Myles Lane were Frank Costello and Gaetano ("Three Fingers Brown") Lucchese. What I did know, from the outset, was that Generoso Pope would have a decisive role in the outcome.

This was nothing special to know if you knew anything about Tammany Hall or anything about New York. But I had a very special relationship with Generoso Pope, he was really a second father to me and had been almost since the day I met him in 1941 when I was 14 and he was 45. The connection was his son, Gene Jr., my buddy and high school classmate at Horace Mann.

I don't know how to explain why a man who practically ran Tammany, was tight with President Roosevelt, was one of the most powerful Italian-Americans in the country would make a little kid his great confidant. But a night didn't go by when I wasn't on the phone with Mr. Pope before bedtime and that was after a good half-dozen calls during the day. We didn't talk about the weather—these conversations roamed from politics to business to intimate personal things. In that way, at least—on the personal stuff—he was closer to me than my father, who was not one to share his innermost thoughts.

Why did Mr. Pope take to me? Unfortunately I'm not much at psychiatry—or maybe it's not so unfortunate—but in retrospect I see my relationship with Mr. Pope as establishing a pattern. All my life I've been able to work well and closely with older, powerful men—Joe McCarthy, Cardinal Spellman, J. Edgar Hoover, Lewis Rosensteil, to name a significant few. It just comes easy to me and to them, and I leave it to others to figure out why. For me facts are facts and enough is enough. So just one early example to indicate why Mr. Pope might trust my judgment when the choice of a United States attorney was up for grabs.

At dinner at his house one night, it must have been 1942, he mentioned that he wanted to buy a New York radio station, WHOM. He said it was worth $400,000, big money in those days. I said, "What's the highest price you'll pay?" He smiled. He asked why I wanted to know. I said, "I'd like to take a crack at getting it for you." He said, "If you can buy it for $350,000 you've got ten grand."

I got the deal done with the help of my uncle, Bernie Marcus, the man whom I loved and who did the time in Sing Sing for the failure of the family bank. Uncle Bernie introduced me to John Harding, general counsel to WHOM, and in record time we had it and I made ten thousand dollars. Mr. Pope was impressed that I could pull this off and I think he was more impressed when at his insistence I kicked back a portion of my commission to an FCC lawyer named, coincidentally, Marcus Cohen. It was pennies to Mr. Pope and it taught me an early lesson about the rich. They seem always to worry more about the buck that got away than the millions they reap.

I never cared about money except to spend it, and never wanted to make it unless there was a reason. My reason then was clear: I wanted to pay for my college education. It was in no way necessary; my parents were well-off and totally generous. But I wanted independence, I didn't want to think I owed them anything that way, I wanted to know that if I cut classes it was on my dough. It makes you free, money does, and when you're free you don't cut classes. Didn't I just say enough is enough? Back to how Irving Saypol became the United States attorney for the Southern District of New York.

I was completely loyal to Saypol despite that he was the very epitome of vanity. Obsequious to his superiors, contemptuous of those under him, wrongheaded, supercilious—the only good thing I could say for him was the only thing that counted for me: he was terrific to me. He put great trust in me, he allowed me to flourish despite my youth. Plus he was an old friend of my family. So when he told me that his own Tammany leader, John Dietz, was backing down, was moving towards Myles Lane—to show you what kind of an ass-kisser Saypol was, he named both his sons after Dietz, their middle names were Dietz—I said, "Let me go see Gene." Meaning Generoso Pope—everybody called him Gene. Of course, Irving said, fine, go to it, my boy.

Mr. Pope said, "Do you vouch for him?"

I said, "Sure. He's a good guy." What did I know about the word "vouch," I was 21 years old. It really meant I was putting my name on the line for Saypol, if it went wrong it could have been my head.

Mr. Pope said, "We hear bad things about him. We hear his word is no good, that we can't trust him, that if he gets in there he's liable to knock our brains out. But you say he's O.K., you vouch for him, yes?"

"Absolutely."

"Then it's done," Mr. Pope said. And followed it with commitments from Carmine DeSapio, the leader of Tammany, and Sammy DiFalco, Secretary of the Hall. So everything was copacetic and I so reported to my boss Saypol.

But a few nights later, Saypol called to tell me that the double-cross was in. That DeSapio had just had lunch with Ed Flynn and submitted Myles Lane as U.S. attorney. Flynn, the Boss, was the most powerful Democrat in the state and one of the top leaders in the nation. He was FDR's man and had put Harry Truman across as vice-president in 1944 when the party dumped Henry Wallace. As the Bronx leader he could, if he wished, have the ultimate say in the appointment of the U.S. attorney for the southern district, because the district encompassed Manhattan and the Bronx. Now Flynn's law partner, Monroe Goldwater, had reported to Saypol that DeSapio was jettisoning him for Lane.

First thing in the morning I called Mr. Pope. He was obviously surprised but quickly turned cold. "I'll take care of this," he said. I went over to his house that night, dying to find out what happened. He told me that Sammy DiFalco had just arrived at the dock after a cruise. That he had sent his assistant, Dominic Florio, to meet DiFalco at the boat. And that I shouldn't worry about anything.

"But what did DiFalco say?" I asked.

"It's what Florio said that counts," Mr. Pope answered.

"What?"

"Florio told DiFalco that I knew about the double-cross, but that I didn't want him, DiFalco, to let DeSapio know I knew. Keep DeSapio far away from Pope, because Pope doesn't talk to double-crossers. Make sure you don't let DeSapio know that Pope is angry. This was my only message to Sammy DiFalco."

I said, "But Mr. Pope, what good does that do? Now DiFalco won't tell DeSapio, and Lane will slide in."

Generoso Pope said, and this was one of the most important lessons of my life, he said: "Roy, two seconds after Florio left the dock, DiFalco was in a phone booth calling Carmine DeSapio. I know, because Carmine has been calling me all day. I'll take his call tomorrow."

Thus, swear an intermediary to secrecy and he'll violate the secrecy. And you'll get what you want.

DeSapio was forced to meet again with Ed Flynn. And to tell him he was putting in Irving Saypol's name rather than Myles Lane's. Flynn wasn't a pushover. "You told me this Saypol character is unreliable, untrustworthy." DeSapio said, "I'll be frank with you, Sheriff"—(everybody called Flynn "Sheriff" because it was his first position, the way they still call, the insiders call,

Ronald Reagan "Governor")—"I hadn't done my homework, but I've done a lot of checking since." Flynn said, "That's the phoniest excuse I ever heard." He said, "I'll think it over."

A week went by without an answer from Boss Flynn. Saypol drove me crazy, he called me thirty times a day. "Call Pope, find out from Pope," like that, constant. Mr. Pope simply said to me, "You don't go chasing something like this." But he seemed confident, though there was no way I could convey this confidence to Saypol.

Saypol got the nod, of course, but it was three or four years before I found out how.

The night before the New York Judicial Convention, I got a call from Saypol, who was in Boston on a speaking engagement. This was after the Rosenberg case, and, though I didn't know it mattered, after Saypol had indicted Frank Costello. Irving said to me, "Call Gene Pope, tell him I want to be nominated to the state supreme court tomorrow night."

The conversation lasted fifty seconds. I didn't know what the hell was up, I was shocked, but I called Mr. Pope and gave him the message. Mr. Pope said, "Why should we reward this double-crosser?" And I didn't know what *that* meant. But Pope added, "Tell him it's done."

The next morning I picked up Irving at the airport and he said, "Do you have everything arranged?" I said yes. I said, "Just give me the names of who you want to nominate you tonight."

It was shortly afterwards that I found out from Mr. Pope what it was all about. And he was surprised I didn't know, he just assumed I was aware of the Costello connection.

"Don't you see?" Mr. Pope said. "He wanted to force us to get him out of the way. That's why he prosecuted Costello, don't you know about this?"

What I didn't know was that Frank Costello was running Tammany for the mob, that Carmine DeSapio was his stooge, that the mob had for years before (and years afterwards) decided the appointment of the U.S. attorney, and that Costello—at Pope's behest—had chosen Irving Saypol. The humbug came when Tommy ("Three Fingers Brown") Lucchese decided to push

Myles Lane. In that mob fight, Lucchese appeared the winner, hence DeSapio's double-cross of Generoso Pope. Poor Carmine, who is one of my best friends, was simply living within a system he did not originate or control. When Costello capitulated to Lucchese, Carmine had to shift to Myles Lane. In the event, Generoso Pope was more powerful than Three Fingers, and Boss Flynn finally shrugged and let it be, he couldn't really care less—once he knew the deal was cleared downstairs.

In the end, it turned out fine for all concerned. When Saypol was elevated to the bench, Myles Lane became U.S. attorney. And it turned out that I was the only player who didn't know what was going on. Which is a pretty good laugh on me when you recall that if it wasn't for me Generoso Pope wouldn't have moved the moving finger for Irving Saypol.

The postscript doesn't do much for my reputation as a young genius. Driving down the FDR Drive with Saypol after Irving had his judgeship, I said, "What's this about Frank Costello making you U.S. attorney?" Saypol said, "You're too young to understand these things."

My father, who remained a political powerhouse while serving on the bench, was instrumental in getting Irving Kaufman his federal judgeship. I was instrumental in getting Irving Kaufman assigned to the Rosenberg case. My father's clout reached into the White House. Mine only reached into the district court clerk's office. But that was the White House when it came to deciding what judge sat on what case. The man to see was Dave Sweeney, the clerk in charge of the criminal calendar.

It was automatic that I'd get to be tight with Dave Sweeney. You don't grow up around Ed Flynn without knowing where the power lies. Judge Kaufman hadn't been on the bench long enough to get cozy with Sweeney, so he turned to me. He wanted the Rosenberg case as much as he wanted the judgeship—and when Irving wants something he doesn't stop, he doesn't leave you alone until you do what he wants.

We were vacationing in Florida, during the Christmas season of 1950. Irving and his wife were in Boca Raton, I was in Palm Beach. We might as well have been in the same room. I think he called me fifty times a day. Call Dave Sweeney, call Dave Sweeney, call Dave Sweeney. If you don't call him some other judge is liable to put pressure on him. Everybody wants this case, you've got to get to it, Roy, call Dave Sweeney. So all right, already, I'll call Dave Sweeney. As soon as I said that, Irving called me so many times I couldn't get through to Dave Sweeney! Make this point, make that point, don't forget this that and the other thing. The big thing he kept emphasizing was the Brothman-Moscowitz trial.

About a month earlier, Saypol and I had tried that one, an obstruction of justice case involving industrial espionage. In many ways, it was a preview of the Rosenberg case, because the two main government witnesses were Harry Gold and Elizabeth Bentley, both of whom were to be critical witnesses against the Rosenbergs. Gold was the courier for Klaus Fuchs, the British scientist at the apex of the Manhattan Project in Los Alamos, and as such he delivered atom bomb secrets to the Soviets. He was also the courier for the Rosenbergs' man in Los Alamos, David Greenglass, Ethel Rosenberg's brother—and as such he delivered the sketch of the bomb to the Russians. Elizabeth Bentley was the notorious "Red Spy Queen" who had decided to tell all.

To repeat, then, the Brothman-Moscowitz case was a dry-run of the upcoming Rosenberg trial. We were able to see how Gold and Bentley fared on the stand, and we were able to see how *we* fared, Saypol and I. On all scores it came up roses. Abraham Brothman and Miriam Moscowitz were convicted, and now Irving Kaufman wanted me to press the victory with Dave Sweeney. "You can tell him that I tried the Brothman-Moscowitz case," Irving said, "and that the Rosenberg case is really a follow-up, so it would be a waste of taxpayer's money to have a new judge, who is not aware of these issues and would have to learn everything from the beginning . . . you understand what I mean, Roy?"

I understood the first time he said it. So did Sweeney. After I pitched him, he said, "Well, your feeling then, Roy, is that this case should go to Kaufman." I said, "I guess that's the point, Dave." He said, "Let me call you back."

I reported this to Irving, it was late-morning, as I recall, and for the rest of the day I got no peace. It was every ten minutes now, the calls didn't stop. Did you hear yet? Do you think you should try him again? Finally, at about ten that night, I relented and called Sweeney at home. He said, "Ah, yes, I had it on my call list for first thing tomorrow morning. It's fine. Tell Judge Kaufman the Rosenberg case is his."

I was delighted to call Irving with the good news. He was impossible but I liked him and was glad I could get this done for him. I was sure we'd get a conviction no matter who the judge was, but still it was nice to be able to put this contract through.

"I talked to our friend in New York," I said to Irving. "It's done."

Irving Kaufman sighed. "Well," he said, "you've really put me in the soup now, my friend. Whatever I do I'm sure to be criticized. There's no way to be popular in a case this fraught with emotion and political overtones. But it's my duty. When you take this job you must accept the consequences."

This was minutes after he had been hustling my ass off to get him the case. I almost threw up, but I stifled myself and played the game. I told him he would do justice, he would perform in the great tradition of the federal judiciary. I guess it ranked with the phoniest conversations of the 20th century.

Back in New York, Kaufman followed with another lollapalooza. He held a pre-trial conference with all the lawyers so he could inform them of all possible conflict questions. He said that he and I were not close friends, but that his wife and my mother had long ties, though he was sure neither would know anything about the Rosenberg case. He said he knew my father, but that this was true of every judge on the federal court. He reminded them that he had presided over the Brothman-Moscowitz case. And then he went on and on, until I signaled him to cut it, it was enough.

I mean, he had made the record and it was clear nobody was going to ask him to recuse, to get off the case. Of course, if they did, he'd have wiped them out, they'd have been in eternal trouble with him, and obviously they knew that. He had this intimidating leer, for one thing, and I must assume they knew he would never get off this case. They'd have had to have a picture of him in bed with Elizabeth Bentley to get him off this one. So the whole thing was a charade, but it served its purpose. Judge Kaufman had given the defense lawyers every chance to object to him, hadn't he?

Before, during, and after the trial, the prosecution team—particularly Irving Saypol and I—were in constant communication with Judge Kaufman. I mean private, or what the lawyers call *ex parte* communication, without the presence of the defense lawyers. Not that the defense attorneys weren't aware that we were talking to the judge; no lawyer worth his salt wasn't aware in those days that prosecutors talked privately to judges about cases. There were a few exceptions, a few judges who would never speak *ex parte*, but most of them did and most of them did it without a thought, it was normal. After Watergate, all of this would change, at least the perception changed, and so I'm sure that readers who were not around before everybody and his brother became sensitive to the Canon of Ethics will be shocked at what I've said about my conversations with Judge Kaufman—and maybe more shocked at what I'm about to say. But this is how it was when I was a young lawyer, and how it remained for years. I make the point only by way of explanation—it's neither an excuse nor a confession. I didn't make the world and I had no intention of tearing it down.

In the past, I've denied having *ex parte* communications with Judge Kaufman, in order not to embarrass Kaufman, who was being harassed by the Rosenberg-Sobell revisionists and attacked by well-meaning people in and out of the media who were seduced by this crowd into thinking that the trial was a frame-up. But now that all their efforts have come to naught—the pile-up of Freedom of Information Act stuff has proven the guilt of the defendants beyond all doubt, not just a reasonable doubt—Irving Kaufman doesn't need protection from me. Probably he never did, and I suppose I should have told it "like it is" from the outset. Because, whatever we did behind the scenes, the Rosenbergs and Sobell were in no way denied a fair trial. Indeed, the only time my private communications with Judge Kaufman really made a difference in the trial was when I prevented Irving Saypol from prejudicing the case, from possibly poisoning the minds of the jurors.

Morton Sobell's lawyer, Edward Kuntz, got Saypol crazy at the end of his summation. It happened that Sobell had fled to Mexico shortly after David Greenglass was arrested. Obviously, he figured the jig was up, but his excuse was, through Kuntz (Sobell didn't take the stand), that he was simply on vacation. We had to get him deported from Mexico, but Kuntz said it was just a sojourn. And then, in summation to the jury, he turned on Saypol and said, "Saypol—if *I* want to go to Mexico, you're not going to stop me." Saypol turned ten shades of crimson, and knowing his bottomless vanity I sensed big trouble ahead.

We adjourned for lunch after Kuntz's summation, and since I had already written Saypol's summation, which was to follow, I went over to Gasner's restaurant. Before I could take bite one, Jack Foley, one of the assistant U.S. attorneys working on the trial, came in and took me outside. He said Saypol was about to expose Kuntz as an ex-Communist. That Saypol was going to begin his summation by reading to the jury an old New York State case where he, Saypol, as chairman of Tammany Hall's Law Committee, had successfully knocked out Kuntz's petitions as candidate for office on the pro-Communist American Labor party line.

I ran back to the courthouse and used the private staircase we had to get to Judge Kaufman's chambers. I told Kaufman it was urgent and he motioned his clerks out of the room. Then I told him what Saypol was about to do. He was livid. He said, "Well, that's nice. After the way this case has gone down, after all the precautions we took to protect the record, he's going to do this? Thanks for telling me. I'll take care of it. We're not having a mistrial here."

Saypol of course knew nothing of this. He walked into court holding the book containing this big deal case of his. Kaufman motioned us to the bench, Saypol and me. He asked him was it possible that that was a book that looked like the New York State Reports? Saypol said sure, he said he intended to read to the jury this decision that would show how Kuntz had "brutally" attacked him in the 1930's when he, Saypol, had attacked Communism. Kaufman said he would take that to mean that Saypol was calling Kuntz a Communist. "I'll declare a mistrial in two seconds if you try that," Kaufman said. Saypol tried to argue but Kaufman waved his hand, and Saypol had to forget about it. The summation then proceeded according to plan, and the rest is history.

Except the unrecorded history, which is what this book is about. To retry the Rosenberg case here, to once again rake over the record and the details and the nuances, would be worse than redundant, it'd be plain boring. I have no interest in discomfiting the recalcitrant or comforting the convinced. My purpose is to . . . ah, hell, my purpose is to let my purpose speak for itself.

The fact is, these *ex parte* discussions with Kaufman were irrelevant to the outcome of the case and were necessary, if at all, because Irving Saypol was driving me to distraction. Kaufman mainly played the role of school principal—he often referred to us as "kindergarten kids." My position was, from the beginning, that the case was solid, that we didn't need to do anything but try it simply and straightaway, that if Saypol only got off my back we'd have a verdict in no time flat. But Saypol wouldn't leave a good thing alone. He carped behind the scenes, he carped in court, he would send me notes and whisper in my ear while I was examining a witness—and it was over this kind of crap that we kept meeting with Kaufman. The trial lasted three weeks, with some ten days of actual testimony, but by the middle of it I wasn't talking to Saypol. Even when we were in Kaufman's chambers, I'd talk to Kaufman and he'd talk to Saypol, and viceversa.

Looking back at all this bickering and craziness, it strikes me as final proof of the guilt of Julius and Ethel Rosenberg and Morton Sobell that we were able to convict them despite what was going on behind the green door.

If I have given the impression that I deserve the credit for the convictions, let me dispel that now. We had a topnotch group of assistant U.S. attorneys and a very fine bunch of FBI agents who did great, yeoman work from beginning to end. We also had

some unexpected help from Manny Bloch, the chief defense
counsel (of which more later). But most of all we had O. John
Rogge, the lawyer for certain key government witnesses. Without John Rogge there might not have been a successful prosecution. Indeed, it is not too much to say that Mr. Rogge broke the
Rosenberg case. Which is the very definition of irony.

Rogge was one of the most prominent radical lawyers in the
country, a real celebrity of the far left. He ran for the Senate in
New York on the same line as Henry Wallace in 1948. The next
year he became vice-president of the National Lawyers Guild,
and a major supporter of the Civil Rights Congress, the legal-
political arm of the Communist party. The prospectus for the
National Guardian (which was left of *The Daily Worker*) was
drawn up in his law offices by Cedric Belfrage, who was later
ordered deported from the United States. And Rogge was a delegate to the Communist bloc World Peace Conference in
Warsaw in 1950. It was there, he later told me, that he finally
realized the vicious totalitarianism of the movement he had so
long embraced.

Rogge represented (among others) David Greenglass, Ethel
Rosenberg's brother. David was a machinist in Los Alamos on
the Manhattan Project. He was the one who turned over the
atom bomb sketch, the secret of the implosion process, to the
Russian courier Harry Gold, who had arrived at his house in Albuquerque with a piece of a Jell-O box and said, "I come from
Julius." Gold had been implicated in London by Klaus Fuchs,
the head scientist on the Manhattan Project—the man who
pleaded guilty to spying for the Russians at Los Alamos. It was
this that got the Rosenberg case going, but if we had to depend
on Harry Gold alone there would have been no conviction of the
Rosenbergs. Because there was a serious problem about Fuchs's
description of Gold, and because the Rosenbergs were smart
enough not to deal directly with him. So without Greenglass
there could have been no case and without Rogge there would
have been no Greenglass.

David Greenglass was forthcoming about Julius, from the outset (thanks to Rogge), but he was naturally reluctant to put his
sister in the same box. The Rosenberg revisionists have made

much of the fact that until about ten days before the trial, David hadn't told us that Ethel had typed up the information about the Bomb. They learned this from the Freedom of Information stuff. I guess they figured we put David under the rack-and-screw or made up the testimony and he then just parroted it for us. What really happened was that John Rogge told me one day that David was holding back on Ethel, that if I talked to him again I might get the true story.

Obviously this didn't mean that all I had to do was walk in and David Greenglass would ring up his sister. It meant I could use leverage I hadn't thought would work before. That is, I could tell David that we knew he was protecting Ethel, and that unless he told us what *he* knew about her activities we could not guarantee that Ruth, his wife, would be safe from prosecution. Until then, she had been an unindicted co-conspirator. It was the only deal we thought we could make, because David was not about to give us Julius without that arrangement. But the understanding had been that he would tell all. Now he was holding back about Ethel. So he had reneged on the deal. Such was my message to him, and he responded with alacrity. Whatever Rogge had said to him—and Rogge never told me, nor did I ask—convinced David Greenglass, and his wife (whom Rogge also represented), to finally tell us the real story about his sister.

It turned out that he resented her terribly. That she was the one who wore the pants in the family, she had recruited him into the spy ring. We didn't bring all this out in court, for tactical reasons—just as we decided not to put David's mother on the stand, though she was quite willing to support David against her daughter Ethel. So the business about the typing was minimal next to what we now knew Ethel was in this espionage ring. And if we didn't know it after talking to David, Ruth, and the mother, we certainly would have known it by watching Ethel Rosenberg in court. She was pulling on defense attorney Manny Bloch's coat, sending messages all over the place, she was the whole show, and there's nothing more conclusive in a courtroom than the demeanor of the witness. Anybody in that room had to know who was the power in the Rosenberg family—and I use "family" as in Corleone.

John Rogge also represented Max Elitcher, and this is my favorite story of the Rosenberg-Sobell case. Elitcher was involved with the Rosenbergs from his days with them at the City College of New York and he was surely part of their spy ring. For us, however, his main importance was as the key witness against Morton Sobell. We had no provable connection between Sobell and the Rosenbergs on atomic espionage, but Elitcher worked together with Sobell to deliver other secrets to the Rosenbergs, and thus to the Soviets. So his credibility was vital to the prosecution of Sobell.

My policy, then and now, as a lawyer, was never to scare my witnesses about cross-examination. I always wait until the last possible moment before telling them what they're really going to be up against. It's simply tough enough to be a witness without having time for too many nightmares. So it wasn't until the eleventh hour that I said to Elitcher, "What will you say when they ask you why you left the Communist party?"

Max Elitcher said, "I'll tell them the truth. I still am a member of the Communist Party."

I thought Irving Saypol would go into cardiac arrest. He threw his arms in the air. He said, "Well, that's what happens when you give a 23-year-old kid the responsibility for a major case." Obviously, I was to blame that Max was still a Communist. Forget about the fact that no one but me thought to ask him the question before he took the stand. I took Irving outside. I was plenty shook myself, but I didn't want Elitcher to know. I told Irving I'd call John Rogge at home, that Rogge would help us here, as he always had helped us.

Saypol resented my relationship with Rogge. This was partly because of Saypol's ego—he wanted to control everything and everybody—and partly because he sensed, correctly, that Rogge had no use for him. Saypol's *conciliatory* speech to our friendly witnesses would always begin with the admonition that "the death penalty is on your head if you don't cooperate." He was just a joy to work with, is all. So when I said I'd get Rogge over, Saypol's response was, "You're awful friendly with Rogge, aren't you?" I said, "What's wrong with that?" He said, "I mean you seem to have a lot of common ground with him." I said, "Irving, do you think he's converting me to Marxism?" He said, "Just that you two seem a little bit too friendly."

Well, I had to keep my mind on the main point. There was no way we could have Max Elitcher get on the stand and say he was still a member of the Communist party. So I called Rogge at home. I said, "John, come down now." Rogge said, "If you say so, I'm there."

He got to our office post-haste. "What's the problem?" he said. I told him, "The problem is, Max thinks he's still a Communist." Rogge said, "Where is he?" I ushered him into the room and I of course walked out. I waited on pins and needles for what seemed like hours but couldn't have been more than a few minutes.

Rogge emerged with a smile. He was a big, easygoing guy, a good-natured guy. He put his arm around me and said, "Max has just left the Communist party."

By the time we went to trial we had so much on the Rosenbergs that I don't believe any lawyer in history could have gotten them off. But Manny Bloch certainly made life easier for us. Not because he was a lousy lawyer—just that he was a 100 percent Communist and so ran the trial according to the party line. And the party line, until a year after the death sentence, was to keep the party out of the case. (To show you how deep this went, there wasn't one Rosenberg placard in the May Day parade of 1952—over a year after the convictions. Later the party switched and played the case to a fare-thee-well, but only after the *National Guardian* had done a revisionist series on the trial—by William A. Reuben, who hadn't attended even one day of the trial.)

Anyway, there is no valid way to explain Bloch's strategy, particularly in regard to the Fifth Amendment—other than that he was following the party line. Thus, he put the Rosenbergs on the stand, and then had them take the Fifth on all questions involving party membership or recruiting. Were they party members? It would incriminate them to answer. Did they recruit David Greenglass into the party? It would incriminate them to answer. Any chance they had went down the drain with these answers, you could see it on the faces of the jurors. And how incredible, when you think about it. Here they were facing a possible death penalty and they're worried about being members of the Communist party! But it's not incredible when you know that the Rosenbergs and Manny Bloch were Communists. They didn't want to incriminate the party. The party was more important than life itself.

Bloch's decision not to cross-examine Harry Gold was also a strategic disaster. In the Brothman-Moscowitz case, Gold had admitted to living a life of lies, and while this figured for a man who made a career of spying, there was plenty of meat for cross-examination on the table. Perhaps because Gold never was a member of the party, Bloch felt there was no point in cross-examining him. In any event, he not only left him alone, he told the jury on summation that everything Gold said was true. One of the things Gold said was, "I come from Julius"—when he received the sketch of the atom bomb from David Greenglass in Albuquerque. Did Bloch think the jury would figure he was referring to Julius Streicher?

Then there was Greenglass's sketch of the bomb, which of course he had to recreate for the trial, since the original had been delivered by Harry Gold to the Russians in 1945. When we moved to introduce the sketch into evidence, Manny Bloch moved to impound the sketch and to clear the courtroom. Bloch was trying to be clever, holier-than-thou; here he was, more patriotic than the government and, by implication, so were his clients. The press protested, claiming First Amendment rights to be present at a public trial. The Solomonic decision by Irving Kaufman was out of the Marx Brothers. The spectators were ordered to leave the courtroom, but the press was allowed to remain!

The sketch, however, was impounded, thanks to Manny Bloch, and this, ironically, was exactly what the Atomic Energy Commission wanted. I know, because I had a knock-down, drag-out fight with the bureaucrats from the A.E.C. who wanted the government to keep the sketch out of the trial, on the ground that it would compromise our national defense. Imagine how dopey that was? Here the whole case was predicated on the fact that the Rosenbergs and their co-conspirators had delivered the sketch to the Soviet Union six years earlier. So who would we be keeping it from? What "secret" could they be protecting? Yet they tried, they went "upstairs" when I practically threw them out of my office. They didn't succeed with my superiors, but they got what they wanted from Manny Bloch. And it wasn't until 1966, on a motion from Morton Sobell's lawyers—Sobell was still trying to get free—that the sketch became public. Even that late in the game, all those years after Sputnik, for heaven's sake, the government was attempting to keep this 1945 sketch a secret. If it didn't actually happen that way, on the record, I couldn't write this for fear that nobody would believe it.

One of the biggest favors Manny Bloch did for the government was to announce to the court, after the verdict, that his clients had received a "fair American trial." I agreed with him, of course, but how was this statement supposed to help his clients on appeal? We were able to use it against the Rosenbergs in appellate courts and in the court of public opinion forevermore. So thanks, Manny, wherever you are.

The death sentences imposed on the Rosenbergs by Judge Kaufman have kept the case alive all these years, and incidentally brought the Communist party and the Pope together for the first time in history. I've already discussed the Communists. In the spirit of all religions, we'll start with God and get to the Pope later.

Irving Kaufman has said that he sought divine guidance in his synagogue before deciding upon the sentences. I can't confirm or deny this. So far as I know, the closest he got to prayer was the phone booth next to the Park Avenue Synagogue. He called from that booth to a booth I used, behind the bench in the courtroom, to ask my advice on whether he ought to give the death penalty to Ethel Rosenberg. We often communicated during the Rosenberg case in this manner; we'd do it through his secretary, who'd tell me where to be at what hour, or if I wanted to talk to Irving I'd tell her where I'd be and when. Mainly I used the courtroom phone booth, which was out of the sight line of visitors who might stroll into the court. Kaufman was always wary of wiretaps, not by the Commies, but by the government, and he was probably right to worry. Certainly, if the Rosenbergs had a communication system like Irving had, they never would have been caught, let alone executed.

In any event, we had a rather extensive conversation on this occasion, which was shortly before the sentencing. Kaufman informed me first that he was giving Sobell 30 years. When I asked him why not the chair, he said because Sobell had not been implicated in atomic espionage. Fair enough, I said. He then said he was having difficulty deciding on whether to give Ethel the chair. There was never any question about Julius; Kaufman told me *before* the trial started that he was going to sentence Julius Rosenberg to death. So we didn't have to discuss him during this conversation, except in relation to Ethel.

Kaufman said he was concerned about a possible public opinion backlash if he sentenced a woman to the electric chair, particularly a mother with two young children. "How do you see it?" he asked.

"The way I see it," I said, "is that she's worse than Julius. She's the older one, she's the one with the brains, she recruited her younger brother into the Young Communist League and into the spy ring, she's the one who typed the atomic bomb documents, she engineered this whole thing, she was the mastermind of this conspiracy. So unless you're willing to say that a woman is immune from the death penalty, I don't see how you can justify sparing her."

I wasn't telling Judge Kaufman anything he didn't know, but he was clearly worried about the impact of this sentence and I understood that. Women were looked upon in an entirely different way in those days, and what was plainly at work here was a kind of reverse sexism, at a time when the word "sexism" hadn't been invented. So I told Kaufman that I could sympathize with his dilemma, but I emphasized that the jury had surely taken her sex and motherhood into account and still the jury did its duty. I ended by saying, "Irving, it's your baby."

More than two years went by between sentence and execution. Every conceivable avenue of appeal was traversed by the Rosenbergs and Sobell, with no clemency or reversal. The most important, historically, was the first appeal in the United States Court of Appeals for the Second Circuit. Because the decision upholding the fairness of the trial was written by Jerome Frank, one of the greatest civil libertarian jurists in American history. From that moment on, I had the complete retort to whatever calumny the Rosenberg revisionists threw at me. Two words. Jerome Frank.

Of course, the Rosenbergs worked all the extra-legal avenues, and they worked them world-wide. As every court turned them down they increasingly went to the streets. Of New York, of Paris, of London, of Rome—and, naturally, the Communist-bloc nations. Pope Pius XII, "out of motives of charity proper . . . without entering into the merits of the case," asked that the death sentences be commuted. This the pontiff did orally through the Apostolic Delegate, the Archbishop of Laodica, during the Truman administration. It didn't become public knowledge until February, 1953, when Eisenhower was president.

By then, I was chief counsel to Senator Joseph McCarthy. Irving Kaufman called me in Washington. He was terribly upset that the Pope had come out for commutation. Knowing my close relationship with Francis Cardinal Spellman, he asked me to call the cardinal, to go and see him, to suggest to the cardinal that the Pope was making a grievous mistake.

I told him that Cardinal Spellman was not likely to contradict the Pope. But Irving was, as always, impervious to logic when he wanted a result. He said that Cardinal Spellman was privately in favor of capital punishment (which was true) and that Spellman could, in a respectful way, a carefully worded way, contradict the Pope.

I knew better, but as I say, Irving could wear you down. So I went to see Cardinal Spellman and I told him what Judge Kaufman wanted.

The cardinal said, "The problem with Judge Kaufman is that he doesn't seem to understand we have two different standards. Judge Kaufman's standard is to carry out a sentence according to the law as he sees it. I respect that. My standard is to extend mercy to human beings, no matter how bad the circumstances.

Indeed, the greater the crime, the greater the call for mercy. That is our Church."

Privately, Francis Spellman agreed with the death sentences. What Irving Kaufman didn't understand was that as Cardinal Spellman his private views were of no account.

In retrospect, I believe both men were right. Judge Kaufman disregarded his fear of public opinion. Francis Cardinal Spellman disregarded his views on capital punishment. And justice was done.

Chapter Five

I went to work for Joe McCarthy in January 1953 and was gone
by the fall of '54. Less than two years. But a lifetime was packed
into it, and more if obituaries tell the tale. Does anybody doubt
how mine will open? "Roy M. Cohn, who served as chief counsel to Senator Joseph R. McCarthy . . ." Which is exactly how I
want it to read. I never worked for a better man or a greater
cause. And while I can wait forever for the obit, I can't wait to let
you in on what it was like to be young and with Joe when Joe was
a one-man commotion, when he sizzled up the American land-
scape like nobody before and nobody since.

I met him at the old Hotel Astor on Times Square on a cold
December night in 1952, a month after Eisenhower swept the
country and the Republicans took both houses for the first time
since 1928. Except for Ike, no politician stood taller than
McCarthy, and even more than Eisenhower it was McCarthy
who swung the Senate to the G.O.P. Since his famous Lincoln
Day address in Wheeling, West Virginia, in 1950, McCarthy

had become the symbol of anti-Communism in America, not to say the lightning rod for the Democratic party, which railed against him as a "native fascist" even as Truman and the Democratic-controlled HUAC and Democratic U.S. attorneys continued to stalk Communists in and out of government.

What had Joe done wrong? He put the blame on the Democratic party for presiding over "twenty years of treason." He thus broke the rule of bi-partisanship, which dictated that it was the two parties against the Commies. Alger Hiss was only for starters. McCarthy accused General George Marshall of selling out China. Marshall, the sainted mentor of Dwight Eisenhower, the former Secretary of State under Harry Truman. George Marshall, imagine it!

For these violations of the rules of the League of Gentlemen, McCarthy posed a threat not only to what he called the "Democrat" party, but to the Republican establishment, which had bi-partisaned and bi-partisaned and lost and lost since memory knoweth not. Ike hated him quite as much as Truman hated him, but Ike wanted to win in '52. And there was no better ticket to the White House than Joe McCarthy. So Eisenhower embraced Joe on a whistlestop in Joe's native Wisconsin just before the election—and never said a word in defense of his "rabbi," General George C. Marshall.

There's an old English ballad that fits here. About a poor but virtuous family from the hinterlands whose daughter goes off to become a rich bawdy gal in London. "They drink the champagne wot she sends 'em," moans the ballad, "but they never will forgive."

Eisenhower and his ruling Wall Street Republican crowd hooked onto Joe McCarthy's star in 1952, but they never forgave. In Ike's case, it wasn't the attack on Marshall he couldn't forgive, it was the exposure of his own disloyalty to the man who had insured his career in the Army. That he later chose the phony issue of the sacredness of the Army to get McCarthy only adds to the irony, and to the show. And what a show it was, the Army-McCarthy hearings. But I jump ahead. Back to the Astor, where it all began, between me and Senator Joseph R. McCarthy (R.-Wisconsin).

I got to the Astor lobby at 10:30 p.m., a half-hour early. My friends will lift an eyebrow at this, or two, since I'm notoriously and unforgivably late for appointments, but this was different, this time I was being auditioned for a top spot on McCarthy's staff. All the trial and appellate experience I had jammed into the past four years may have prepared me for the job I was looking for, but it didn't do a thing for my nerves. All of a sudden I felt like any other 25-year-old kid, I was just jumpy as hell.

Of course, I wasn't just any kid come to interview for a big job, cold off the streets. I came with recommendations that meant plenty to Joe McCarthy. In my corner were George E. Sokolsky, the most powerful conservative political columnist in America; Richard E. Berlin, president of the Hearst Corporation; and Robert M. Morris, a New York judge who left the bench to fight Communism and was now chief counsel to the U.S. Senate Internal Security Subcommittee.

McCarthy was addressing a patriotic group in the ballroom that December evening, and I was sitting outside the big hall waiting for the doors to open, which would be my cue to hustle up to his suite. I was Johnny-on-the-spot, but still when I got up there a crowd was milling around the corridor and pouring into the living room. I panicked that I was somehow going to get lost in all of this and I darted about looking for Bob Morris, who had arranged this meeting.

Finally I spotted him, rosy-cheeked as ever, a pleasant smile that seemed to say "relax," and the next thing I knew we were in the bedroom with a bunch of black-ties and gowns and Joe McCarthy. Who was wearing pants, suspenders, socks, shoes— and nothing else. Joe McCarthy in hair-shirt!

Bob Morris led interference like a pulling guard. And had to shout to get Joe's attention. "Roy Cohn," he said. "Here's Roy Cohn." McCarthy leaned through a few bodies and grabbed my hand, a big, infectious smile on his famous map. "I wanted to see for myself," he said, "whether you're the genius they say you are, or if you just have good press agents." Obviously, I was supposed to smile or laugh or something, but I blew it. I think I gave him a cold fish shake and mumbled a few dummy things. Altogether awkward, Jeezus it was embarrassing. When he said

I should stand by, he'd be in touch, I felt like I was really in one of those theatrical auditions. Thanks, we'll call you, we've got your number.

And there was no call for days and days. I waited and waited and hoped and hoped, until finally the holidays approached and I went listlessly down to Boca Raton, Florida. Where the phone at long last rang. But it wasn't Joe McCarthy. Sokolsky calling. George Sokolsky, my main rabbi. In hushed tones, George said, "Stay where you are, don't leave the phone, McCarthy's calling any minute." And hung up. He loved mystery, George did, and he was positively *devoted* to king-making. He was going to get me the job as Chief Counsel to McCarthy's Senate Investigating Committee, that was his contract, and all I had to do now was wait by the telephone. It was some contract. All I had in my way was Bobby Kennedy, whose old man was one of McCarthy's top supporters. But I had George, and who was the founding father next to George Sokolsky? Just ask George!

Or just ask me, though I wasn't thinking so positively as I waited for much longer than "any minute" for McCarthy's call. The fact was, however, that George had only a few months earlier put me across as special assistant for internal security to the attorney general of the United States.

In the summer of 1952, my doctor decided I needed a vacation, after three non-stop years in the courtroom. So I booked a trip with my mother on the maiden voyage of the *United States* to Europe, sailing on July 3. As the ship steamed down New York harbor I was summoned to the telephone room. I didn't even know ships had phones, that's how sophisticated I was at age 24. The call was from James P. McGranery, Truman's last attorney general and one of George's innumerable best friends. Sokolsky had mentioned something to me about working for McGranery but I hardly listened, much less took it seriously. Now McGranery wanted to know if I'd come to Washington to be his special assistant for internal security.

Flustered, I told McGranery that I was on my way to Europe for an international bar conference. He laughed. "One of those tax dodges, huh?" he said, in his gruff way. "How long you gonna be gone?" I said a month. He said, "Stay two weeks, then fly home. I'll expect you in Washington the very next day."

Judge Irving Kaufman was on the boat and I consulted him. He said not to do it, not to go near Washington. "It's a jungle there, all you'll get is aggravation and misery." As I would discover years later, Irving was exactly right about the capital, but I knew Irving and I figured he didn't want me to go because I'd get too much publicity there in a spot like that. So he clinched it for me. Two weeks later, I flew back with Mother and was in Washington on the appointed day. My father came too, and so did my friends in the press—I had the attorney general's ante-room packed with reporters and photographers waiting to record my swearing-in rites.

It didn't go over too well with McGranery's top honchos, particularly with his press chief, G. Frederick Mullen. Mr. Mullen was a dynamo of activity while we waited in the ante-room, and I noticed that he was buzzing over a press release with the attorney general's leading assistants. I didn't like the smell of it and I thought I'd better make a move or forever hold my peace. "Can I see the release?" I said. No answer, but very unfriendly glances. The attorney general came in, and I repeated my request. No answer. McGranery didn't seem to know what was happening. Again I asked to see it. Finally McGranery said, "Well, what's the secret? Show it to him. And by the way, show it to me, too."

The press release announced my appointment as an attorney in the internal security section of the Justice Department—a far cry from the man in charge, from what I had been promised. But McGranery said nothing. I had to think fast. If I let this go down I'd be a schmuck, I'd prove Irving Kaufman right, and right away. Plus I'd be nobody, I'd be finished to begin with. So I took the Eleventh Commandment: When in doubt, call Sokolsky.

George was livid. "That's the bureaucracy for you," he said, his voice rising in anger. "Before you're even there, they want to cut you down. Now listen to me. Go back into the room, tear up the press release, and say you're leaving, say there'll be no swearing-in."

I swallowed hard, thinking of my parents and the assembled

press. But I had to stick with who brought me here. I said, "All right, I'll do it. Do we all just leave then?"

George said, "No, of course not. Start to leave, yes. And as you're walking toward the door, the attorney general will call me on the phone—and when I get through with him, there will be a different scenario."

I did what he said, I tore up the release and I "apologized" to McGranery for how his staff had mishandled both of us. I started for the door. McGranery said, "Wait a minute. Wait a minute, please. Give me the courtesy of five minutes alone in my office and I'll have this all straightened out."

Ten minutes later, McGranery's private secretary came out and signaled to me. "There's an urgent call for you in the private office," she said.

George was all business. "O.K.," he said. "I just rewrote the release and Jim has accepted it. Go in there and take the oath."

With that history, I shouldn't have worried about a thing once Sokolsky said to sit by that phone, Kennedys or no Kennedys. And in a few minutes McCarthy was on the wire. "Roy," he said, "I'd like you to be chief counsel to my Senate Investigating Committee."

Bobby Kennedy, who had to settle for assistant counsel, never forgave me for landing the top job; he thought it was coming to him by birthright. In fact, birth was all he had going for him— and it was almost all he needed. Despite the fact that he never tried a case or conducted a hearing, that he had absolutely no experience in dealing with subversives, Joseph P. Kennedy pressured McCarthy relentlessly, and nobody could put on the heat like Papa Joe. He'd been a friend and confidant and big-scale contributor to McCarthy and now he was presenting all his markers for Bobby. Why didn't it work? I never asked McCarthy, but I have a theory or three.

I had the professional credentials—Remington, the Rosenbergs, the hundreds of convictions without an acquittal as assistant U.S. attorney, the short but important stint as special aide to McGranery. I had the backing of the Hearst papers, and of course I had Sokolsky, and Bob Morris, who was McCarthy's first choice for the job. I knew my way around the press and had a proven knack for public relations that had benefited by bosses and the cause of anti-Communism. And I was Jewish. Joe McCarthy was anything but an anti-Semite, he was a friend of the Jews and the new State of Israel. There was a growing slander abroad in the land, however, that McCarthy was a Jew-hater, and he was sensitive to it and outraged by it and he wanted to deflect it. I was the obvious answer, and the alternative—the son of the well-known, well-documented anti-Semite Joseph P. Kennedy, the former pro-Hitler ambassador to the Court of St. James's—was the last person McCarthy needed to head his committee.

And yet, I doubt that all of the above would have been enough to buck Joe Kennedy—had not Joe Kennedy already cashed in his ace marker on McCarthy. I refer to the 1952 senatorial election in Massachusetts, where John F. Kennedy was running against incumbent Senator Henry Cabot Lodge, Jr. In Massachusetts, McCarthy could have outpolled anybody but God, and he was "pick-em" against God, especially in certain sections of Beantown. It was urgent to keep McCarthy on the sidelines if young Jack was going to defeat the popular incumbent Lodge in a year that clearly promised a Republican landslide. Had McCarthy campaigned for Lodge, which Lodge desperately wanted, he'd have taken enough Catholic votes away from Kennedy to swing the election. But he stayed out, as a favor to Joe Kennedy, and Jack won by Joe McCarthy's five-o'clock shadow. Now, a month later, McCarthy didn't have to do anything grand for the founding father. So is history made, and so was I made. One wonders what the course of our country would have been had McCarthy gone into Boston and wiped out JFK? Or had he instead appointed Bobby as chief counsel. Would Bobby Kennedy have become a liberal icon had he been Joe McCarthy's right hand during his "witch-hunt."

I found out early on that Bobby was my enemy within the McCarthy committee. My source was one Francis D. ("Frip") Flanagan, the committee's "general counsel," a title I put in quotes advisedly. McCarthy inherited Flanagan, who'd been general counsel to this committee, formally known as the Senate

Subcommittee on Investigations, for years. Joe could have
dumped him, of course, but Frip had about a dozen kids, which
practically guaranteed him a lifetime job with McCarthy, who
loved children and was totally a softie when it came to these
things. Frip was an ex-FBI agent and a nice guy, but the only
argument I ever heard for keeping him around was that he had
all those kids. It was never a question of having all those brains.
Joe left him with his title and made Bobby Frip's assistant. It
made for a funny scene when Joe announced his appointments.
One of the reporters said, "Senator, Mr. Cohn has just been
confirmed as chief counsel, is that right?" Joe said, yes. "And
Bobby Kennedy is assistant chief counsel?" Joe said right. "And
Mr. Flanagan remains general counsel, is that correct?" Joe said
correct. And the reporter said, "Well, can you tell us, Senator,
what everybody is supposed to do, and who's in charge?" Joe
laughed and said, "I don't know, but you figure it out and then
let me in on it."

Anyway, one day somebody told me to talk to Frip Flanagan,
that he had some info for me. He sure did. He told me I had a
real enemy in Bobby Kennedy. I asked why. No particular reason, Frip said. I asked why again.

"Well," Frip said, "first of all, he isn't crazy about Jews. Second, you're not exactly a member of the Palm Beach polo set.
And thirdly, you've got the job he wanted."

I thought these were pretty strong reasons for a guy to dislike
me, and I got sort of leery of Bobby. Then one day the door
opened, my office door, and Bobby Kennedy was standing
there, alone. He just had pushed the door open but he hadn't
crossed the threshold. I said come in. He hesitated for a split
second and then he came in and I stood up and then I turned
around to sit down again and he was still standing.

"You know," Bobby said, "you're a real mystery man."

"I am?"

"Yes."

"Why, are you investigating me or something?"

"No. But some people, like Morton Downey [the Irish tenor
and Joe Kennedy's confidant], think you're the greatest guy.

Other people think you're a real danger to my career. I don't know who's right and who's wrong."

I didn't know what to say and I said so. "Am I supposed to make a confession or a denial, what do you expect me to say?"

Bobby just stood there, he looked me up and down as if he were shopping. I thought I was being measured for something.

I said, "I don't know what your career is or what you want it to be. But I have no interest in it pro or con, so you can forget about me, I can't be a danger to you if I'm not thinking about you. As far as what kind of guy I am, well I suppose in my own eyes I'm a rather nice guy. Somebody else might tell you the opposite."

Kennedy just stared at me, still measuring me, and then he turned and walked out of my office. A rather strange and poignant scene, I thought then and I think now. It was the only conversation I had with Bobby. He was supposed to be my assistant, but McCarthy had him working a separate vein, so I had no commerce with him. Bobby investigated the trans-shipment of American goods to Communist China and other Iron-Curtain nations. It was illegal here to trade with these countries; every flag ship had to sign documents swearing that none of the American goods picked up on our shores were going to Communist countries. What would happen, however, was that the Greeks would swear to it and would abide by the letter of the law. They'd simply take the goods to Portugal, and then another ship would pick the stuff up and move it to China. It was big business—and the British were particularly in it up to their necks—and nasty as hell considering that we were in the middle of the Korean Police Action and plenty of American munitions were going to Red China.

Bobby held some hearings—ironically, one of the people he cross-examined was Aristotle Onassis—and he did a good job. He showed that in the three years since the outbreak of the Korean hostilities western Allied trade with China and other Communist nations exceeded two billion dollars. But despite this shocking disclosure, it was becoming plain that the Eisenhower administration wasn't about to do anything to stop our wonderful

Allies from making money by trading with our enemies. So Bobby Kennedy composed a letter to Secretary of State Dulles for McCarthy's signature, that burned right off the page. I've written tough letters since, and read a few, but you can hope and wait and I guarantee you won't find one as rough as this baby Bobby worked up for Joe. It tongue-lashed the State Department and the White House and threatened to expose everybody concerned.

McCarthy was in Bethesda Naval Hospital for treatment of an old leg injury, but he was happy to sign the letter. Copy to the White House. Where it set off firecrackers.

Wrote White House Chief of Staff Sherman Adams in a memoir years later: "If Eisenhower answered it with a statement of policy regarding trade with the Communists, as McCarthy was demanding, he could avoid neither antagonizing the British nor stirring up criticism from anti-Communist groups at home." How get out of this muddle? Vice-President Nixon to the rescue. Nixon telephoned Joe at the hospital and Joe agreed to withdraw the letter. It was a shrewd move to use Dick Nixon for this contract. Joe would never have listened to anyone else in the Eisenhower administration. Not that he agreed with Nixon, he just did him a favor. Typical Joe McCarthy, and this time, one of the rare times, Ike's people figured him out right.

Anyhow, this was essentially all Bobby Kennedy ever did on the McCarthy committee, and although substantively it didn't come to much, this obviously wasn't Bobby's fault. He left the committee in July, 1953, and returned, as minority counsel, in time for the Army-McCarthy hearings. He wasn't finished with me—he was never finished with me—and as we'll see I wasn't finished with him.

People are forever asking me what I'd do differently if I had my life to live over again. I disappoint them, because I wouldn't change much, and most of those who ask this question appear eager to hear confessions. I have no sense of overriding guilt concerning my past, I look back with a clear conscience. But there is one thing I'd do different. I sure as hell wouldn't have taken that trip with my friend G. David Schine in the spring of 1953.

This journey to Europe, to check out the State Department's Information Program, was a worse public relations disaster for Dave and me and Senator McCarthy than the program we were investigating was for America. And that's saying a mouthful, since State's idea of promoting the U.S.A. was to flood its libraries with pro-Communist, anti-American books.

G. David Schine was an unpaid consultant to the McCarthy committee. His lack of salary had nothing to do with his value, only with his bank account and his patriotism. His family owned a chain of lucrative hotels and theatres, but as a young man recently out of Harvard, Dave was more interested in fighting Communism than in joining the Schine empire. He wrote a pamphlet, *Definition of Communism*, that defined his views, and in fine capitalistic fashion, he used the Schine chain as his distribution center. Every hotel room had it, the way others had the Gideon Bible. I met Dave in one of the Schine hotels in Florida, either the Roney Plaza in Miami Beach or The Boca Raton. I don't remember which, and I don't remember whether I read his pamphlet in my room. Both of us were about the same age and both of us were close to Walter Winchell, who always wintered at the Roney, so I suppose it was the Roney, if anybody cares. The thing was, we hit it off immediately, and I later encouraged him to join the McCarthy committee.

It was some favor I did him. He was clobbered on The Trip as a book burner, a junketeering gumshoe. He was the butt of cartoonists the world over, and jokes and jokesters—and worst of all, always in tandem with me. It was Cohn and Schine as in Abbott and Costello or Laurel and Hardy. And that was for starters. A year later, Dave was the apparent cause of the Army-McCarthy hearings. For lagniappe, the sensitive liberals who decried "McCarthyism" spread the rumor that Cohn and Schine were Jack and Jill, a slander that continues to this day, no matter that Dave married Miss Universe and is the father of seven children. That he has remained my friend, for all of this, is all that needs to be said about his character.

McCarthy sent us to Europe to find out what the International Information Administration was doing to put America's best foot forward in the fight for men's minds in the Free World. Millions were being spent by the State Department for this frankly propagandistic program and Joe was properly interested in what kind of bang we were getting for our bucks. We discovered quickly that what we were getting was banged. These overseas libraries were fairly teeming with anti-American, pro-Soviet books written by Communists and fellow-travelers. Conversely, very few anti-Communist books were stocked. It was scandalous and exactly opposed to the purpose of the libraries; but when the smoke cleared Dave and I turned out to be the scandal.

To show you how naive we were, we thought it was a routine trip, the kind congressmen take all the time, a fact-finding mission. It was about as routine as a liver transplant. Journalists followed us around like fireflies, our every move was recorded—with an inventiveness, complete with plot-turns, that made Hecht and MacArthur look like dullards. We were the Katzenjammer Kids with black hats, terrorizing good and decent State Department careerists, disrupting the diplomacy of the United States, destroying the Bill of Rights, the Declaration of Independence, while defacing Miss Liberty herself.

We were so fearsome we made people come up with great lines. As one State Department drone supposedly said to another, "See you tomorrow, come Cohn or come Schine."

Most of this stuff originated with the European press, which viewed McCarthy as the reincarnation of American isolationism. It was true that McCarthy was supported by many people—most notably Joe Kennedy—who had opposed American involvement in World War II. But Joe McCarthy was anything but an isolationist: his preoccupation was to keep Western Europe and Asia from falling to Communist control. His attacks on Truman, and now on Eisenhower's State Department, were based on the failure of America to achieve these goals. Any schoolboy should have known this, but what are facts in the face of hysteria? Only distortion grows in such soil, and when it comes to distortion nobody does it like the Brits.

Schine and I planned to make a visit to the BBC, where we

hoped to study the outstanding job the official British network had done in broadcasting behind the Iron Curtain. The English newspapers ran headlines that we were going to "investigate" the BBC! They raised such a tumult that the subject was brought up in Parliament, where a Laborite, one G. Wigg, rose in the Commons and asked the assistant postmaster general, whose department controlled the BBC: "Would the Honorable Gentleman extend to these gentlemen, [Cohn and Schine] the customary British welcome, but would he also assure them that we should regard it as thoroughly reprehensible that any visit to this country should be used as an occasion to gather evidence to prosecute and deliberately smear liberal-minded persons in America?"

The assistant postmaster general replied, "No application whatever has been made to the BBC or to the post office for any facilities for these two gentlemen."

Did this end the matter? The *Daily Mirror* screamed: "WITCH-HUNT BOYS GET COLD FEET." The *Daily Mail* ran with, "McCARTHY'S BOYS 'PUT OFF' BBC PROBE." And the *Manchester Guardian* reported upon our departure from London: "Mr. Cohn and Mr. Schine have arrived, investigated and departed. They landed at Northold shortly after two-o'clock and left punctually at eight, protesting to the last that they had never intended to investigate the BBC. . . ."

It was hardly news, of course, that the British establishment was soft on Communism. Dr. Klaus Fuchs, the key atomic scientist at Los Alamos—and a central figure in the Rosenberg spy case—gave a full confession to Scotland Yard, pleaded guilty, was given a slap on the wrist by the British courts and was later allowed to go in peace to East Germany. This has often been used by the Rosenberg revisionists to show how "brutal" the U.S. courts were in executing Julius and Ethel Rosenberg— consider how much more "civilized" are the British, goes the line. But the British, by this example, only exacerbated their (and the Free World's) problems, as witness the shocking Burgess-Maclean-Philby spy ring that surfaced in the late 1960's, and the revelations, quite more recently, of the traitor Sir Anthony Blount, who after *his* confession continued to be the cock-of-the-walk in his posh London clubs. One might hope that the Brits would learn from all of this, but instead they prefer to berate as "jingoists" all those who bring it to their attention.

If the British reaction to our trip was historically understandable, the same could not be said about the reception we got in West Germany from our own people. At least we had the right to expect that the office of the High Commissioner of Germany (HICOG) would be interested in promoting American interests, rather than in denigrating our country and propagating Communism. We expected much too much. The HICOG from the outset of our short trip spied on us, leaked lies and sought only to cover up its own pro-Commie backside.

As we discovered, they had plenty to hide.

Item. HICOG authorized and paid for the publication of a book entitled *Synchronoptische Weltgeschichte*, a world history written by two Germans, dealing with modern times and intended for wide use in German schools and for distribution by our State Department as a part of its information program to fight Communism. It was sheer Communist propaganda, extolling Stalin and Mao as "statesmen" and blasting Churchill as an "aristocrat" who "has tried to unite the states of Western Europe against the Soviet Union in dependence on the United States."

Item. HICOG subsidized the Frankfurt edition of the newspaper *Neue Zeitung*, installing as its editor Hans Wallenberg, who had backed the Communist line during the Hitler-Stalin Pact, and who now was using five active Communists as writers for the paper. This ran American taxpayers a bill in the millions each year. While HICOG was publishing its own newspaper in Frankfurt.

The man in charge of our information program in Germany was Theodore Kaghan, who held the auspicious title of Acting Deputy Director of the Office of Public Affairs of HICOG. Kaghan set the press against us, put an "escort officer" on us who daily leaked stories to the papers about our "exhorbitant spending" (I once picked up a $25 check for dinner for four, including this "escort" spy) and hit us with a name that smeared us as good as could be done. "Junketeering gumshoes," he called us and it hurt. But in the end, Kaghan couldn't avoid the consequences of what he had done to the image of America. The Communist "world history" was terminated, the money for *Neue Zeitung* was terminated, and in short order, Kaghan's resignation was accepted by State.

So we accomplished something, in substantive terms, and not only in Germany. The McCarthy committee unanimously backed our findings of Communist infiltration of our libraries, and the entire information program was redefined and clarified by order of President Eisenhower.

Why then did I say the one thing I wouldn't do again in life was take that trip with Dave Schine? Because we played directly into the hands of our enemies by allowing ourselves to be portrayed as a couple of Rover Boys, unshaven hit-men out to do in American Democracy. We weren't ready for the propaganda assault, we were indeed Innocents Abroad, and we thus harmed our cause, no matter that we saved millions of dollars and straightened out an insidious "propaganda" program.

Were we book burners? In a way, I guess we were. Confronted with more than thirty thousand works by Communists, fellow-travelers and unwitting promoters of the Soviet cause on the shelves of America's overseas libraries, we decided to do something about it. The whole purpose of these libraries and reading rooms was to sell America to Western Europe, that's what we were paying for. One could argue—but how many liberals did?—that this in itself was wrong, was jingoistic, was playing the Ugly American. But having made the decision to fight for the minds of men during the Cold War, why lead with our chin? Why beat up on America and extol totalitarianism? This wasn't the New York Public Library we were talking about, where free circulation of ideas is the reigning virtue. Our job, on behalf of the McCarthy committee, was to see that the taxpayers weren't footing the bill for anti-American propaganda. The issue was salesmanship, not censorship.

If that be book burning, so be it. But whosoever says so ought to be prepared to say the same about Harry Truman, who instituted the program with exactly the purpose in mind of selling America to Western Europe. And to Ike. As Robert Donovan wrote in *Eisenhower: The Inside Story*: "He was opposed to suppression of ideas. He believed, however, that the United States should not pay for books to be put on shelves abroad which advocated a system of government that would destroy the United States. Books advocating communism, he felt, should be excluded. . . ."

Who could argue the point? Well, you should have been in Europe for those thirteen days in April 1953 with Cohn and Schine.

Chapter Six

There was no more natural man for staff director of the Mc-
Carthy committee than J.B. Matthews, the Methodist minister
who had practically invented the House Un-American Activities
Committee in 1938 and whose name was synonymous with anti-
Communism. Yet within two weeks of his appointment by
McCarthy, J.B. Matthews had brought down on our heads the
Protestant clergy, the National Conference of Christians and
Jews, the Democrats and Republicans in Congress, and the
White House itself. I guess everybody but the Teamsters
Union, and nobody bothered to poll the Teamsters, so maybe
them too.

One sentence did it, but what a sentence it was. In the July,
1953, *American Mercury*, Matthews led off an article with this
gem: "The largest group supporting the Communist apparatus
in the United States today is composed of Protestant clergymen." As it turned out, Matthews never wrote the line, but
nothing was as it appeared to be in this strange scenario.

The wire services picked up the story before the magazine hit the stands, and it didn't take a genius to know it would be an instant *cause célèbre*. Clearly, Matthews had to be off-the-wall to hit the Protestant clergy with this broad-brush. I was startled, and worried, and so was McCarthy. He said to me, "The clergy, better than any other group, know that Marxism can't be reconciled with religious faith."

But once we read the entire piece in *American Mercury*, which of course had been written before Matthews was hired, we thought we could shrug it off as a mere *contretemps*. The article, about 4,000 words long, pointed out that only a small minority—7,000 out of 250,000 ministers, or 2.8 percent—were Red-tainted and most of these were innocent dupes of Communists. Matthews explicitly stated that "the vast majority of American Protestant clergymen are loyal to the free institutions of this country and to their solemn trust as ministers of the Gospel."

Of course, nobody cared about the rest of the article. Who reads the second sentence? The heat was on and it was coming from everywhere, including some of McCarthy's most fervent supporters, who wanted him to dump Matthews without further ado. The Democratic minority on the McCarthy committee jumped at the opening and were at Joe like sharks at a pool party. McCarthy said to me, "You better handle this yourself." He wasn't about to jettison Matthews. He was loyal to a fault. I took his words to mean, "Check it out up and down and see how we can save the guy."

The first thing Matthews told me was that he didn't write the lead, that it was edited-in by Jack Clements, who ran *American Mercury*. Matthews said he didn't know about the editing until he read the magazine, and that when he called Clements on it, Clements said he had "reworded" the lead to give the article greater impact. As soon as I heard this, I asked Jack Clements to come to Washington to talk this thing over.

McCarthy was at the meeting, but he wanted me to take charge so I put the question directly to Jack Clements. "Did you write this opening line in without consulting with Matthews?" He said yes. He didn't hesitate. I thought to myself, fine, this is going to be easy. Clements, after all, had asked Matthews to do the article, *American Mercury* was on our side 100 percent, and now Clements was man enough, in front of McCarthy and Matthews, to say he had made up this lead sentence.

"Well, then, Jack," I said, "we seem to have no problem. Just write out a brief statement saying that you rewrote the lead in the mistaken but honest belief that it was true to J.B. Matthews' position, but that now you're convinced it was not what the author meant. You can say that you tried to check it out with Dr. Matthews, but you couldn't reach him and deadline pressures caused the error. O.K.?"

To my amazement, Clements turned me down cold.

"Can't do it," he said. "It would destroy the credibility of *American Mercury.*"

"C'mon, Jack," I said. "The magazine will survive this and so will you. I think the way I outlined it, it will sound like an error in judgment, honestly arrived at during deadline pressure."

"No chance," he said. "Forget it. Sorry. But that's it."

I blew up. I told him he was a coward, that he had no right to sit back while another man was being ruined because of what he wrote and the other man hadn't even seen. It's a matter of human decency, I said. But Clements didn't have the capacity to understand human decency.

Afterwards, I discussed with Matthews the possibility of him giving a statement, but he said nobody would believe it. He was right, of course. Even if Clements had issued a statement we'd have had to produce the manuscript with his writing on it, the way everybody was going after us on this story.

Even so, McCarthy wanted to keep Matthews, the last thing he wanted was to throw him to the dogs. One of Joe's great qualities and great strengths—maybe it was the finest thing about him—was his loyalty to people who worked for him. And it extended to all those in and out of the government who provided him and the committee with information—often at the risk of their careers or even criminal prosecution. Nobody who ever gave stuff to Joe McCarthy was given up, nobody, no way. Which is why he had the greatest network of informants in the history of the Senate.

But the hullabaloo over Dr. Matthews was too much, the dogs

already had Matthews. Joe didn't worry about his enemies, his enemies would have guaranteed Matthews his job forever. The trouble was, the article violated so many of his friends. The Protestant clergy were the main supporters of Communism in the United States? And now Matthews couldn't deny it without looking like a liar.

Finally, McCarthy told me what had to be done. We were on a plane flying up to New York from Washington. "I want to talk to you about Matthews," he said. I said, "What do you think?" He said, "Get him out of here. Don't let anybody know I did anything to move him out. I'll express shock and I'll say I want to reject his resignation. Fix it up that way. But get him out."

J.B. Matthews was a perfect gentleman. He knew it wasn't me asking him to go, a 26-year-old kid, but he said nothing against McCarthy, he simply agreed and signed his resignation letter on the spot. Had we released it at once, I probably wouldn't be writing about this incident today. What we didn't know was that the White House was on the verge of setting up a public hanging for Matthews. Or rather for Joe. The White House didn't give a damn about Matthews, only Joe. In the event, they beat us to the presses by minutes.

What happened was this. Emmet John Hughes, Ike's principal speech writer, and Deputy Attorney General William Rogers (later Nixon's Secretary of State) arranged a telegram of protest to be sent by the National Conference of Christians and Jews to Eisenhower concerning the appointment of Matthews, signed by clergymen from Notre Dame, the Union of Hebrew Congregations, and the Presbyterian Church.

Since Hughes was worried about time—McCarthy could get wise any minute to the public outrage over Matthews and fire him—he pushed Sherman Adams, Ike's Chief of Staff, to draft a reply to this set-up letter from the Reverend Clergy. And the reply was there, on Hughes's desk, before the telegram arrived from the National Conference of Christians and Jews.

There was only one problem. Nobody had informed Eisenhower. So now they had the reply, they had the telegram, but they didn't have Ike's signature. What they did have, was word that McCarthy was about to announce the resignation of Matthews, it was buzzing all over Capitol Hill.

Rogers frantically called Hughes at the White House. "For God's sake," he said, "we have to get that message out fast, or McCarthy will beat us to the draw." The whole plot would have gone up in smoke had we gotten the word out first. Everything was arranged to make it appear that McCarthy had knuckled under, that he was firing his old friend in response to Eisenhower's reply to the National Conference of Christians and Jews. But how to arouse Ike in time? This was always tough, whether the President was sitting feet on desk in his office or playing golf.

To buy the needed minutes, Nixon was put on the case, good old reliable Dick. He buttonholed Joe in the Senate Office Building and kept him in conversation about all sorts of crap—it was never hard to keep Joe talking—until Hughes signalled the all clear to Rogers who gave the sign to Nixon. Just in time, because Joe was on his way to give the story of Matthews' resignation to our friend Fulton Lewis, Jr., for his radio broadcast.

So the story came out the way the White House wanted it. McCarthy had bowed to the pressure of the good men of the Eisenhower administration, to all good men and true of the National Conference of Christians and Jews.

It was a brilliant maneuver, and we were caught short. Does it sound like invention, a paranoic fantasy of mine? Well, I didn't know the details until I read them ten years later. In Emmet Hughes's book, *The Ordeal of Power*.

In the event, the Matthews affair didn't harm McCarthy with the public, for all the administration's stratagems and deceptions. Six months later Joe had a 50 percent approval rate in the Gallup Poll with only 29 percent opposed. But if we had known how the White House had set up this telegram, we could have been helped by the case. We might have anticipated the extent to which Ike was willing to go to get Joe—and that might have saved us in the Army-McCarthy hearings a year later.

There was a bizarre footnote to the Matthews story, for which I don't depend on secondary sources like Emmet Hughes, you should forgive the expression. This one was me alone, me and

Ayn Rand, the author of *The Fountainhead* and *Atlas Shrugged*. Miss Rand was of course the New Moses of the Right and I was properly impressed when she pulled me aside at a Georgetown cocktail party and said, "You're late." I said sorry. She said, "I've waited for you. I knew you'd come and I wanted to meet you. There's a question I must ask. But not here. We must have lunch, soonest." I said sure.

She came right to the point, I didn't have a chance to order a drink. "Why did Joe McCarthy sell out to the Communist party?" Just like that.

I laughed, but she repeated the question, which was an accusation, no fooling around.

I said, "Lady, I don't know if you've been drinking this morning, but otherwise there'd be no good explanation of why you'd make this statement."

"The Matthews case," Ayn Rand said, all business.

"Huh?"

"He sold out J.B. Matthews to the Communists. I want to know why!"

I said, "Miss Rand, if that's what you want to believe . . ."

"I *know* it," she shot back. "I want to know *why*."

"I'm telling you it's pure baloney what you're saying. Ideologically, McCarthy is one hundred percent with Matthews, that's why he hired him. He didn't create the situation, he was forced into getting rid of Matthews, there was no way out."

"The Commies got to Joe, and you're protecting him."

Well, it was quite a lovely lunch.

I saw Ayn Rand a couple of more times over the years. Each time she'd wave her finger at me and say, "You're going to tell me the truth some day." The poor lady went to her grave believing that the Communist party reached McCarthy and that's why J.B. Matthews had to go. Oh well, nobody's perfect.

McCarthy put a question to the United States Army in December, 1953, for which neither he nor the country ever got an answer. But it was probably the most popular question of its time, and before much time was up the pursuit of the answer led Joe and the committee down alleys and up highways and through biways that finally culminated in the great Army-McCarthy hearings which glued 20 million Americans to their TV sets for 36 afternoons in the spring of 1954.

And the question was, "Who promoted Peress?"

The subject was a 36-year-old Queens dentist named Irving Peress, a round-faced slightly balding fellow who had applied for a commission in the Army in the spring of 1952. As part of his application, he certified that he was "not and never had been a member of any foreign or domestic organization, association, movement, group, or a combination of persons advocating a subversive policy or seeking to alter the form of Government of the United States by unconstitutional means." This certification was required by the Doctors Draft Act of 1950—a point that should be noted by the revisionists who claim that everything that ever happened that they didn't like concerning loyalty oaths began with McCarthy. McCarthy had nothing to do with this, though he would have approved of it, obviously; this was all good old liberal Harry Truman's doing and bless him for it.

Anyway, after Peress got his captaincy in the Army Dental Corps he had to fill out another Defense Department form, a loyalty certification. But here he took the Fifth Amendment on three separate questions regarding membership in certain subversive organizations. Nonetheless, he was ordered to active duty effective January 1, 1953, and assigned to Brooke Army Medical Center at Fort Sam Houston, Texas. After four weeks of basic training he was ordered to proceed to Fort Lewis, Washington, for further assignment to the Far East command at Yokohama, Japan. When his wife and six-year-old daughter took sick, Peress received emergency leave and he never did go to Japan. While home he applied for and received reassignment to Camp Kilmer, New Jersey, 30 miles from New York.

Meanwhile, First Army's G-2 (Intelligence) had received Peress's loyalty forms and ordered an investigation into why he had taken the Fifth. After investigating him, G-2 recommended to the Pentagon that Irving Peress be dismissed from the Army as a security risk. But the Army apparently couldn't find Irving Peress. The file traveled around the country looking for him— for nine months.

While this journey to nowhere was proceeding, Captain Peress wrote a letter (dated September 9, 1953) requesting a promotion to major. Under the law he was entitled to an automatic promotion based on his age and experience. On October 23, he got it. Who promoted Peress? The order was signed by Maj. Gen. William E. Bergin, "By Order of the Secretary of the Army." But that was bureaucracy, pure and simple. And bureaucracy pure and simple had missed up on a letter dated two days earlier from Brig. Gen. Ralph W. Zwicker, commanding officer of Camp Kilmer. Zwicker recommended that Peress be relieved from duty without delay.

So here was Peress's own C.O. asking for his head, while the Army promoted him.

So what? Who could care less if a dentist got promoted? Does a cavity have politics?

Later, liberal jokesters would have fun with these questions. But what this showed was the incredible laxity of Army security. It was this same type of laxity during World War II that permitted David Greenglass to be taken into the Army and assigned to the A-bomb project at Los Alamos, where he was perfectly positioned to turn the secret of the bomb over to his sister and brother-in-law, the Rosenbergs. Now, ten years later, nothing had changed with the Army. Only the security of the United States was in greater danger than ever before.

Obviously, nobody was suggesting that Stalin had dropped a dentist into Camp Kilmer. It wasn't Irving Peress we were interested in, but those in the Army who had ignored his Communist background and permitted his promotion. If it could happen to a dentist, it could happen to a scientist, and while the point was clear to everybody it didn't stop the establishment pundits (like Richard Rovere) from attempting to trivialize the issue by playing on the bicuspids.

Yet nothing could show the importance of the case more than naming the man who tipped McCarthy to Peress. Joe, true to his code, never revealed his identity, though as we shall see, the provocation was extreme. I do it now because confidentiality is no longer relevant and in light of what happened later the revelation is historically important. The leaker was none other than General Ralph Zwicker, whose famous (or infamous) confrontation with Joe made him a hero to all of McCarthy's enemies and led inevitably to the big showdown between the Eisenhower administration and McCarthy.

In the beginning, however, it was Zwicker who, convinced that the Army was planning a full-scale coverup of its scandalous security system, alerted McCarthy to the Peress case. And he did it in a way that dramatized the sick bureaucratization of the United States Army: he had McCarthy call him at a pay phone!

Here was a hero of World War II, one of the top generals in the nation, afraid to talk on his own telephone. And the cloak-and-dagger stuff continued. After he gave Joe the brief outline of the case, I was dispatched to get fully debriefed by Zwicker's young aide. Not at Camp Kilmer. At the bar of the Sherry-Netherland Hotel in New York.

Immediately afterwards I spoke to John G. Adams, the counsel to the Army, giving him Peress's name. A few days later, Adams told me he had checked it all out and was taking action. McCarthy said fine, we'd leave it to the Army, at least for a while; we'd see what they'd do with this. It was early December, 1953. By the end of January, when nothing had happened—and Joe hardly missed a day asking me what was up about Peress—McCarthy said to me: "I don't believe the Army is planning to do a damned thing. The committee has to move on it now. Have a subpoena served on Peress."

On January 30, Major Peress appeared before us in executive session. And took the Fifth on every question.

Two days later, two things happened. Peress met with General Zwicker and requested an immediate honorable discharge from the Army. And McCarthy (who didn't know about this request) sent a letter to Secretary of the Army Robert Stevens suggesting a thorough investigation by the Army to determine who was responsible for the Peress commission and promotion, with court martials to follow, and the court martial of Peress.

Stevens was traveling in the Far East, so the matter was handled by John Adams. On February 1, after we learned of the

possible immediate honorable discharge, we urged Adams to reject this route. On February 2, Major Peress got his honorable
discharge.

Joe was furious. He caught the returned Stevens at his home
that night and let him have it right between the eyes. "You're
trying to cover up a scandal, Bob, and I won't have it, you're not
going to get away with this, Bob." He told me, "When those
bastards want to move fast, they can shuffle those papers quicker
than you can see them."

McCarthy, of course, never wasted time, and on February 18
he opened hearings in New York. At the public session that
morning, Irving Peress's Communist activities were detailed by
Ruth Eagle, a New York City policewoman. Miss Eagle, a cop
for eleven years, had for the past two and a half years posed as a
member of the Communist party on special undercover assignment from the Police Department. She testified that Peress had
acted as a liaison between a Communist cell and the American
Labor party; that he submitted lists to her of ALP members who
were Communists and other ALP members whom he was
organizing; and that he attended the Leadership Training
Course of the Communist party.

In the afternoon we went into executive session to hear General Zwicker. We had every reason to believe Zwicker would be
a cooperative witness. Not only was he the one who tipped
McCarthy to Peress (as if that wouldn't have been enough reason) but a few days before the hearing Zwicker told our chief in-
vestigator, former FBI agent Jim Juliana, that he was opposed to
giving Peress an honorable discharge and that he had been in
communication with the Pentagon on the case. Plus, at lunch,
just before his testimony, he couldn't have been more amiable
and friendly to Joe. Zwicker would tell us who was responsible
for the outrageous mishandling of the case, no doubt about it.

Well, you trust and the next thing you need is a truss. Zwicker
suddenly knew nothing, except how to back and fill and dissem-
ble and lie. First he said that on the day Peress got his honorable
discharge he (Zwicker) didn't know that Peress had refused to
answer any questions before the McCarthy committee. Then he

conceded he knew that much, but he said he didn't know the questions referred to Communism.

McCarthy: "General, let's try and be truthful. I am going to keep you here as long as you keep hedging and hawing."

Zwicker: "I am not hedging."

McCarthy: "Or hawing."

Zwicker: "I am not hawing and I don't like to have anyone impugn my honesty, which you just about did."

McCarthy: "Either your honesty or your intelligence. I can't help impugning one or the other, when you tell us that a major in your command who was known to you to have been before a Senate committee, and of whom you read the press releases very carefully—to now have you sit here and tell us that you did not know whether he refused to answer questions about Communist activities. I had seen all the press releases, and they all dealt with that. So, when you do that, General, if you will pardon me, I cannot help but question either your honesty or your intelligence. One or the other. I want to be very frank with you on that."

Later McCarthy asked Zwicker a "hypothetical question," which encompassed all the facts involved in the Peress case, centering on what Zwicker would do about a general who ordered an honorable discharge for a man who had taken the Fifth when confronted with evidence of serious Communist activities.

Zwicker plainly didn't want to answer it, and began moving and ducking and playing will-o'-the-wisp. McCarthy decided to pin him.

McCarthy: "All right. You will answer that question, unless you take the Fifth Amendment. I do not care how long we stay here, you are going to answer it."

Zwicker: "Do you mean how I feel toward Communists?"

McCarthy: "I mean exactly what I asked you, General, nothing else. And anyone with the brains of a five-year-old child can understand that question. The [Committee] reporter will read it to you as often as you need to hear it."

Zwicker: "Start it over, please."

After the reporter read the question, Zwicker finally answered. "I do not think he should be removed from the military."

Joe exploded. Face flushed, his voice rising, he leaned toward Zwicker and said: "Then, General, you should be removed from any command. Any man who has been given the honor of being promoted to general and who says 'I will protect another general who protected Communists' is not fit to wear that uniform, General. I think it's a tremendous disgrace to the Army to have this sort of thing given to the public. I intend to give it to them. I have a duty to do that. I intend to repeat to the press exactly what you said. So you know that. You will be back here, General."

The outburst plagued McCarthy the rest of his life. His enemies were able to use his harsh words against this war hero for every phony reason under the sun. Not the least of which was to give a patina of legitimacy to that fake of all fakes, the Army-McCarthy hearings.

Of course, he was right about Zwicker, just as he was right about the underlying principle involved in the case. But it was, on its face, a political blunder of the first order—and as we'll see, it becomes more astonishing in light of what McCarthy knew about the forces who at that moment were poised to cut him down.

Was it a mere temper tantrum? But for all his famous outbursts he was always in fine control of his emotions. Was he a self-destructive, hyper-driven nutball? Forget about it.

The answer lies in the genesis of the Peress affair. Zwicker brought the case to Joe. Now Zwicker had instantly turned into an ass-covering bureaucrat. Somebody, therefore, had reached Zwicker, had scared the hell out of him. What made this unacceptable to Joe—who otherwise would not have been slightly surprised—was that he couldn't blow the whistle on Zwicker. Because Joe's underground was sacred to him, he had never given anybody up who provided him with information about the Communist menace, or perfidy in government, or anything else, for that matter.

So when Zwicker turned on him, McCarthy had no outlet for

his frustration—except to call Zwicker unfit to wear the uniform. And a good part of the reason he was unfit was that he violated the honored position of a McCarthy underground fighter.

I never asked McCarthy if this was it, because until now I never put the whole thing together. But it makes sense, doesn't it make sense? And nothing else makes sense.

Substantively, McCarthy was totally vindicated in the Peress affair. Two weeks after Zwicker's appearance, President Eisenhower admitted that the Army had made "serious errors" in handling the case and promised that the Army would make the necessary reforms so as "to avoid such mistakes in the future." Then Charles E. Wilson, the Secretary of Defense, said that Peress should never have been commissioned, and thus not promoted and should not have received an honorable discharge. The Pentagon then thoroughly overhauled its security regulations to prevent another Peress case. As Secretary of the Army Stevens explained to the Armed Services Committee: " . . . First, any person known to be disloyal or subversive will not knowingly be taken into service either in a commissioned or enlisted grade. Second, a person in the service found to be disloyal or subversive will be discharged. Third, if any person while in the service commits subversive acts, he will be brought to trial by court-martial . . ."

The brass weren't happy about this result, to say the least. Nor was it our first run-in with the Army. Between August, 1953—four months before the Peress case began—and October, 1954, we held extensive hearings concerning the security system at the Signal Corps installation at Fort Monmouth, hard by Camp Kilmer in Jersey. We heard 71 witnesses in executive sessions and 41 at open hearings. These were bitterly criticized by the Army and the establishment press: it was, we were told, a waste, a farce, a fruitless exercise, because we uncovered no active espionage ring, we produced no Rosenberg protégés, no masterminds at work funneling our secrets to the Kremlin.

McCarthy, admittedly, brought much of this on by making overblown claims, as was often his wont. He told the newspapers that the Monmouth investigation "has all the earmarks of extremely dangerous espionage," and ominously suggested that Julius Rosenberg himself had created a spy operation at Monmouth that "may still be in operation."

While we did not produce another Rosenberg, we uncovered a system so dangerously lax that the civilian personnel employed by the Army had been infiltrated by subversives, that this infiltration extended to the secret radar laboratories at Monmouth, and that the FBI for years had been warning Army officials of people with Communist affiliations at work in the secret installations.

The Army was hardly cooperative. In fact the brass did all it could to block the investigation. Except for one man, Major General Kirke B. Lawton, the commanding officer. General Lawton helped us every way he could to expose Communist infiltration in his command. But the Pentagon took care of Lawton. As soon as they recognized that he was aiding us, they ordered him to report to Walter Reed Hospital for a medical examination. Where he was found to have a physical disability he never knew about. After several weeks of confinement to elaborate and comfortable quarters, Kirke Lawton was given a "disability" discharge from the U.S. Army.

So the Army didn't like us to begin with and now that we had the imprimatur of the Eisenhower administration in the Peress case, they seethed with resentment. They weren't going to let McCarthy get away with being right, or what's a military establishment for? Let the Pentagon admit "errors"; the Army would jump on Joe's miscue in the Zwicker case.

As it turned out, the Army had plenty of allies. Right there in the Eisenhower administration. Right there at the top. The highest levels, as they say.

Chapter Seven

In the eyes of the Eisenhower administration and the bi-partisan congressional leadership, McCarthy, as 1954 approached, was a rolling hand grenade. Hardly a day went by when he wasn't at Ike, whom he considered a lightweight without the stomach to fight Communism. And when he wasn't at Ike he was at Ike's people, his hero George Marshall, and his old comrade-at-arms Zwicker, the whole damn Pentagon put together. The Democrats were of course guilty of presiding over "twenty years of treason." Now Eisenhower, as his first year ended, was added in, it was "twenty-one years of treason." And now the Republicans were labeled as the party of "appeasement, retreat, and surrender." Not all Republicans, just the Eisenhower wing, but there it was. And while Joe never meant any of this literally, his popularity was so high that none of the hyperbolic targets were smiling it off; you couldn't convince them that McCarthy was just trying to wake up the American people. They feared him as the most charismatic politician since FDR, a man who was a sure thing to influence the off-year elections of '54; if nobody stopped him he'd likely bring a right-wing Republican bloc to Congress, at the expense of the Democrats and the liberal Republicans. Where he would go from there . . . that question shook them, the White House, the two-party Establishment and their sycophantic press. It shook them out of their Brooks Brothers shoulders.

What to do? Maybe they saw open warfare at the end of the line, but they were afraid of it and I'm sure they didn't even want to think that way, not right away anyway. So in the waning months of 1953, a couple of efforts were made at what you might call accommodation.

The first, a kind of passing shot, was told to me by George Sokolsky. Milton Eisenhower, the President's intellectual brother, arranged a Manhattan lunch with George and it was obvious from the outset that he had been sent by the White House, if not by Ike himself. All he talked about was Joe, and finally he made the pitch. "What can be done to work things out?" Knowing, of course, how close George was to McCarthy. But George cooled him, let him know that Joe was not in the mood for deals, he wanted the White House to help him root out Communists in the Army and the government-at-large. So Milton went home empty-handed, and it really was an amateur set up. I mean, did they think it could be done on that level?

Well, it didn't take long before they came at Joe directly, or at least more directly. We went to a party, Joe and I, at Bazy Tankersley's house—Bazy being Mrs. Ruth McCormick Tankersley, publisher of the Washington *Times-Herald*, and niece of Col. Robert McCormick, publisher of the Chicago *Tribune*. By pre-arrangement, and at his request, White House aide I. Jack Martin was at the party. He had called Joe and said he wanted to talk to him somewhere away from Capitol Hill. Bazy's house was perfect, a big suburban house, and Bazy was an old friend of McCarthy's. Martin, a jovial guy with a famous sense of humor, was a trusted White House liaison man and troubleshooter. He had been the administrative aide to Senator Robert Taft, and after Taft's death, the administration grabbed him to handle the conservative Republicans on the Hill.

As soon as we walked into the party, Jack Martin grabbed Joe and took him downstairs for a private confab. Twenty minutes later, Martin looked like the greeter at the mortuary. Joe was jovial. He took me aside, and said: "This one really takes the cake. Poor Jack has to give blood to Ike or he'll be out of a job. Listen to the deal they offered me: stop all public hearings and hold only executive sessions. The minutes of the executive sessions will be taken to Ike personally. He will read them closely and take what they call 'appropriate action' on the administrative level against the people named in the testimony."

I said, "What'd you tell him?"

McCarthy replied, "It was rough. I thought about it for almost a full second before I told him no."

It was an incredible proposition from any vantage point. Governmentally, *constitutionally*, it was unthinkable. The whole point of our system of checks and balances would be destroyed by a deal that would have a Senate investigations committee cut out the public and submit its findings only to the executive branch it was created to investigate. McCarthy told this to Martin and added that given Ike's outlook the findings would find their way only to the President's wastebasket.

Politically, the notion was so unrealistic, so crazy as to make one wonder whether the White House was *compos mentis*. Here was McCarthy, riding high on an issue so close to the American people as to dominate household talk in the country, forget about the Congress. And Eisenhower apparently thought that at this moment, Joe McCarthy would capitulate. It made me worry plenty about what he was thinking the Russians would do.

On the way home that night, Joe said his "No!" would infuriate Ike. "I guess I'll just have to lead a life deprived of tea and watercress sandwiches on the White House lawn," he laughed. I laughed with him. Little did either of us know that they were about to prepare something quite unlike a tea party for us. Well, maybe like the Boston Tea Party.

They seem always to come at you from a place you least likely expect. With us, it was G. David Schine. When he came to work for the committee, at my behest, Dave was 4-F, owing to a slipped disc. In the fall of '53, during the Fort Monmouth hearings, Drew Pearson, that old implacable foe of Joe, moved that disc right up Dave's backside—and ours. Pearson pushed Schine's draft board in California to reopen the case and in November Dave was ordered into service. And Dave wanted to go, he was never comfortable with the 4-F classification. It was my idea that he apply for a commission and in the meantime complete his pending work with us. I shoulda stood in bed, the way things worked out.

But it made every kind of sense—if you were living in a vacuum. Dave was a natural for a commission, and if he hadn't been working for McCarthy he'd have been an automatic. Consider it: Schine was a Harvard graduate, he'd served two years in the U.S. Merchant Marine, he had run a large business and had worked effectively for a congressional committee. The average guy didn't need a quarter of those credentials to earn a commission, even the average Communist.

I often wonder where we'd all have been if Irving Peress had somehow managed to slip into the McCarthy committee rather than the Army, and then Drew Pearson had jumped on his case. Certainly, in view of what happened to Dave, Peress would never have been commissioned. And so nobody could have promoted Peress, at least not to more than sergeant.

They drafted Dave as a private and put him in Fort Dix. His application for a commission was routed through what ordinarily would be considered normal channels. That is to say, the Defense Department kept a staff on Capitol Hill for the sole purpose of processing applications for commissions from legislators, administration officials and others on behalf of people they believed qualified. So McCarthy put Dave's papers through, and I followed up on it. Ordinary, right? Like the shot at Fort Sumter.

The first warning I got about impending trouble came from Senator Stuart Symington, the Missouri Democrat who sat on the McCarthy committee and whom Joe would label, during the Army-McCarthy hearings, "Sanctimonious Stu," a savage but all-too-true sobriquet that poor Symington never could shed. But this "happening" I'm about to describe came months earlier, in January 1954 in Symington's office. I don't remember why I went in to meet with him, but the rest I remember like yesterday.

Symington gave me what Damon Runyon would have called a "hundred dollar hello" and motioned me to a chair beside his desk. He was a tall, imposing figure, a handsome man whom everybody said "looked like a president." What this meant, what it always has to mean, is that he looked like a Hollywood version of a president, the way Gregory Peck looks like a president. (McCarthy saw something different; he somehow spotted Symington as movie light-comedy star Gig Young, and in these insights nobody was better than Joe.)

Anyway, after seating me, Symington walked to the door, closed it carefully, returned to his desk, leaned forward slightly, looked at me steadily, paused dramatically and said: "Crossfire." Very softly. "Crossfire." I said nothing, I didn't know what the hell he was talking about. He waited a few seconds and said it again, ever so softly. "Crossfire."

I said, "Senator, I gather this is supposed to mean something to me, but it doesn't register. Could you tell me—I mean—what is this all about?"

He leaned toward me again, raising his voice slightly, as if I hadn't heard him. And said, "You have to worry about a crossfire."

I laughed nervously. "I'm afraid, Senator, that I just haven't a clue."

"Now, you're a bright young man," he said. "Soon you're going to know what I mean." And then once again, "Crossfire."

He walked me to the door and his good-bye was: "Be careful, you may be caught in the crossfire."

I said, not knowing what else to say, "Is there anything I can do?"

Symington said, "If you can, I'll let you know."

A few days later, he phoned me at Park Avenue, where I lived with my parents when I wasn't in Washington. He didn't say hello, he didn't say his name. He said only, "Resign."

"Resign, Senator? Why should I resign?"

"Crossfire." And hung up.

It made my day.

I didn't find out what "crossfire" was all about until late February. But within a couple of weeks, the Dave Schine angle came into focus. First because of rather insistent needling about Schine and his Army career by the Democrats on the committee; and later a major escalation by the administration.

Aside from Symington, the other Democrats on the committee were John McClellan of Arkansas and Henry "Scoop" Jackson of Washington State. With the new year, they were back in attendance for the first time since July, where they had walked out over the J.B. Matthews affair. It was phony as a three-dollar bill, this walkout, it was strictly for publicity; they were trying to make hay out of our embarrassment over J.B.'s trouble. The reason they gave was that Joe was "domineering," as if they just found out that he was the chairman. But walk they did, and so they weren't around for the Monmouth hearings or the Peress case. Now they were back, and with their very own minority counsel, Robert F. Kennedy, Esq. And what they wanted us to do—McClellan actually asked Joe for this—was to end the Army investigation altogether. That was of course out of the question. So they took to bugging me about Dave Schine and the so-called "undue pressure" I was putting on the Army on his behalf.

From beginning to end, from top to bottom, it was baloney, this charge that I was seeking favored status for Dave Schine, that I was threatening to "wreck" the Army through the McCarthy investigations if the Army didn't bow to my will and "take care" of my "buddy." The facts were the opposite: the Army decided to block Dave's commission in retaliation for his work on our committee and was using him as hostage in an effort to stop our investigation of the Army.

Did I make calls on his behalf? Certainly. More than usual? Certainly. Was I sometimes harsh in my talks with Pentagon bureacrats? Certainly. Was I looking for "preferential treatment" for "my pal"? Certainly *not*. I was looking for ordinary treatment for Schine, the same treatment anybody off the street would get. But the Army had blackmail in mind. That's why I made the "too many" calls and used "too tough" language. Yes, Dave was my friend, I had brought him into the committee, where he had done yeoman work for no pay, and now he was being punished by Army brass and who-knew-who-else because of it, which is to say because of me. I'd have been less than human if I didn't try to straighten out this injustice. What would *you* have done?

Here's what they did.

John Adams, counsel to the Army, a guy who was tight with me, who talked all the time about going into law practice with me in New York, spent three hours with Joe McCarthy on the night of January 22, 1954, at McCarthy's home. I was taking a few days in the Florida sun, a little R & R from Irving Peress and the Fort Monmouth investigations.

As soon as Adams left McCarthy's house, Joe called me. He said that Adams had started the conversation by asking Joe to cancel the subpoenas we had served on the members of the Army's Loyalty and Security Screening Board. We naturally wanted to question the members to find out how security risks like Peress managed to get through the supposedly tough barriers erected by the administration. Adams told Joe that the Eisenhower people considered the subpoenas as an attack on the authority of the executive branch, that what we were attempting here was to control the board's decisions. This was nonsense, and Joe told him so, but soon it was clear that Adams had other fish to fry.

When it got down to the dirty, Adams put it like this:

1. I was to get out, and the investigation of the Army was to cease.

2. If we refused, we would be destroyed by a report on my "improprieties" in the Schine matter.

3. If we agreed, there'd be no problem in giving Dave Schine a soft berth in the Army.

Joe gave him no definitive reply, but he gave me one on the phone that night. No. And promptly no. But Joe was disturbed. "This has got to be coming from the top," he said.

He was right, though we wouldn't know how on-target he was until well into the McCarthy-Army hearings. Thus it turned out that the night before Adams met with McCarthy, there was a secret conference in Attorney General Herbert Brownell's office. It was run by Ike's chief of staff, Sherman Adams, and was attended by UN Ambassador Henry Cabot Lodge, Deputy Attorney General William Rogers, White House Assistant Gerald Morgan, and John Adams himself.

It was here that Sherman Adams (later to be disgraced by revelations that he took a vicuna coat from a Mr. Bernard Goldfine in return for favors as the President's "door-keeper") gave John Adams (no relation) his marching orders. Which specifically included instructions to prepare a white paper detailing my "pressures" upon the Army in Schine's behalf. Not to be made public, not unless McCarthy failed to see the "reasonableness" of the thing. That is, use it as a club, and surely Joe would dump Roy and then McCarthy would be fangless.

I could take that as a compliment—the truth is, while I was very valuable to Joe, mainly because I was organized and he wasn't, I was eminently replaceable—but modesty aside, it remained the White House strategy right up to the Army-McCarthy showdown. In their minds, if they got me, they'd have him.

Of course, they weren't quite ready to pull the trigger on this ultimatum of John Adams. Remember, this was January and Joe's Gallup Poll was 50 percent. It was a signal, the toughest yet, but a signal. Before this they had been content with approaches ranging from accommodation to appeasement to bribery.

A month later, hard on the heels of the Zwicker-Peress situation, another attempt at accommodation was made—and it turned out to be the last. It was called the Chicken Lunch, and not because of the menu, which appropriately was fried-chicken. This one was arranged by Senator Everett Dirksen (R.-Illinois), a member of our committee, a good friend, a good conservative. It was to be a "secret" lunch attended only by McCarthy, Secretary of the Army Stevens and the Republican members of the committee. It turned out to be as secret as the Army-Navy game. The whole press was outside Dirksen's office and as soon as the lunch was over, poor Stevens was looking for a sick bag.

Stevens, who had mainly been cooperative with the commit-

tee, agreed at the lunch to remain cooperative. He said he'd
give the committee the names of everybody who had a hand in
promoting and honorably discharging Peress and he agreed that
we were within our rights in questioning General Zwicker.

Just fine with us, and exactly right for Stevens to do, on the
merits. But what merits counted here? The press trashed Stevens for "capitulating" to Joe, and within hours the White
House aides had drawn up a face-saver for Bob. He would
never, he said, allow his officers to be "browbeaten" and he had
assurances from the committee that it wouldn't happen again.

It was crap, and McCarthy immediately said so: he shot Stevens down on the spot. Nobody will get special treatment, Joe
said, military or not. "I very carefully explained to the Secretary
a number of times," McCarthy said, "that he was Secretary of
the Army and not running the committee."

The peace move collapsed. And the war was on for real.

Three days after the Chicken Lunch, on Sunday, February
27, 1954, I at long last learned what Symington meant by
"crossfire." And I learned it from the most impeccable establishment source in the nation: Arthur Krock, the venerable *New
York Times* columnist. Krock wrote that the White House was
counting on Republican members of the committee to join with
the minority Democrats in a move to "sever" me. I'd be caught
in the "crossfire," he said, because I had encouraged McCarthy
to go after the Army in order to help Dave Schine. The other
Republicans on the committee were being urged to "restrain"
McCarthy from such "outbursts" as those against General
Zwicker. The best way to restrain him was to dump me.

It was as though Krock had wired Joe's meeting with John
Adams, and for me it was worse—he was clearly stating the
plotline of the White House and the Eisenhower wing of the
party.

Then, on the heels of this, came the famous Annie Lee Moss
case, which to this day, regardless of the evidence, is served up
by McCarthy haters as proof that he was in the business of destroying innocent people.

Annie Lee Moss had been employed in the Pentagon code

room. We discovered evidence that she was an active member of the Communist party. I was in charge of this case, and I brought it before the committee. We produced a formidable witness, Mrs. Mary Stalcup Markward, an undercover agent whom the FBI had placed in the Communist party. She testified that Annie Lee Moss was listed as a member in the Washington, D.C., region in the 1940's.

I called her to the witness stand. She denied the charge. There must be another Annie Lee Moss, she said.

I told the committee, "There is only one Annie Lee Moss FBI file and only one Annie Lee Moss Department of Justice file." We also had a second witness who corroborated the testimony and other supporting evidence.

What we didn't have was Joe McCarthy. Or any other Republican senator. I knew Joe wasn't around, he was ill, but somehow I hadn't noticed that all the other Republicans were absent that day.

Senator Symington jumped in. "I believe you are telling the truth," he said to Mrs. Moss. Out of nowhere he said that; talk about crossfire. Then he said that if the Pentagon wouldn't keep her he'd personally give her a job, even though "I may be sticking my neck out." The *beau geste* brought a storm of applause from the audience.

Senator McClellan, chairing the meeting in McCarthy's absence, blasted me. It was a disgrace, he said, for me to drag this poor woman before the committee when there was no basis for my accusation. More applause.

The anti-McCarthy press made the most of it. A national headline explosion ensued. Annie Lee Moss was a black woman, to boot, and so everybody could feel piety here. Edward R. Murrow made her the heroine of one of his programs, stressing the theme that even a poor innocent Negro woman can, through mistaken identity, be wrongfully accused of Communist ties.

But our informant, Mrs. Markward was right. The FBI and Justice Department were right.

The trouble was, they weren't proved right until 1958, four years later. And by then who cared? It went virtually unmentioned in the press. So today, I'm still hit with, "But you crucified an innocent Negro woman, you destroyed Annie Lee Moss!"

Emboldened by the media outburst over Mrs. Moss, Secretary of Defense Charles Wilson invited McCarthy to lunch a couple of days later. He told him that a lengthy, thoroughly documented report had been compiled, showing that Roy Cohn had been exerting terrible pressure on the Army to give favored treatment to David Schine.

"I had barely pulled my chair up to the table when he hit me with this garbage," Joe told me. "The end of it was, he wants your resignation or he'll be 'powerless' to keep it from getting out."

I said, "What did you tell him?"

"What do you think I told him?" Joe said. "I told him to go to hell."

A couple of hours after this, after the McCarthy-Wilson luncheon, Joe and I ran into Symington in the corridor of the Senate Office Building. In hushed tones, conspiratorial as a Hitchcock villain, Symington said that he and the rest of the committee had just received a "strictly confidential" report detailing our "improper activities" on behalf of Schine. As he turned away, he whispered to me, as he had two months before, "Crossfire!"

I told Joe, "This 'strictly confidential' report will be leaked to the press in ten minutes."

I was wrong. It took two hours.

We held a strategy meeting that night at McCarthy's house. The stories hadn't broken yet, just the leak had happened, the news would be on the stands in the morning. Joe of course was at the meeting, and his wife Jean and Dave Schine, and Edward Bennett Williams and a public relations man named Carl Byers.

Byers wanted us to issue a release immediately. He kept saying, "We've got to get something out." I said, "Hey, it's now nine o'clock at night. Most papers have gone to bed. What are you going to get, two lines in a five-column story? Better that we give them the first full shot out of the box and call a press conference for tomorrow. Today is their day, tomorrow will be ours."

It seems to me elementary to do it this way, and yet every day you read denials that get swallowed up in the "charge" story. I can always see brilliant public relations minds change when that happens. (I do know a few good P.R. men, but I think most of them just stay true to the pledge they made to their mothers, that they'll never work for a living.)

Anyhow, I managed to convince everybody else that it was best for us to hold our considerable fire power and I left the P.R. man talking to himself. I went back to my hole-in-the-wall apartment at the Carrol Arms hotel, I called my mother to warn her about the news and assure her we'd be on the scoreboard real quick, and then I took a sleeping pill. Which didn't work too well, my head was spinning all night. When I finally fell under, the door started banging and wouldn't quit. 7:30 A.M.

It was Tony Lewis, my old pal, standing there sporting a bunch of newspapers with *The New York Times* right on top. Tony wasn't yet with the *Times*, he was a budding genius on the Washington *Daily News*. But he had the *Times* out there for my wiped-out eyes to see. Nobody could miss it. A four-column headline, leading the paper:

ARMY CHARGES McCARTHY AND COHN
THREATENED IT IN TRYING TO OBTAIN
PREFERENTIAL TREATMENT FOR SCHINE

The story ran three pages and carried the whole government case, a 34-page report detailing my alleged "pressures" on the poor old U.S. Army. Jeezus. I hadn't figured on it, not a war headline, not all this stuff, three pages, Jeez.

With that, the phone rang. Larry Spivak of "Meet the Press." Would I come on a week from Sunday night?

I said, *"This* Sunday night, Larry."

He said he had a cabinet member on this week. I told him, "I have to get out there at once or my story will never get heard."

He called back in a few minutes. "I've cancelled the Secretary," he said. "You're on Sunday night."

Tony, meanwhile, wasn't there as a delivery boy; he wanted an exclusive interview. Of course I was happy to do it and happier still to read his lead in the morning paper. "Roy Cohn, clad in undershorts . . ." I wasn't clad in anything, so there was Tony dressing me up a little. We were still good friends and I don't remember any flak from him about my career. I know he no longer accused me, as when we were kids, of being too liberal; but he didn't accuse me of being a reactionary either.

Later that morning, McCarthy counter-attacked. We had been keeping our own memos—though no eavesdropped conversations on tape as the good clean Bob Stevens had done, as well as the White House gang. Instead of our pressuring the Army on behalf of Dave Schine, the Army was trying to do everything to silence us. And we had the documentation.

Item. Stevens on November 6, 1953, asked us to hold up our Army hearings and go after the Navy, Air Force and Defense Department instead. When we said we had no evidence on any of these departments, Stevens said, "Don't worry, there's plenty of dirt there."

Item. John Adams on December 9, 1953, told me he knew about an Air Force base loaded with homosexuals and that he'd give it to us if I'd tell him which Army project we were going to investigate next.

Item. John Adams referred to Dave as "hostage," to one of our investigators, Frank Carr, who on December 9, 1953, memo'd Joe: "I am convinced they will keep right on trying to blackmail us as long as Schine is in the Army."

And these were typical of many more efforts to shut us down. Clearly, the Army didn't feel "pressured" by anything I did for Dave; they were keeping Dave from his deserved commission in order to silence Joe.

I scored well on "Meet the Press," I was able to put the Schine business in a little bit of perspective. The most popular charge that had been made against me in the Army report was that I tried to get Dave off KP duty. Now that's something that could get any red-blooded American annoyed, there being nothing more sacred than that good old equalizer, KP. And I agree, I think everybody in the Army ought to peel potatoes once in a while, including the generals. But now they had painted me as a power broker who would go so far as to get a buddy off this onerous duty. Here was my answer on "Meet the Press":

"As a memorandum in our file reflects, that was the weekend before the deadline on filing the Overseas Information Program report which Schine wrote. That was a Sunday and there had been an agreement in advance that he could use that day to work on this report. They reneged on that agreement, and that was the only purpose of my communication with the Army. At no time did I or anybody else on the committee ever suggest that he should be relieved from KP or any other unpleasant duty that any draftee had to go through and I don't think he ever would have wanted us to make such a request."

I was asked if I had threatened to "wreck the Army," a charge that had made headlines and was designed to portray me as a vicious, dangerous head case. Of course I didn't and of course I couldn't and that's all I said but because it was true it seemed to have hit a nerve. Letters and telegrams poured in, most of them favorable.

The studio was flooded with phone calls after the show and I took two of them. My mother said, "Do you realize that your tie was crooked for the whole program?" Bob Hope said, "Anytime you want a job, just call me up. You were great." Hope said he was watching the show with Senator Symington, who agreed that I was terrific.

But a few days later the committee called me in for a meeting, and the minute I walked in the room I smelled a lynch party. Now Symington wasn't pleased at all. He wanted to know why I hadn't obtained the committee's advance permission before I went on television. Par for the course for Symington, you could never ever get mad at him.

McClellan was something else again. He didn't like me from day one, not because he was soft on Communism, he was very tough on Communism. No, what McClellan didn't like about me had to do with an ancient disease he had picked up. He was a

Bible belt Jew hater, John McClellan was, and the more he ad-
mired my work the more he couldn't stomach the fact that here
was a Jew doing it. So he hit hard.

"What is this business with television appearances," he said.
"This is a private matter between you and the committee."

I wasn't entirely unready for this. I had good information that
the committee wanted to vote me out in executive session, nice
and quiet and clean. They had the votes. The "crossfire"
Symington had warned about was in the person of Senator
Charles E. Potter (R.-Michigan), who pretended to be a good
conservative supporter of McCarthy's, but was a sycophant to
the White House crowd. He would provide the fourth vote and
I'd be gone and presumably Joe would be defanged. That was
the plot until "Meet the Press" upset it, and now McClellan was
giving vent to his frustration—and I shot right back.

"A private matter, Senator?" I said. "When I'm smeared on
every front page in the country, with the connivance of certain
members of this committee? It's no private matter to me, it's a
very public matter and if you think you're going to bury me
without my saying a word, you're all wrong. I'm going to go out
and tell the press that I want open televised hearings."

A threat like that from me would have gone nowhere had my
TV appearance not been a huge success. But the committee read
the papers and I had enough support now, from the public and
the press, to guarantee against a swift, secret execution. So they
went along, it would be public, it would be televised. And that's
how come the Army-McCarthy hearings became the instant
leading soap opera of the decade.

The funny thing is, Joe wasn't even around when these
portentious fireworks occurred. He was in Arizona. I was on my
own, and I did what came naturally. I fought back and they
backed down. But they didn't back away. They were after Joe,
nothing would stop them. Only they wouldn't have succeeded if
it hadn't been on television. They tell me that mine is known as
a Pyrrhic victory. If there ever was one.

Roy Cohn, columnist George E. Sokolsky (center) and Senator Joseph McCarthy confer at a breakfast meeting prior to a hearing of McCarthy's Senate Investigating Committee. (UPI/Bettmann Newsphotos)

Senator Joseph McCarthy announces the appointment of Roy M. Cohn as Chief Counsel for his Senate Investigating Committee. They are seen here conferring with Francis D. ("Frip") Flanagan (right), longtime General Counsel for the Senate Subcommittee on Investigations. (UPI/Bettmann Newsphotos)

Roy Cohn huddles with Republican Senator Karl Mundt during a hearing of the Senate Investigating Committee. Rumors had it that Republican members of the committee were asking for Cohn's resignation or removal. (UPI/Bettmann Newsphotos)

Senator McCarthy expresses confidence in his Chief Counsel at a press conference. (UPI/Bettmann Newsphotos)

Roy Cohn is sworn in as a witness before the Army-McCarthy hearings on May 26, 1954, just before the hearing recessed as the committee concluded with testimony from the Army side. Army counsel Joseph Welch (wearing bow tie) is seated just beside Cohn. (UPI/Bettmann Newsphotos)

Roy Cohn testifies before the Senate Investigating Committee concerning an alleged "doctored" photograph showing Army Secretary Stevens with Pvt. G. David Schine. Directly behind Cohn are General Miles Reber (left, rear), Maj. General Robert Young (foreground), Army counsel Joseph Welch (bow tie), and Army Secretary Robert Stevens. (UPI/Bettmann Newsphotos)

Army Pvt. G. David Schine (left), Senator Joseph McCarthy, and Roy Cohn at the Army-McCarthy hearings, June 7, 1954. (UPI/Bettmann Newsphotos)

Out of the spotlight, Roy Cohn does his homework as he prepares a case. (UPI/Bettmann Newsphotos)

Roy Cohn with friend and client George Steinbrenner, owner of the New York Yankees, during a Yankee victory party at New York night spot Studio 54. (UPI/Bettmann Newsphotos)

Roy Cohn with clients Ian Schrager (left) and Steve Rubell, owners of Studio 54. The disco owners were found guilty of tax evasion and were sentenced to three and one-half years in prison. (UPI/Bettmann Newsphotos)

Roy Cohn, with unidentified guest, hosting a New Year's Eve party at Regine's, New York City, December 31, 1984. (Copyright © 1984 by Ron Galella)

Roy Cohn (right) with (from the left) radio personality Barry Farber, Roger Wood, executive editor of the New York *Post* , and author Sidney Zion.

Roy Cohn with columnist and celebrity chronicler Earl Blackwell and fashion columnist and writer Eugenia Sheppard, at a book party for them. (Copyright ©1980 by Ron Galella)

Chapter Eight

Kids today would surely call it unreal, the Army-McCarthy hearings. Because it was a fabulous media happening, loaded with villains, heroes, suspense, crazy plot turns, and corn higher than Oscar Hammerstein's eyes.

But unreal it was, in the real sense.

That is, it had nothing to do with what it said it was doing.

The Army-McCarthy hearings were advertised as an investigation into whether Joe McCarthy and Roy Cohn attempted to force the Army to give special privileges to Dave Schine. Or whether the Army used Schine to blackmail McCarthy into stopping his probes of the Army.

But the real purpose of the whole shebang was to wipe out McCarthy. Joe knew that, I knew that. We thought we'd win, is all. And we almost did. In true American fashion, almost don't count; what does count is that we keep the hearings in perspective, that we understand they were an illusion, it was all show biz. That way, I can write about them without throwing up.

127

The hearings opened on April 22, 1954, and ran for thirty-six days stretched over seven weeks. They might as well have cancelled the spring for all anybody seemed to care about the birds, bees and baseball while this show was on the air. Twenty million watched it on television every day, and this was in the relatively early days of TV. It was easily the top attraction of the era, leaving the World Series and the Kefauver Crime Hearings of 1951 in the dust. The mind boggles at what numbers would have been achieved had the TV audience been as large as it was even five years later, and had the hearings been held in prime time. In the event, it seemed that whosoever could watch it did watch it, down with work and the gross national product. The pollsters were too backward to check the impact on the birth rate, but it must have approached ground-zero. Who had time to play around when all this action was happening day-in, day-out, come Cohn or come Schine?

In the capital, where of course face is all, it was get into the hearings or die of disgrace. Perle Mesta, who ran the town's social calendar, the Hostess with the Mostess, called off her parties. "I couldn't compete with this," she told the press. But while Perle managed to get in, and with an entourage no less, it was wait and hope for almost everybody else. A good part of the reason was that Senate wives had first dibs, and this was a big break for our side, or at least for me. The Republicans were in the majority, and so commanded the best seats, or at least the best view. And this turned out to be right behind the Democratic members of the committee. I spent a lot of hours on the witness stand and the Democrats probably thought I was gifted with extrasensory perception.

The truth is, it was Mrs. Styles Bridges and her cohorts. They sat there looking over the shoulders of my interrogators, and when they saw a tough question about to pop, I'd get a nod and then I'd wink to one of our people strategically placed near the ladies and presto! I'd have a note with the upcoming query right in front of my nose. Better than the CIA, my conservative women, better by far.

I suppose they figured I needed help. Everyone would have figured it after my hapless cameo appearance as a witness early in the proceedings. This was the "cropped picture" incident, which thirty years ago needed no more introduction than that, and probably still conjures up sharp images for those who watched the show.

Dave Schine had had a photograph taken with Secretary of the Army Robert T. Stevens at Fort Dix. It was a jolly, smiling picture—and that was the main reason we wanted it in evidence. Because it was taken at a time when Stevens claimed he was bitterly angry at Schine for using pressure tactics to get soft treatment. The other reason we wanted it in evidence was that Stevens had denied taking a picture with Schine at Fort Dix.

I remembered there was a picture and I asked Dave about it and he said it was on his office wall in New York. He made a trip to the city to get the photo, arriving back in Washington during the first day's hearing. Jim Juliana, one of our assistants, whispered to me that the picture was here and I told him to have copies made.

When the picture was placed in evidence, four days into the hearings while Stevens was testifying, Joseph M. Welch, the brilliant, pixyish Boston lawyer representing the Army, charged that the photo had been "doctored." The next day he produced the original—and it caused a national sensation. Because cut out of the picture that we put in was Colonel Bradley, the commander of Fort Dix. Ours, said Welch, was "an altered, shamefully cut-down version" intended to show only Stevens and Schine together.

It was nothing of the kind. Stevens and Schine were standing next to each other, looking into each other's eyes. Bradley was standing next to Schine, his presence had absolutely no relevance.

So why was he cut out of the picture? Because Don Surine, a member of our staff, thought that's what we wanted and could see plainly that it made no difference if Bradley was in or out of the picture. Don had been told to make copies by Jim Juliana and since he was friendly with the technicians in the photocopying unit of the Senate Office Building he asked for two copies of the original and two of only Schine and Stevens. He only gave us the latter, again because he understood that what we needed was a picture of Stevens and Schine. I hadn't seen the original and neither had the committee counsel, Ray Jenkins.

Obviously, if the cropped version had changed the meaning of the picture in any way we'd have been guilty as sin. And utterly stupid, to boot, because we didn't have the negative so we would have had to assume that we'd be caught out. But there was no difference: who cared if the base commander was standing by? If anything, it looked worse for the Army, because Bradley was smiling too.

But Welch made the most of it, and it was plenty. Even today many people believe we doctored up that picture, that it was "typical McCarthyism."

But I said I was a lousy witness. Welch put me on the stand to testify about the picture and about the work Dave Schine did for the committee. And I blew it. Not because I lied or got confused, nothing like that. I made the terrible gaffe of being a wise guy, of being brash, smug, pompous and petulant. You want more? I was rambling, garrulous, repetitious. And worst of all, I tried to trade quips with Joe Welch, who only had forty years of trial experience on me and a rapier-like wit that I couldn't match if I lived a hundred and twenty years.

One example will do it. Welch said, "I think I observe on Colonel Bradley's face a faint little look of pleasure. Do you, sir?"

I answered: "I would say I knew that Colonel Bradley had a good steak dinner shortly afterward. Perhaps he was anticipating it."

Welch swallowed me up, and broke up the house. "If Bradley is feeling good about a steak dinner," he said, "Schine must be considering a whole haunch of beef."

Joe McCarthy grabbed me at the lunch break. "You were about the worst witness I ever heard in my life," he said. This time Joe wasn't guilty of hyperbole, you have my word for it. Symington overheard Joe laying me out; we were waiting for the elevator, and Joe was hitting me point by point. Symington said, "Don't be so hard on him, Joe. I'll give you fifty dollars for his brain any day." All I could think was that he'd be overpaying.

I learned from this humiliating experience. When I took the

stand for extended testimony weeks later I was a different person and I think even my enemies would concede that I acquitted myself well. But my title as the world's worst witness had long since passed into the bumbling hands of the Secretary of the Army, who was so pathetic he became known around the country as Poor Bob Stevens; it was as if Bob were his middle name. He was far and away the best witness for our side, and if Joe hadn't acted up so much and screwed up, we'd have won hands down on Stevens's testimony alone.

But that's not why I had affection for Poor Bob Stevens. He endeared himself to me, despite the fact that he was doing his best to destroy me, because it was obvious that only a basically decent person could be such an ineffectual liar. I mean, he couldn't keep a lie afloat long enough to finish it.

I always thought he wanted to root out Communists and subversives from the Army, that left alone he would have helped us in our efforts. And at first he did cooperate. But the sharks in the Pentagon and the barracudas in the White House were too much for an Ol' Boy Network guy like Stevens, who didn't prep at Andover and graduate from Harvard to become a rebel. So when his bosses pushed he moved. First they got him to try to co-opt us by spreading the red carpet, socially and officially. When that failed, they took him down the blackmail trail, where he was not only out of his league, but utterly out of character. Had he been of the ilk of his superiors, he might have been a terrific witness against us. But Poor Bob Stevens was the classic example of a good man in a bad trade. A rare breed, particularly in government, and hardly the stuff out of which persuasive perjurers are made.

Stevens spent fourteen days on the witness stand, most of the time under the grueling cross-examination of Ray Jenkins, counsel to the special committee. Jenkins was "discovered" by Senator Dirksen while Dirksen was on a visit to Knoxville, Tennessee. By then, Jenkins was 57 years old, had tried 500 criminal cases without losing a single client to the electric chair (and in those days the electric chair was a pretty steady worker, a fine client of the Tennessee Valley Authority). He had a lantern jaw, a craggy head topped by dull-red hair that he wore in a crew cut, and a reputation for determination and fairness. Politically, he was a middle-of-the-road Republican of the Taft wing, though in 1940 he had served as presidential campaign manager for Wendell Willkie. Born poor, he worked his way through the University of Tennessee Law School, and now he was one of the wealthiest attorneys in the state and surely the most colorful. On Dirksen's recommendation, the committee hired Jenkins and they couldn't have made a better choice.

I never saw a performance to compare with his. Since he was the committee's lawyer, he considered himself to be the attorney for the Republicans and Democrats, for the Army and McCarthy. So on direct examination, he would take a witness through his testimony as if he were the witness's best friend, forget about only being his lawyer. Smoothly, almost lovingly, he'd bring out the best in the witness. Then, with direct examination finished, he'd become Mr. Hyde—and watch out! Clarence Darrow couldn't have been tougher on William Jennings Bryan in the Monkey Trial than Ray Jenkins was on everybody. As someone said about Jenkins's astonishing role-switching: "He is totally impartial. He is unfair to both sides."

Stevens wouldn't have been able to stand up to a law student, much less a super lawyer like Jenkins. All of his allegations of "improper pressure" made in the press before the hearings and again on his direct examination fell apart under Jenkins's cold, pursuing cross examination. Far from being threatened by us, Stevens revealed himself to be a man who saw nothing unusual or wrong in anything we did, and who, in point of fact, went far out of his way socially and officially to win the favor of McCarthy, Cohn and Schine—the very people he was accusing. Moreover, though he had always maintained his cooperation with our investigations of the Army and denied any attempt to stifle it, he admitted under cross examination that stopping our probe was his only clear aim, once his efforts to pacify us failed. Jenkins got him to concede that he wanted the investigations suspended for as long as possible—the Pentagon must have shuddered at this admission—and then Joe took over the questioning. After Stevens ducked and dodged sixteen straight requests from Joe to clarify his attitude, he finally nailed the Secretary on the seventeenth try:

McCarthy: Now, can you tell us today, whether or not you wanted the hearings at Fort Monmouth suspended?

Stevens: I wanted them suspended in order that the Army could carry out the hearings themselves and make progress reports to your committee and stop the panic that was being created in the mind of the public about Fort Monmouth on a basis not justified by the facts.

McCarthy: How did you finally succeed in getting the hearings suspended?

Stevens: How did I finally succeed?

McCarthy: Yes. They are suspended as of today. We both agree to that, I believe. How did you finally succeed?

Stevens: They aren't suspended, as far as I know.

McCarthy: Are the hearings still going on?

Stevens: Are they still going on? You know about that.

McCarthy: You know that the hearings were suspended the day you or someone filed your charges against Mr. Cohn and myself. You know that, don't you? Let's not be coy.

Stevens was on the stand fourteen days. After the first few days, however, Senator Dirksen, pained at Stevens's sorry performance, convinced that it was doing the administration much harm and the country no good, decided to try and end the spectacle as soon as possible. For starters, he proposed that the number of witnesses be limited, but this was shot down by the Army. Joe Welch announced, "We were unable to invent a magic formula for shortening the hearings. . . . I have been forced to say that I think the American people will demand and should have the long, hard furrow plowed."

Undeterred, Dirksen went to work on a plan to end the public hearings at once. The witnesses would be heard in closed session, with public release of all testimony. Why would the Army go for this if it wouldn't agree to so modest a proposal as limiting the number of witnesses? Because there was something in the plan that could have saved the faces of all concerned—at the expense of only two necks. Mine and John Adams's, the Army's lawyer.

It is truly said that there are no secrets in Washington. If ever an exception proved the rule this was it. With all the press swarming over the Army-McCarthy doings, the deal that would have turned the whole show off TV never made the papers and never made the television newscasts.

And the deal was this: Adams and I were to resign simultaneously with statements that would say we were taking the step at a personal sacrifice to end a stormy public display that we believed was harming the nation. Our move would save the taxpayers' money and serve the commonweal.

Senator Dirksen didn't come to me directly with this proposition. I was called by a friend, a prominent business executive, who in turn was approached by Tom Coleman, a powerful Republican leader from Wisconsin. Coleman, an original McCarthy backer, remained close to Joe and at the same time stood well with other segments of the Republican party, including the White House.

I wasn't overjoyed but I had to be realistic. We were winning big but we wouldn't always have Poor Bob Stevens on the stand. Who could foresee what might happen in the interminable days to come? And the hearings were already a nuisance, a colossal bore (I somehow couldn't focus on how much the public seemed to be entranced with the show) and surely the most monumental absurdity in our history. I told my friend I'd go along but I'd have to get Joe's O.K.

We had a staff discussion. McCarthy saw the wisdom of stopping the theatre, which he wasn't enjoying despite the points he had made against Stevens. He said he'd hate to see me leave, but the alternative was a chaotic mess up ahead for the whole country. "Besides," he said, "nobody is going to win this thing, and it may continue till God knows when. Meanwhile all that work is piling up undone."

I try to recall how I felt then, but I can't. I mean, I'm sure I'd have liked it better if Joe had said to tell them all to go to hell, the way he did when Defense Secretary Wilson made my head the price of peace. But here I was advocating the deal, how could I complain? I know I wasn't bitter, but I'm sure I wasn't happy either.

Anyway, in a couple of days, on a morning when the hearings were in recess, I was installed in a suite at the Mayflower Hotel and told to remain there until I received a call informing me that the deal was accepted by the Army. In the meantime I was to prepare a statement explaining my resignation.

It was a rough day, a lonely day, I knew now what Irving Berlin meant by his evergreen, "All Alone by the Telephone." Lunch had no taste at all, and I wasn't much of a drinker or I'd have been good and loaded. I paced, but how much can you pace? Occasionally the phone would ring with "progress reports" that inevitably indicated no progress. Thus: Adams undecided but will do as bosses wish . . . Stevens thinks plan has merit, but . . . Pentagon chiefs in huddle . . . things look bad . . . things look good.

I kept fixing up my statement, using wads of legal paper, yellow legal paper, and I couldn't help thinking of the import of color. I ordered dinner, but couldn't touch it. Darkness hit. Nothing. Finally, my business friend, my intermediary, called. He said, "Go home. The Army has killed the deal. Very bad judgment but they did it, and that's that."

I was too numb to be relieved or upset. But Senator Dirksen was furious. He went to the White House and asked the administration to insist that the Army go along. But the White House said no dice. If that's the way the Army wanted it, that's the way it had to be.

The idea that the Army was acting autonomously was plainly ridiculous, but Dirksen, ever the optimist, proceeded as if it were so, and the next day he unveiled a new plan to the committee, a compromise that would shorten the hearings and get them off the screen expeditiously. He proposed (1) that the public sessions be limited to the rest of Stevens's testimony and McCarthy's; (2) that all other witnesses be heard in executive session; (3) that Jenkins report on whether any others should be heard in public; and (4) that McCarthy, at the conclusion of his testimony, be authorized to resume his Army investigation on matters not related to the present controversy.

The Republican members were enthusiastically for the Dirksen plan, reflecting Republican opinion in the country, which was all for ending the show. Even Mr. Crossfire, Senator Charles Potter, was in favor. Since the Republicans had a 4-3 majority on the committee, approval should have been easy. But

Chairman Karl Mundt (R.-South Dakota) had promised earlier to oppose a stoppage to public hearings if any of the principals objected on grounds of fairness.

After his usual hemming and hawing, Poor Bob Stevens sent in his objection. Feeling honor bound, Senator Mundt voted with the Democrats, and the Dirksen plan failed.

The press generally played this as a principled stand by Stevens, who was said to have stood alone, defying all pressures of his party and the President himself. If this had been true it would have ranked as one of the miracles of the twentieth century. Of course, it was pure bull. And years later, when White House Press Secretary James Hagerty's diaries were published, the real story surfaced.

"Ike wants hearings open and televised," Hagerty wrote, on May 11, the day of the committee vote. Why? Because he knew the Army was losing and a compromise would be viewed as surrender. Furthermore, he figured that closed sessions would benefit McCarthy, who "would use his old trick of coming out . . . and telling reporters anything he wanted. He would have a forum and the Army would not."

Everett Dirksen didn't need to wait for Hagerty's memoirs. Late on the day his proposal was defeated he sent a message that he wanted to see me. Early the next morning, I arrived and could see by the way he ran his fingers through his tousled hair that he was mad as hell. He summarized his efforts to persuade the administration and the Army to accept his plan. Then, his mellifluous voice rising from the deep, he said: "Roy, I've just about had it with these people. I'm fed up with them. I offered them a chance to get off the hook and they were stupid enough not to take it."

Dirksen proceeded to tell me that he had certain facts in his possession that directly contradicted some of the Army's charges. Thus, on January 22, 1954, the same date on which John Adams had gone to McCarthy's house to demand that the subpoenas for the loyalty board members be cancelled and that I be delivered up, both Adams and White House aide Gerald Morgan had first come to see Dirksen.

"They said to me, 'kill those subpoenas,' " Dirksen told me.

"They said if the subpoenas weren't stopped, charges about you and all the others would be made public."

"Did they actually make that threat?"

"Not openly," Dirksen said. "But the implication was plain. They spoke about how the entire committee might be made to look in the eyes of the nation if those charges came out."

"That's blackmail, Senator," I said. "Can these facts be brought out at the hearings?"

Dirksen replied: "In the interests of the country and all the participants I tried to stop this fiasco. I knew if it continued I would be honor bound to give facts within my knowledge. The Stevens group has demanded continuance of the hearings, and it is at their peril that the facts must now emerge."

Dirksen, who talked in private as he did in public, now talked in public as he did to me. He took the witness stand and told the story of the Morgan-Adams meeting and about a meeting he, Dirksen, then had the next day with Mundt, Potter and McCarthy at Joe's office. Where he "thoroughly aired" what Adams and Morgan had told him, including the stuff about Cohn and Schine, which he had heard for the first time from Adams.

Once Dirksen took the stand, Mundt and Potter had to do the same. Mundt said that he too was visited by John Adams on January 22, was told about my alleged efforts to win preferential treatment for Schine and was asked to use his influence to stop the subpoenas. Potter, on the same famous day, was approached by one of his close friends, Deputy Army Counsel Louis Berry, who came with the same story.

So now there were three senators backing up our contention that the Army was blackmailing us and threatening the committee, rather than vice-versa. But it remained for the Army itself, through John Adams, to let the White House cat out of the bag.

Like all witnesses under Ray Jenkins's direct examination, Adams was going along swimmingly, portraying me as an ogre who would do anything to get soft duty for Dave Schine, and claiming that when I couldn't move the Army I got McCarthy to subpoena the loyalty board members. This was as incredible as anything the Army claimed. Could anybody believe that McCarthy needed a reason like that, or any reason other than

anyone's refusal to cooperate, in order to issue subpoenas? But
that's what Adams swore and then, inadvertently, he told the
truth.

Adams: On January 21, I met in the attorney general's office
with Mr. Brownell, Deputy Attorney General Rogers, Presidential Assistant Sherman Adams, White House Assistant Gerald
Morgan, and UN Ambassador Henry Cabot Lodge. . . . I re-
counted the details of the loyalty board ultimatum [the subpoe-
nas] and at Mr. Rogers' request I described the problem we
were having over Private Schine and how the two matters
seemed to me to be related. . . . Governor Adams [Ike's chief-
of-staff Sherman Adams] asked me if I had written a record of all
the incidents with reference to Private Schine . . . and when I
replied in the negative he stated he thought I should prepare
one.

With this blunder, the rose was off the bush. No longer could
the Army claim that it was fighting solo to keep Schine on KP,
that it had acted independently in a brave struggle against
McCarthy and Cohn. The White House was quarterbacking this
game to get Joe and had been all along. Any child could see it
now—or would for sure if Jenkins and the committee members
were to cross examine Adams, and then call the others at the
Justice Department conference to bear witness. Obviously,
something had to give. What gave was the separation of powers.
Under the guise of protecting the separation of powers, in the
wake of Adams's testimony, President Eisenhower made the
Mafia rule of *omerta* a constitutional principle. Nobody in the
executive branch, he decreed, was permitted to testify to Congress about anything he or she discussed within the executive
branch.

Nothing close to this had ever been done before by a President of the United States. And you don't have to take my word
for it. I don't make a habit of quoting Arthur Schlesinger, Jr. But
here he is, in his book *The Imperial Presidency*:

"On May 17, 1954, Eisenhower made the most absolute assertion of presidential right to withhold information from Congress
ever uttered to that day in American history."

Presidents since Jackson, Schlesinger noted, had claimed

their own conversations and communications with aides and cabinet members as privileged, without serious dispute from the Congress. "What was new," he said, "was the idea that this privilege extended to everybody in the executive branch."

Thus, without a scintilla of constitutional grounding, the President imposed a blackout that prevented the committee, and us, from blowing the Army out of the water, from showing beyond all doubt that the whole "case" was manufactured in the White House in order to stop our probe of the Army and ultimately to destroy McCarthy.

I asked Joe that night why he thought Ike would go this far. McCarthy said, "Too much was coming out and he had to stop the show." With that, he handed me Arthur Krock's column of May 16, the day before Ike put the lights out. Krock, no friend of Joe's (to push an understatement) wrote:

> It may be that when the testimony has been completed, Senator Joseph R. McCarthy's national influence will have suffered the heavy injury which is the hope of many. But if that is dependent on the proof that his investigation of security risks in the Army was unusually ruthless, was the direct consequence of the Army's refusal of certain favors for Private G.D. Schine, and was pursued for the purpose of discrediting the Army's former commander, now in the White House—whatever the cost to national security—the testimony so far has not supplied it.

Eisenhower, who liked to say about McCarthy, "I won't get into the gutter with that guy," had gutted the Constitution, simply to avoid further embarrassment in an already losing war. Of course, once a president violates the Great Charter in pursuit of the "good fight," it gets to be a habit with him. As Mr. Schlesinger points out: "The Eisenhower directive ushered in the greatest orgy of executive denial in American history."

From 1955–1960, there were by Schlesinger's account at least 44 instances when officials in the executive branch refused information to Congress on the basis of the Eisenhower directive— "More cases in these five years than in the first century of American history."

It goes without saying that neither Schlesinger nor his liberal-left cohorts complained about this usurpation during the Army-McCarthy hearings. "The detestation of McCarthy," Schlesinger writes, "was by this time so universal that few noted the absolute sweep of Eisenhower's claim." Forget about Schlesinger's notion of the universe, this had nothing to do with "few noting" what Eisenhower had done. They noted it all right; they happened to like it, because they happened to hate Joe. So *The New York Times* and the Washington *Post* were ecstatic—they loved what Ike did, they had no problem at all knowing what he did, or "noting" it. It was simply that the end justified the means.

And this by people who said, *ad nauseam*, that they agreed with McCarthy's ends, but didn't approve of his means.

Twenty years later, when President Nixon invoked executive privilege to try to end the Watergate investigation, the same people who cheered Ike booed Dick. (But it wasn't vice-versa, it wasn't just a case of whose ox is gored. By and large, the conservatives didn't stand with Nixon—and of course, his own Supreme Court justices unanimously rejected his claim of privilege on the famous tapes, and so made his resignation inevitable.)

Don't get me wrong, I wasn't bitter then and I'm not bitter now. I was surprised at the extent of liberal hypocrisy, sure; after all, I grew up around liberal Democrats. And I guess I didn't expect them to side so vehemently, or even at all, with the Army. Who ever heard of liberals being pro-military?

The Eisenhower directive (it would be four years before William Rogers, then the attorney general, would pin the fancy title "executive privilege" on presidential blackouts) caused so much consternation among the members of the committee that the hearings were recessed for a week to see if Ike's mind could be changed. Even Senator McClellan called the order a "serious mistake," adding: "If such an order was to be issued, I think it should have been issued long ago and we could have known then that a part of the truth possibly would never be available to this committee. We could have determined then whether we would undertake these hearings under those conditions."

Of course, no blackout order was needed until John Adams blurted out the truth, but we couldn't expect McClellan to go that far.

Senator Dirksen made the point that if the hearings continued under the presidential order, the committee would be in the "unhappy position of litigants in a lawsuit where proof on one side could not be fully established." Then, characteristically, Dirksen urged the recess to "explore the full impact of the executive order to determine whether or not there are any modifications or exceptions to it."

Dirksen went to the White House and tried to persuade Eisenhower to back off, of course to no avail. In retrospect, it was naïve, to say the least, of Dirksen to think the President would listen to reason, or history, or logic. For whatever Ike and his lieutenants tried to say about the lofty "principle" of executive secrecy, principle had nothing to do with it. Eisenhower and his men knew full well what we'd have done to his advisers had they taken the witness stand. And that's all there was to the whole business: flat-out cynical politics. You don't beat that with principled arguments, you beat it with a head-on challenge, right out in the open. In this case, it would have meant suspending the hearings while waging a constitutional battle against the President in the courts.

But the truth is, none of us pushed it, and I don't know why. We didn't even seriously consider it. Perhaps it was because what Eisenhower did was so outrageous, unprecedented, it caught us all unawares. Or maybe we knew the Congress had no stomach for it. Whatever, it's a pity. I'm sure we'd have won, no court would have upheld so extreme an assertion of presidential power, certainly not the Supreme Court. And then everything would have been different, not just the Army-McCarthy show. A Supreme Court decision putting the President in his constitutional place would have been a fine lesson for future chief executives.

In the event, we were back in session a week later without having laid a glove on Eisenhower. And I had no time to contemplate constitutional law. I was the lead-off witness for our side and I spent a good part of the recess fighting off pressure from my friends, from my father, from McCarthy, to get a lawyer. I'd have said the same to anybody else. I would have parroted the adage, parroted now to me, that he who is his own lawyer has a fool for a client. I'd have noted that it was no shame to have counsel, that every other witness at the hearing had a lawyer by his side, including the Army's lawyer, John Adams. And I'd have said all of these things even if I were certain that the person I was advising was bound to be a great witness.

In my case, everybody already knew I was a lousy witness, I'd proven myself in the "cropped picture" incident.

So McCarthy said: "Roy, run, don't walk, to a lawyer! Get Eddie Williams." Edward Bennett Williams, still in his early thirties, already had a reputation as a great trial lawyer.

My father said, "Get Charlie Lockwood or Paul Windels." Lockwood was a retired New York Supreme Court justice and Windels a former Corporation Counsel of New York City, both men of integrity and courage.

George Sokolsky told me: "Don't be stupid, get a lawyer." It was unanimous.

But it wasn't out of contrariness that I didn't get a lawyer. It was a calculated decision, arrived at coldly.

If it wasn't obvious at the start of the hearings, it was crystal clear by the time I was set to open the defense case that what we were involved in was pure theatre. This was not a search for truth that would be decided on the evidence. The jury was the audience, and the audience was twenty million strong. Who won and who lost would be determined by which side put the song across best. Joe Welch knew that from opening day, and so did Symington—and so did McCarthy, who often told me that the people would decide guilt or innocence based on what they saw. He was too right, as it turned out for him. But he knew it from the outset. It took me a little longer to catch on. Once I did, there was no question but that I had to go it alone up there.

What could a lawyer do for me, except make me look like a guy who needed a lawyer? What did lawyers do for Poor Bob Stevens and John Adams? What did all those brass hats sitting behind them do for them? Just made them look like they needed brass hats, that's all. I was determined to sit up there by myself, no counsel, no advisers, no briefcases full of documents.

To that end, I spent all my free time—after my initial debacle on the stand—practicing. I told nobody about this; how could I tell my friends that I sat before my mirror every night answering my own questions, studying my demeanor, listening to the inflections in my voice? I wasn't going to make the same mistakes again. This time I'd be calm, deferential, withdrawn, unruffled, and I'd speak only to the point, no more garrulous crap.

And no more Mr. Wise-Ass, either. At McCarthy's house on the eve of my testimony, Willard Edwards of the Chicago *Tribune* said, "Roy's greatest handicap is the general feeling that he's a cocky young bastard, and he should strive to remove that impression." Well, I am that, I *am* one, I said, but don't worry about it, I said, I won't be that way on the stand.

I was true to my word. I took everything Mr. Jenkins in his Hyde-suit threw at me, and I was such a sweetheart I could have won the "goody-two-shoes" award. And then I did the same with Mr. Welch. In view of what happened while Mr. Welch had me under cross-examination, I wish I hadn't kept my promise so faithfully. Maybe then, maybe if I'd been my shoot-em-up fiery self, Joe McCarthy wouldn't have walked into the deadliest one-two punch since Joe Louis flattened Max Schmeling.

So the famous Fisher incident, which lasted fifteen minutes—and practically obliterated everything that came before or after. When Joe Welch cried the country cried with him!

Frederick G. Fisher, Jr., was a 32-year-old associate in Welch's Boston law firm, Hale and Dorr. When Welch was hired by the Army, he decided to bring Fisher in as his assistant. When Fisher confessed to him that he had once been a member of the National Lawyers Guild—Attorney General Brownell called the Guild "the legal mouthpiece of the Communist party"—Mr. Welch sent Fisher back home to Back Bay, back to Hale and Dorr.

The story made the papers in mid-April, a week before the hearings opened. *The New York Times* even ran a picture of Fisher together with Welch's explanation concerning the Lawyers Guild.

On June 7, after my sixth day on the witness stand, Welch and I found ourselves walking together, quite alone. He said,

"There's a little matter I'd like to talk to you about sometime. I think you're the kind of person to whom I can talk off the record about it."

I thought I could talk to him the same way, I sized him up as a horse-trader. I said, "And there's something I'd like to talk to you about privately."

"Well then," Welch said, "let us make 'sometime' now."

We went into an empty committee room and closed the door.

"Do you want to go first, or shall I?" Welch said.

"I'll do it," I said.

A couple of days before, Welch had made mention of my old draft status. I knew where he was going, and though I had nothing to hide, I also knew it could be embarrassing to me, simply by him asking questions. The liberal press had already made intimations that I was a draft-dodger. I told Welch that there was no truth to it, and he agreed, but he said he was under pressure from his "client" to work it over.

The truth was this. I had been appointed to West Point in 1945, but had flunked the physical exam. A year later, I flunked it again. Not that I was a ninety-pound weakling, but I couldn't do the hundred-yard dash carrying a man on my back, and I couldn't throw a softball a hundred and forty feet either. Call it vanity, but I didn't want twenty million people to know this.

Following the West Point rejection, I was classified 1-A, and shortly afterward drafting was stopped in the New York area. It was resumed in June, 1948, but by that time I had enlisted in the National Guard as a private. In September, 1949, I was promoted to sergeant and two years later moved up to warrant officer. In February 1952 I was commissioned a first lieutenant in the Judge Advocate General's Corps.

What was wrong with all this? Nothing, except the National Guard, exempted me, automatically, from the draft. Obviously, those who wanted to smear me, could make what they wanted of this.

Welch said, "Let me suggest a trade. I'll tell you my *quid pro quo*."

And it was that we say nothing about Fred Fisher's membership in the Lawyers Guild. He didn't want it broadcast to twenty million people. I said if he didn't hear from me to the contrary, we had a deal. He'd drop my draft stuff, including the West Point business, and we'd leave Fisher out.

That night, I went to McCarthy's home and gave him a full run-down of my talk with Welch. And Joe approved the trade.

Two days later, seemingly out of nowhere, McCarthy thrust Fred Fisher into history. It looked like a temper tantrum, and in a way it was, but it didn't come out of nowhere. Joe was trying to protect me from Welch, even as I was sitting there pleased with myself for not letting Welch get under my skin.

Welch had been at me for days, taunting, needling, haranguing, throwing everything he had at me in an effort to get me to blow my cool. He wanted to show the American people that I was indeed as advertised by the liberal press: McCarthy's baby hit-man, exactly the kind of young punk who'd threaten to "wreck the Army" unless the Army bent to his will.

When I didn't bite, however, Welch began to look like the bully he was trying to paint me as, and at one point he admitted as much. "Mr. Cohn," he said, "my mail and telegrams reflect, sir, that you are held in gratifyingly high esteem in this country. There apparently are a good many people who think I was unfair to you yesterday."

But he couldn't stop trying to bait me because he had nothing else to go with. It was obvious to all but the totally committed anti-McCarthyites that the Army's case had been manufactured. So now Welch, in what must have been a last desperate attempt to shake my composure, swung to a line of questions designed to demonstrate that I had been lax in getting Communists out of the Army!

Instead of these painstakingly long investigations and hearings, why didn't I just rush into the Pentagon and yell, "We've got some hot dope on Communists in the Army"? Why didn't I grab Stevens by the lapel and say, "Sic 'em Stevens"? How could I sleep at night knowing there were Commies around, why didn't I go get 'em out of there "before the sun goes down"?

Rather than upset me, I was delighted that Welch was down to this kind of clowning; he was like a pitcher whose arm had gone dead.

"May I add my small voice, sir," he said to me, "and say whenever you know about a subversive or a Communist or a spy, please hurry. Will you remember these words?"

Was I supposed to jump out of my seat and grab him by the throat for this big bad needle? And yet this really got McCarthy's goat, this dopey little noise of a query had Joe at his mike, blurting out, "Mr. Chairman, in view of that question . . ."

Mr. Mundt said, "Have you a point of order?"

McCarthy said, "Not exactly, Mr. Chairman, but in view of Mr. Welch's request that the information be given, once we know of anyone who might be performing any work for the Communist party, I think we should tell him that he has in his law firm a young man named Fisher whom he recommended, incidentally, to do work on this committee, who has been for a number of years a member of an organization which was named, oh, years and years ago, as the legal bulwark of the Communist party. . . . I have hesitated bringing that up but I have been rather bored with your phony requests to Mr. Cohn here that he personally get every Communist out of government before sundown. . . ."

I tried to stop him the second he opened his mouth. I shot him a terrible look, I mouthed "No, No" to him, I scribbled a note to him reminding him that this was the subject we'd committed to Welch we wouldn't touch: "Please respect our agreement as an agreement, because this isn't going to do any good." But there was no stopping him. The best he could get himself to say was, "I know Mr. Cohn would rather not have me go into this."

Joseph Welch let him carry on, let him punch himself out. And then:

"Until this moment, Senator, I think I never really gauged your cruelty or your recklessness."

His eyes filming over, Welch took the audience through the story of how he had asked Fred Fisher if there was "anything funny" in his background, and upon learning that Fisher had joined the Lawyers Guild while at Harvard Law School and stayed with the Guild "for a period of months after," he, Welch, had said, "Fred, I just don't think I am going to ask you to work on the case. If I do, one of these days that will come out and go over national television, and it will just hurt like the dickens."

The Senate Caucus Room was hushed, and presumably so was the entire TV audience. Welch, his voice dripping with emotion, looked at McCarthy and said:

"Little did I dream you could be so reckless and so cruel as to do an injury to that lad. It is true he is still with Hale and Dorr. It is true that he will continue to be with Hale and Dorr. It is, I regret to say, equally true that I fear he shall always bear a scar needlessly inflicted by you. If it were in my power to forgive you for your reckless cruelty, I would do so. I like to think I am a gentleman, but your forgiveness will have to come from someone other than me."

McCarthy couldn't drop it now if he wanted to, and all I could do was sit by and hope against hope that he wouldn't make it worse. Of course, he made it worse.

"Mr. Welch talks about *this* being reckless and cruel," he said. "What hypocrisy! He's been baiting Mr. Cohn for hours . . . I just gave this man's record, and I want to say, Mr. Welch, that it has been labeled long before he became a member, as early as 1944."

Welch stopped him here, with the statement that stole the hearing: "Let us not assassinate this lad further, Senator," he said. "You have done enough. Have you no sense of decency, sir, at long last? Have you left no sense of decency?"

The tension in the room snapped. The spectators burst into applause, the newsmen burst into applause. Chairman Mundt gaveled and gaveled but who could gavel down the air itself?

Joe McCarthy had snatched defeat from the jaws of victory and Joe Welch had made the most of it. With his wondrous felicity of language, Welch left a lasting impression among many people that McCarthy was nothing but a rotten bastard who deliberately sought to wreck a fine young man's life. As a lawyer, I had to admire his skill. But it was pure nonsense.

McCarthy wasn't going after Fisher, the Fisher story had already made *The New York Times* without McCarthy's help. He was going after Welch because Welch was going after me.

McCarthy was reckless alright, but only in walking into Joe Welch's lethal one-two punch. As for inflicting a lifelong "scar" on Fred Fisher—I would have liked a dozen scars like that. He became an overnight folk-hero and could have stayed one had he had the desire and spark. Nothing could have hurt him, particularly at Hale and Dorr, and nothing did, and Welch knew this, if for no other reason than he controlled Hale and Dorr. That Joe Welch was able to make the country cry over Fred Fisher proved not only that he was a natural actor—he later played a judge for Otto Preminger in *Anatomy of a Murder*—but also that he understood "McCarthyism" far better than the eponym of the term.

His final touch, after the hearing adjourned for the day, was to stand in the corridor outside the Senate Caucus Room, weeping copiously into a handkerchief. Page one across the world, but nobody else shed crocodile tears.

Of all the ironies connected with the Army-McCarthy hearings, none could beat the fact that Joe McCarthy knew better than anybody else that public opinion would deliver the real verdict. During a lunch recess, early in the game, he said to me: "People aren't going to remember the things we say on the issues here, our logic, our common sense, our facts. They're only going to remember the impressions."

So his enemies walked off with the good impressions, while thirty years later I have to remind everybody about logic, common sense and facts.

Here was a man with warmth, humor, loyalty, a man who loved people, who was forgiving almost beyond the bounds of reasonableness. And here was a man who came across, at the most important crossroad of his life, as villainy incarnate—a dictatorial, brutal, obstructive, utterly humorless bully with a perpetual five o'clock shadow that gave new dimension to the word "menacing."

Just why McCarthy couldn't see what he was doing to himself, while being brilliantly critical of everybody else's performance, is either easy to analyze or beyond analysis. The obvious psychiatric answer is that people tend all the time to go blind when looking at themselves. And maybe that was it. But it's too pat an explanation. Joe was too complicated for such a five-and-dime answer. And yet the alternative is. . . . I don't know, perhaps the occult?

What I do know is that I knew, and all of us around Joe knew, he was doing miserably. But we never told him. Here he was, screaming "Point of order," until it became a national joke—and we didn't tell him to cut it out. Here he was, constantly complaining about being interrupted, when he was doing most of the interrupting. And we didn't tell him. Here he was repeating himself so often that a buddy of mine said one day, "Joe was not only redundant this afternoon, he said the same thing twice." And we didn't tell him once.

Why not?

Well, we were busy; every night after the session we were inundated with countless details, we were setting up the next day's events.

How could we be bothered with post mortem discussions of McCarthy's demeanor when we had to worry about tomorrow, when we didn't even have time to watch the nightly kinescope reruns on TV?

But the truth was, we didn't have the guts. I know I didn't, and I'm sure the others were just as scared to tell this national figure that he was screwing up. I mean, here I was just a kid, and who was I to say anything, especially since I wasn't asked?

Would it have mattered? If we all had the courage to tell him it sure would have mattered. Joe Welch certainly couldn't have done the Fred Fisher number had Joe McCarthy been even half the McCarthy we knew. It took a lot of self-destruction to get set up for that line about "decency." And that was the line that made the lasting impression.

Still, I don't buy the general opinion that the hearings "killed off" McCarthy. Sure, they hurt him badly, they precipitated his downfall, but there was a more fundamental reason for his decline. By the time the hearings ended, McCarthy had been the center of the national and world spotlight for three and a half years. Communism may go on forever (God forbid!), and subversion (God help us!), but America's attention span is something else again. No public man can remain indefinitely at the center of controversy. The people always look for new thrills. And McCarthy had nothing new to offer, just more of the same. He was Johnny-One-Note in a country that got bored with symphonies.

If this sounds like second-guessing, consider that Richard Nixon didn't even mention subversives, didn't mention Alger Hiss, in his 1960 presidential campaign.

Of course, McCarthy's enemies were not so philosophical, they wanted him dead yesterday, not on some inevitable tomorrow. But they didn't kill him off at the hearings, surely not according to the committee's verdict. In a strict party-line vote (even "crossfire" didn't fire) the Republican majority cleared McCarthy of the charge that he brought "improper influence" to bear on Schine's behalf. The Democrats, while attributing "inexcusable actions" to both McCarthy and me, blasted Stevens for "inexcusable indecisiveness" and said that he and John Adams merited "severe criticism" for "appeasement."

Given McCarthy's screw-ups, this was a victory indeed, no matter that it came across as a yawn to the public. But on the day the verdict arrived—August 31, 1954—a special Senate committee opened hearings on a resolution to censure McCarthy. The timing was probably coincidental, but not the purpose. This time they were going to get Joe, this time there'd be no fooling around.

"You're the kid who came to the party and peed in the lemonade," Senator William Jenner (R.-Indiana) told McCarthy. As such, he had to go. "We can't strike out this time," an eminent Eisenhower Republican senator told me one night at a party. "Unless we get rid of your boy, he's going to be a mighty big thorn in our side."

Indeed. For whatever I might have thought about the long run, the White House knew that McCarthy still commanded 35 percent support in the Gallup Poll *after* the Army-McCarthy hearings. The Eisenhower crowd had only to look back to 1912 to see what happened when the party split, when Theodore Roosevelt bolted and ran on the Bull Moose ticket and thus elected Woodrow Wilson. This was exactly on the minds of the

the Republican establishment as it looked to the 1956 elections, and saw the possibility of Joe McCarthy leading a right-wing third party ticket. And while this might have made the Democrats salivate, they hated Joe too much to try and play it cute. He'd done himself in with them for all time with his "twenty years of treason" line, which of course he never meant literally. The Democrats, understandably, weren't interested in parsing it, they weren't letting him off the hook now that they had him on the line.

So it was a foregone conclusion, the censure of McCarthy; and for saying that, for calling it a "lynch party," he was bi-partisanly condemned by the Senate—it was one of the two reasons given in the censure resolution. The other, that he abused members of the Subcommittee on Privileges and Elections, was just as phony, and to discuss it, or the protracted hearings on it, would be to give it credibility and that, frankly, *would* make me throw up.

In any case, by the time the censure hearings began, I was long gone. Right after Army-McCarthy, in June, I went on National Guard duty at the Kessler Air Force Base in Biloxi, Mississippi. When I got back, it was clear that the committee was going to dump me, "crossfire" me, courtesy of the three Democrats plus Senator Potter. Joe wanted me to stay on as his administrative assistant, and my initial tendency was to stick.

My family wanted me to leave; they thought I'd done well and that by and large the public was sympathetic to me. I was to discover that between "by" and "large" there was a ravaging, boundless hatred that would only become more vituperative after McCarthy died (in 1957) and I was the only symbol of the evil incarnate left to kick around. I say this without complaint but with bemusement over the virility of the anti-McCarthy, anti-Cohn virus, which seems to be genetically transmitted by liberals. Much of it, I believe, is the result of good old liberal guilt. That is, the more they find out about such great heroes as Franklin Roosevelt, who only abandoned the Jews of Europe, and Harry Truman, who stacked the Supreme Court with anti-Communist conservatives and who began the whole loyalty-security program, and of course LBJ and Vietnam, the more they love to pour all their frustration on me as stand-in for McCarthy.

Anyway, I listened to my family and decided to quit and go back to New York to practice law. I'm not sorry I left, but I have always regretted the manner of my leave-taking. I could have forced the committee to fire me, making Crossfire Potter go on record, which his devious nature deplored. And I should have done so, as quitting was against everything I was ever taught. To go quietly is to go cowardly. It bugs me to this day that I hauled off and left without making those bastards do the dirty job themselves, out in the open.

Well, done is done! And I wonder if it ever occurred to me that I'd never be back in public life again? Not to say that my life became anything but public. Often more public than I liked, as in indictments, as in public trials.

I'll get to them; we're not hiding anything here. But first I want to put to bed a couple of myths about Joe McCarthy, and about Bobby Kennedy.

The central myth, the one you hear and read about all the time, is that Senator McCarthy didn't care a whit about Communism, that he was a political opportunist who stumbled onto it and finding it a good thing just rode with it, that he had no sincerity, that it could have been *anything*, any issue that turned out to be popular.

Now there's no question that when first he got to the Senate in 1946 and for some years afterward, he didn't know Communism from a hole in the ground. But when he got into it, when he began reading and talking to people like Whittaker Chambers and J.B. Matthews, he was at first incredulous, unbelieving, and then shocked and outraged; he became totally committed to anti-Communism and there wasn't an ounce of insincerity in it. So I state flatly that of all the things that have been said about McCarthy—and some things maybe are true and others half-true—the one that's an absolute falsehood is that he didn't believe in what he was doing, that he was a self-seeker using Communism as a political tool.

Actually, he'd have had to be nuts to think it would help him politically when he started in 1950—the worst time to be an anti-Communist, when the press and the intellectuals were so against the exposure of left-wingers and Commies. Politically it was equivalent to taking a speedboat out to board the *Titanic* when it hit the iceberg. But in any event, smart or not, it wasn't phony, and Joe never wavered once he made the commitment.

Nearly as central is the myth that McCarthy was responsible for everything that happened in the fight against domestic Communism. Were Hollywood screenwriters and actors blacklisted? McCarthy did it. Were newspapermen and authors purged? McCarthy did it. Did a television actor commit suicide? McCarthy again.

But the media probes had nothing whatever to do with McCarthy; they either preceded him or were held in the House, and Joe was never in the House; ipso facto he was never head of HUAC, believe it or not. This isn't to say he opposed these investigations—you and I agree he was all for them, and for the blacklists as well. But he didn't do it. And he didn't investigate the press, either. In fact, he was dead when Senator Eastland (D.-Mississippi) conducted his press hearings in 1958. As for suicides, I keep hearing that people jumped out of windows because of Joe and because of me, too. I don't appreciate that, my sense of humor doesn't reach that far, nor my sweet nature. It's a flat out lie and a very lousy lie, and the marvelous thing is that the liberals who float it don't think they even have to provide the names of the putative suicides. McCarthy did it, McCarthyism, that's what killed so-and-so. I'll lay odds till Doomsday that most people who saw Woody Allen's film, *The Front*, were certain that when Zero Mostel went out that hotel window, McCarthy did it. And Cohn too. They did it, yessir.

And if you confront these fair-minded souls, and show them they lie, they just shrug. Hell, the ends justify the means, who cares, eh baby?

And so another myth: the liberals say they loved our ends, they just didn't like our means, our methods.

Well, our methods were far from perfect. McCarthy sensationalized evidence, he often shot from the hip, he made overly dramatic statements, he didn't always do his homework, to say the least. But with all of that conceded, I say without hesitation, that our treatment of individuals, our respect for constitutional rights, was better than most congressional investigating committees and fundamentally superior to most prosecutors.

Our committee gave witnesses and "suspects" rights they didn't enjoy in a court of law. Every witness that came before us, for example, had the right to have a lawyer beside him at all times—a privilege never granted in grand jury investigations. We used executive sessions, insulated from the press and the public; hundreds of persons were called by the McCarthy committee every year who nobody ever knew had been summoned, because they had satisfactory explanations for alleged illegal conduct, and so were dismissed without harm to their reputations. Show me a district attorney who does that! They leak like a sieve to the press. Imagine a public official called before a supposedly secret grand jury, and nobody hearing about it.

I don't buy the liberals' line that they only opposed McCarthy's methods. I believe most of them opposed his ends—which was to expose and bring to justice Communist subversives. If it were the methods they didn't like, why didn't we hear from them when Kefauver investigated the mob? Well, we did hear from them. We heard cheers. And later, when McClellan went after the Teamsters, the liberals ran to orgasm. And the McClellan committee, with Bobby Kennedy as chief counsel, violated civil liberties on a wholesale basis.

In my years as prosecutor and counsel to McCarthy, I never tapped a wire, never used any kind of eavesdropping equipment, I never inserted an informer into a lawyer-client conversation, I never used "mail covers"—the opening of letters sent to targets of investigations—in short, I never did any of the things Robert F. Kennedy did as a matter of course, both in his position as Senate counsel and attorney general. I was a veritable William O. Douglas next to Bobby Kennedy. So who's the liberal icon? Just guess. So much for "ends and means."

Yet Bobby, in his book *The Enemy Within*, says that he left the McCarthy Committee in 1953 because he didn't approve of our methods.

"Most of the investigations," he wrote, "were instituted on the basis of some preconceived notion by the chief counsel or his staff members and not on the basis of any information that had been developed. Cohn and Schine claimed they knew from the outset what was wrong; and they were not going to allow the facts to interfere. Therefore no real spadework that might have destroyed some of their pet theories was ever undertaken. I thought Senator McCarthy made a mistake in allowing the committee to operate in such a fashion, told him so and resigned."

Apart from the fact that this really described Bobby's methods, not ours, here is Kennedy's resignation letter to McCarthy, dated July 29, 1953:

> Please accept my resignation as assistant counsel and deputy staff director of the Senate Permanent Subcommittee on Investigations, effective as of the close of business July 31, 1953.
> With the filing in the Senate of the Subcommittee Report on Trade with the Soviet Bloc, the task to which I have devoted my time since coming with the subcommittee has been completed. I am submitting my resignation at this time as it is my intention to enter the private practice of law at an early date.
> I have enjoyed my work and association on the subcommittee, and I wish to express to you my appreciation for the opportunity of having served with your group.
> Please accept my sincere thanks for the many courtesies and kindnesses you have extended to me during these past seven months.

Bobby, of course, never did go into private practice. He hooked up with the bi-partisan Commission on Organization of the Executive Branch of the Government—the Hoover Commission. And then came back to the McCarthy committee as counsel to the Democratic minority, just in time for the Army-McCarthy hearings. Where we had our famous fight. Or rather, non-fight.

It happened on June 11, while McCarthy was on the witness stand. Near the close of the day, the discussion turned to a plan for selling democracy that had been prepared by Dave Schine before he joined our committee as consultant. The plan listed fifteen channels through which democracy might be promoted in areas into which Communism was spreading. Its basic aim was to "inspire native leaders everywhere to express democracy in every field of social action and to develop democratic groups and parties." In short, a precursor of Jack Kennedy's Peace Corps.

Bobby, however, saw it as a way to get at me, by ridiculing Schine's report. He kept feeding gibe-questions to Senator Henry "Scoop" Jackson (D.-Washington). Schine, for example, had written: "We must create a 'Demiform' or association of democratic parties on the basis of mutual cooperation free of the charge of American imperialism." Jackson inquired scoffingly: "Isn't the word 'Demiform' pretty close to 'Cominform'? Aren't some of the people going to get mixed up?" This broke Jackson up, and he was hot now, he kept going, as Bobby kept feeding him Henny Youngman lines.

Schine had written that it was important to encourage the clergy to play a role in the support of Democracy. Jackson, grinning, wanted to know: "Is he going to infiltrate the clergy?" Fits of laughter, on and on, until the session was adjourned, right after the Bobby-Scoop Show ended. I was pissed off. I didn't need this burlesque, especially from Kennedy, whom I knew was secretly entirely on McCarthy's side and hated the fact that I was sitting where he wanted to sit.

I gathered up my papers at the adjournment, and as I walked out I came face to face with Bobby. I told him he was unfair, and that he was full of crap. His voice rose, he warned me that I wasn't going to get away with it and I was going to be stopped.

People lingered to listen, but Bobby paid no heed. "Look," I said, "apparently there is only one way to settle this," and I started to swing. Two men grabbed me, Bobby moved away, and nobody got hit. Lucky for me. I wasn't a mountain climber or touch football player, he'd probably have beaten hell out of me.

The next day, the papers headlined it, and said I had threatened to "get" Scoop Jackson and when Bobby told me to fuck off, the "fight" began. Well, I was used to this press stuff by then, but it didn't mean I had to like it. And I did have to answer it, which was worse. I did it through Senator Mundt, the chairman, who told the press he had known of our feud for a long time. "I don't know why and I don't care why," he said. "It is something that has no place in the hearings and it isn't going to have a place in the hearings. They are just popping off and they can stop it."

We could and we did.

Then one day John F. Kennedy became the President of the United States. And Bobby became the Attorney General of the United States. God be with me.

And He was.

But He tested me. Watch and see how He tested me.

Bobby as attorney general. Oh, Wow!

Chapter Nine

The day Bobby Kennedy was made attorney general, I called Jim Juliana, the only person who ever worked for us both. He was my assistant counsel on the McCarthy Committee, and Bobby's assistant when Bobby became chief counsel to Senator McClellan's "Get Hoffa" committee.

"Jim," I said, "I don't want to bother you with this, I haven't spoken to Bobby in years, I can't imagine he's sitting around thinking about me. But just between us, Jim, what's his attitude towards me?"

Jim Juliana said: "Hoffa's number one. You're number two."

I don't recall that my stomach sank or anything like that. But I sure didn't go out and buy a new suit.

Even an editor of the *Harvard Law Review* could figure out that somebody who was second to Jimmy Hoffa on Bobby Kennedy's hit list was not going to have the life promised by Mr. Jefferson in the Declaration of Independence. And I wasn't exactly an agrarian idealist. By 1961, when Bobby took over the

Justice Department, I was running a pretty active law firm in New York, and that's not all I was doing. I was a major fight promoter, I had a gossip-column list of famous clients, I traveled the world in style—let's face it, I was practically indictable for being Roy Cohn.

An Attorney General of the United States with a target in his sight-glass is potentially as deadly and inevitable as a guided missile. Through his U.S. attorneys he controls all the federal grand juries in the country. Grand juries have long been the institutional rubber stamps of prosecutors but while most states impose certain restraints on them, in the federal system anything goes. A federal grand jury can indict on hearsay alone. This means that an FBI agent, for example, can simply read his report to the grand jury, citing anonymous sources, and the grand jury can indict and the indictment will stand. Under federal law—and again this does not apply in most states—a grand jury can indict and a petit jury can convict a defendant on the uncorroborated testimony of a so-called accomplice. That is to say, anybody who can make a deal with the government can "rat out" whoever the government wants ratted out—and if the jury believes his story and he's tried and convicted, the conviction will be upheld on appeal, on the accomplice's word alone. Never mind that his "word" wouldn't be worth a six-cent verdict in a municipal court automobile accident case. Never mind that he's got a record two arms long. Never mind that he's probably going to walk free after the trial, though he admits to being part of the crime itself. His word alone can convict someone who never got a parking ticket. Indeed, prosecutors normally flaunt the criminal record of the accomplice: after all, they say, what was this "unblemished" defendant doing with this killer, this swindler, this destroyer of the poor and the innocent!

Of course, I knew the game by heart. As a young assistant U.S. attorney I convicted my share of people on uncorroborated accomplice testimony. But it was one thing to make use of the tools at hand—however unfair the tools may be—and another, quite another thing, to employ the extraordinary powers of the federal government in pursuit of a personal vendetta. That I never did. I never hated anybody enough to do that, and if I were attorney general I can't imagine bothering; if I was up there all my enemies would be yesterday's newspaper, I couldn't care less about them. But if Jim Juliana was telling me the truth—and he was my good friend, so, unfortunately, I had no reason to disbelieve him—this was certainly not the attitude of Bobby Kennedy.

Well, all I could do was wait, and I waited nearly three years. That it took Kennedy all that time to indict me, and on a phony charge, says more about my clean living than my reputation needed. I mean, part of my mystique depended on people thinking that I was getting away with every kind of shady deal; but with Bobby after me, how could I be involved with *anything* and not be nailed? I'm kidding, of course, but I think only my mother knew I was that honest.

Actually, Bobby made his first direct hit on me in September, 1962, a year before the indictment, and he did it through the Internal Revenue Service, which the attorney general is not supposed to control, and usually doesn't—but "usually" had nothing much to do with anything once the President's brother was the attorney general. Anyway, I owned a fight promotion company named Championship Sports, Inc., with my law partner and best friend, Tom Bolan, and we put on the Floyd Patterson-Sonny Liston heavyweight title bout in Chicago on September 25, 1962. Liston whacked out Floyd in about two minutes—which was longer than it took Bobby to knock us out of the box office.

The IRS seized all the proceeds of the fight, both the live gate and the closed-circuit theater gate. They did it under a fascist procedure known as a "jeopardy assessment." I say "fascist" advisedly, for it has nothing whatever to do with democracy. The government can simply grab money by saying, as it said here, that it was worried that Championship Sports wouldn't pay its taxes. The taxes weren't due until the following year, and no proof existed that we were going to dead-beat the government. Moreover, everybody's end was seized—the fighters', the theater owners', the managers'—in that way, I suppose, Bobby and his boys were very democratic, they screwed everybody equally. Now, of course, they didn't claim to own all the money, they simply escrowed it into court and it was up to us to sue for it. Eight years later we were still owed $435,000 and had incurred over $50,000 in fees and expenses. And while the government conceded that most of the funds had to be returned to us, we were told to wait in line. No wonder the New York *Daily News* editorially blasted the government for this being one of the most "high-handed examples of unbridled Big Brother power." And to think that I hadn't even touched Bobby that day in the Senate corridor. Imagine if I'd landed a lucky punch.

Long before the Patterson-Liston fight, I began to receive phone calls from dozens of lawyers in New York tipping me off that clients of theirs had been asked by the United States attorney what they might be able to say against me. Most of these people didn't even know me, but if they were potential witnesses or defendants charged with white collar crimes, they were pushed to furnish information, told that things would go better for them if they could implicate me in some way.

The U.S. attorney with all this interest in me was Robert M. Morgenthau, appointed by Bobby in 1961. Morgenthau had his own reasons for wanting to put me away, which he always denied, but which I thought quite natural. In 1953, the McCarthy Committee investigated the incredible turnover of United States occupation-currency printing plates to the Soviet Union after World War II. It was the first time in history that the United States had parted with its currency plates, and the turn-over allowed the Russians to print hundreds of millions of dollars of American obligations without accountability to America. The scheme could not have been effectuated without the signature of the Secretary of the Treasury—Henry Morgenthau, Jr., the father of our new United States Attorney for the Southern District of New York.

Henry Morgenthau's principal aide in Treasury was Harry Dexter White, later revealed as a Soviet spy—not by Joe McCarthy but by the Attorney General of the United States, Herbert Brownell, who got the information from the FBI files. White had tremendous influence over Morgenthau—enough so that despite vigorous objections by Budget Director Daniel Bell, Morgenthau directed that the money plates be turned over to the Russians.

I was, of course, chief counsel during these hearings and our committee issued a report unanimously condemning Morgenthau. As noted, Robert Morgenthau has steadfastly denied that his father's case had anything to do with his investigations of me—which investigations resulted in three indictments and three acquittals. But then, Morgenthau has steadfastly denied that either he or Bobby Kennedy conducted a vendetta against me.

For years, it was Morgenthau's word against mine. I had the acquittals, sure, but Morgenthau had his friends and I had my enemies. You didn't have to believe vendetta if you didn't want to, and if you wanted to, what did it really matter once I was cleared and Morgenthau was out of office? It really was yesterday's newspaper and I was satisfied to leave it at that. And then, out of the blue, in the October, 1976, issue of *Commentary*, under the title "Memoir of a Prosecutor," there appeared a full-out confessional by one of Morgenthau's former assistants, Professor Irving Younger of Cornell Law School. It was pure dynamite, proof of everything I'd said in my *j'accuse*, and even more than I suspected.

Younger wrote that in the late summer of 1961 he was summoned to Morgenthau's office and introduced to Robert F. Kennedy himself. Kennedy said nothing, just nodded a hello, and Morgenthau did the talking.

"The Department," said Morgenthau, "has a special interest in Roy Cohn."

This, wrote Younger, was no news to him since it had been the gossip of the office for months.

"The Department," Morgenthau continued, "thinks it would be a good idea to consolidate all of our Cohn activities in one assistant. I'm designating you. Review the files. Follow up. Go wherever you have to. Your job is to find out whether Cohn is guilty of something. The Department wants Cohn."

Younger said: "I'll get him."

Nine months later, Younger reported to Morgenthau as follows:

"I'm licked. If he has violated the law, I can't find it."

This after he had traveled half the world to uncover me. "I had been to Europe twice, to Central America once, and to various places within the United States," Younger wrote. "I had studied every official file in which Roy Cohn was mentioned. I had put Cohn before the grand jury. I had devoted myself single-mindedly to investigating Roy Cohn, and the result was nothing."

He also, as he readily admitted, offered a deal to a prospective defendant if he'd give me up and then tried to "break" him with a conviction and jail sentence in the hope that *then* he'd turn me over. He had the FBI bug a hotel room where one of my friends, a lawyer, would hopefully say something against me to a Swiss crook who was given immunity and safe passage in New York for the sole purpose of setting me up. He used surveillance teams, he used my income tax returns—legally confidential and not supposed to be turned over to the U.S. attorney—he made and broke promises when necessary. In other words, he did every-thing conceivable to put me away, without regard to ethical con-siderations, without regard to the Constitution.

The difference was that Irving Younger wasn't proud of him-self and was willing to say so in print. "It was the power of power," he concluded. "If I possibly could, I was going to be the one to do the job the Department wanted done. Not once did I stop to think what it was a Department of."

And finally the irony of ironies. Having left the Department of Justice after giving up on me, he ran into one of his old bosses while attending to a client in the Federal Courthouse on Foley Square.

It was William G. Hundley, head of the Department's Orga-nized Crime Section, and very tight with Bobby. Hundley said he'd been meaning to call Younger, and did he have a second to talk?

"Listen Irv," Hundley said, "what about your resignation?"

"What about it?"

"We've heard that you were forced out for being too tough on Cohn."

"That's not true. I resigned because I'd been in the office long enough. It was time to move on to something else."

"Well," said Hundley, "if you say so, O.K. But the Depart-ment thinks maybe Cohn got to Morgenthau."

Morgenthau finally got a grand jury to indict me on September 3, 1963, a forty-page, ten-count indictment charging me with perjury, obstruction of justice and conspiracy to commit the perjury and the obstruction. It was an incredible reach, it was really scraping the bottom of the barrel, especially in view of what they had spent many months trying to prove: That I had bribed the chief assistant United States attorney back in 1959 to buy off the indictments of a couple of Las Vegas crime figures and other assorted sleazebags in the then-famous United Dye case. In the end, the only thing the Kennedy-Morgenthau axis succeeded in doing was to turn the name of the case into the Roy Cohn case. That and costing the government a fortune in time, money and credibility, plus letting the convicted culprits out in the bargain. But they put me through the grinder pretty good, so maybe it was worth it to them.

The underlying indictment—out of which I emerged as the "principal" years later—was brought by Morgenthau's Republican predecessor, S. Hazard Gillespie. It was a major stock swindle case, involving as main defendants the following:

Alexander Guterma, president of United Dye and Chemical Corporation. Guterma was an arch-swindler and was accused here of artificially manipulating and illegally trading company stock.

Allard Roen, a Las Vegas bigshot, a relative of the old syndicate gangster "Nigger" Rosen, and owner of an oil-pipeline company, whose stock he had illegally traded for United Dye.

Sam Garfield, a convicted illegal gambling-house operator and behind-the-scenes partner of big-time underworld figures.

Sidney Barkley, a man with a long criminal record, who ran a "boiler shop"—a brokerage house that ground out phony stock, which he sold through a high-pressure telephone campaign. Barkley's "maiden name" was Beckerman, which name he thought better of after the case. He is once again Sidney Beckerman, only now he's a well-known Hollywood movie producer, who for a time in the 1970's was president of Allied Artists.

Allen Swann. He was a lawyer for United Dye.

This crowd's criminal manipulation and illegal sale of stock led to the longest and probably the most expensive criminal trial in legal history until then, lasting from February to December, 1962. It was tried by Morgenthau's assistant, Gerald Walpin, who described it as a case in which a handful of conspirators had swindled "thousands of people out of millions of dollars."

And who could deny it? Certainly not the swindlers. They all pleaded guilty in the end. And in the end, they all walked free, every one. By Morgenthau's recommendation!

How could such a thing happen? Easy. They testified against me. Obviously, only a paranoic would claim a vendetta against a prosecutor who let go those who swindled thousands out of millions. Obviously, a little background music is required.

On August 25, 1959, Alexander Guterma and others were indicted by a federal grand jury of conspiring to sell United Dye stock fraudulently, and with committing mail fraud against people who purchased the stock. But the "others" did not include Garfield, Roen, Swann, and Barkley. Shortly afterwards, a superseding indictment named all of these worthies, and under this indictment Morgenthau's office tried them all—and they all pleaded guilty. Morgenthau, to repeat, had indicted nobody, Gillespie did that. After John Kennedy won the presidency, Morgenthau inherited the indictment, the *superseding* indictment, and proceeded to try and convict the culprits.

It was only after the trial, and after the guilty pleas, that the Four Horsemen—Garfield, Roen, Swann, Barkley—decided to save themselves by concocting a story against me. And the story was that I had arranged a bribe to Morton Robson, the chief assistant U.S. attorney under S. Hazard Gillespie, to keep them out of the original indictment.

That indictment had been returned on August 25, 1959, but according to the tale they told, Robson didn't cash in on the bribe until after Labor Day. This alone should have indicated something to Morgenthau—Who fixes a case and *then* tries to collect?—but neither this anomaly nor any other that was to turn up in this strange and strained effort to get me would ring any bells, turn on any red light. Such is the way when the decision to go is made in advance of the proof—facts are not seen, much less allowed to stand in the path of righteousness.

So (as they told the story), I called Sam Garfield at the Pierre

Hotel in New York sometime after Labor Day and told him that the "man" in the U.S. attorney's office who took care of the case would be going to Vegas to collect his fifty grand and that he should be given two-thirds of it. Garfield then called Allard Roen in California and told Roen to go to Vegas and take care of the matter. Roen agreed, but there was one snafu that had to be overcome: Garfield didn't know the name of the U.S. attorney who was coming out to pick up the cash. Because I had forgotten to tell him!

Therefore, Garfield called me and said, "Roy, you forgot to tell me the name of the guy coming out for the money." I said, "Robson." Garfield called Roen back and said, "Robson." So, Roen with the name in hand, and the cash, returned to Vegas, and one balmy fall evening a man came over to him and said, "I'm Robson." Roen then put the $33,000 in a "letter-sized envelope," took Robson into the elevator that runs up a couple of floors to a hotel dining room, and handed the envelope to Robson on the way. What happened to the rest of the fifty grand? Garfield said he gave it to me at a later date.

Again, simple logic should have told Morgenthau how idiotic it was to assume that the number two man in the most important federal prosecutor's office in the country would go to Las Vegas to personally collect a bribe. The story was not only palpably false, it was provably false.

Robson had never been in Las Vegas in his life. Further, on the day Roen testified he was there, Robson was in New York and could back it up beyond all doubt, not just a reasonable doubt. It turned out he was moving his family from one apartment to another that day, and he had signed receipts from the movers and witnesses galore to prove it.

Moreover, Robson was not the man who made the decision to omit the Four Horsemen from the original indictment. The decision was made by Gillespie, without consultation with Robson. Gillespie thought that further investigation was required to strengthen the case against the Garfield-Roen group, and when that was done they were added as defendants in the superseding indictment.

Who was the source for this? Hazard Gillespie. He told it to

Morgenthau when Morgenthau was trying to make the bribery case against me in the grand jury. Now Mr. Gillespie was not only the former U.S. attorney; he was one of the most distinguished lawyers in the country. And he and I had never met. You would think, then, that Morgenthau would tell the grand jury what Gillespie told him. Indeed, you would think he'd put Gillespie before the grand jury. Of course, he did no such thing. In fact, he tried later to prevent Gillespie from testifying for me at my trial! He actually subpoenaed Gillespie's books and records and threatened to invoke some kind of nonexistent cockamamie idea of "executive privilege" against Gillespie should he attempt to testify.

Well, Hazard Gillespie was not a man to be intimidated. He took the stand at my trial, and as Homer Bigart put it in *The New York Times*, Gillespie's testimony "struck at the heart of the government's case."

But I jump ahead. What happened at the grand jury level was that Morgenthau saw that no matter how much control he had over the jurors, there was no way he could make a bribery case stick against Robson or me or anybody. So he again called me before the grand jury and tried to salvage his crusade by trapping me into a perjury charge. I probably set a record as to the number of questions I was asked—4,851. They covered every phase of my personal and professional life. I had no doubt at all that he'd come up with an indictment, and if I had any hope it was put away one night just before the grand jury's term was to expire.

I got a call from Hale Boggs, then one of the top members of the Democratic leadership in the House of Representatives. Boggs was a friend of mine and a friend of the President. And the President told him that Morgenthau was insisting on going ahead—saying that he had an iron-clad case against me—and that Bobby was not about to stop him, and that Jack Kennedy, though he didn't like to see this happen to me, couldn't control Bobby.

I said, "Well, Hale, you know, I'm not in a position to be making grandiose statements, but if the President of the United States can't control his brother, he's in pretty bad shape."

This is not to say that if Jack Kennedy had another attorney general I'd have been in the same spot. We were never enemies and when we occasionally met we were always cordial, even friendly. I particularly remember his warmth when I ran into him a few years after my corridor scene with Bobby. We were both guests of C.Z. Guest at an April-in-Paris ball at the Waldorf. Jack said: "I'm sorry you and Bobby are always at each other's throats. I think you've got a great deal of ability and I like the job you've done against Communism. The fight between Bobby and you hasn't carried over to us."

Anyway, as I said, when the indictment finally came down it was the pits. To make any sense out of the charges, I'll have to briefly go over what actually did happen.

I met Garfield and Roen at the Desert Inn in Las Vegas in 1959. I was on vacation with one of my closest friends, William Fugazy, then president of the Diners Club, Fugazy Travel and now of Fugazy International. Roen had a piece of the Desert Inn, and other Vegas hotels, and Fugazy did extensive business with him on package tours and promotion. He introduced me to Roen and Garfield in the cocktail lounge of the Desert Inn, and it turned out to be the most expensive drink I ever had.

Roen told me he'd been called to an interview by a staff member of the Securities and Exchange Commission in connection with the stock sales of United Dye. He had no lawyer at the time (his attorney, Allen Swann, was not a New York lawyer and was himself potentially involved) and so Roen asked if I could get him a short adjournment. I did it by calling the S.E.C. staff lawyer and sending a confirmatory letter. It was a simple accommodation for a friend of a friend.

Garfield came into the picture later, when the United Dye case was forwarded to Morgenthau's office for prosecution. Garfield asked me to check if he was a target. I spoke to the chief of the criminal division who referred me to the assistant handling the case. And he told me there was a strong possibility that Garfield would be indicted. I told Garfield to get a lawyer, but not me, since I never represented a defendant in a criminal case. I suggested Murray Gottesman, and he hired Murray.

Garfield claimed that his lawyer, Swann, had told him he

could unload the United Dye stock under an exempting regulation. Since that would be a terrific defense, I advised that Swann explain this to the grand jury. Just before his appearance, Gottesman and I reviewed Swann's testimony with him at Garfield's suite in the Pierre.

Now, you may ask, why am I going on about these rather silly-seeming details? And the answer is—get ready for this one—the perjury count in my indictment was that I lied when I said I met with Gottesman, Swann and Garfield at the Pierre. By itself the thing would have been so minor that even if true who'd make a federal case out of it? But if I committed perjury on that I should have been committed to an institution. Because by the time I testified in the grand jury, Garfield and Swann had pleaded guilty in the United Dye case and had made a deal with Morgenthau. Why would I make up a story about meeting with two people who could contradict me in a minute? And remember, by the time I went to the grand jury Morgenthau had given up on the so-called bribery. So what motive would I have had to commit perjury with the bribe charge dead in the water?

I was also charged with obstruction of justice, for allegedly telling clients and friends who testified before the 1962–63 grand jury that "it is not a crime not to remember." To top it all off—or bottom it—Morgenthau threw in a conspiracy charge, and to make it travel he threw in poor Murray Gottesman, who really needed this wonderful client I gave him. The charge here was that Murray and I conspired for me to commit perjury and obstruct justice. I told you it was the pits. But on these pits Mr. Morgenthau took me to trial—twice. The first trial ended in a mistrial when a juror's father died during the deliberations. Three months later we were back again, and this time we were acquitted on all counts, and in a trice.

But Morgenthau and Bobby lost more than the verdict. They managed to get the American Civil Liberties Union to support Roy Cohn!

It all happened because Charlie the mailman got sick one day. Charlie wasn't my mailman, he was Tom Bolan's mailman— Tom, my partner, close pal and one of my lawyers in the trial. Tom had lived with his family in Cambria Heights, a Queens suburb, since postwar days. And Charlie had always delivered the mail. But on this day, a substitute carrier rang the bell. Mrs. Bolan came out and found the guy scratching his head and studying a yellow card. He handed it to Tom's wife, saying he didn't understand what it meant. Mrs. Bolan did. It was a confidential direction to the mail carrier to deliver the Bolans' mail to his supervisor. In other words, a mail cover.

We immediately moved to quash the indictment. Gerald Walpin, Morgenthau's assistant prosecutor in charge of my case, filed a sworn affidavit flatly denying any knowledge or responsibility for this "mail cover." Morgenthau put in his own affidavit supporting Walpin. But Judge Archie Dawson ordered a hearing. And under direct questioning by Judge Dawson, Walpin admitted he not only knew of the mail cover but had ordered it himself. And admitted that not only was Tom's home mail being intercepted, but so was mine, both at the office and at home.

Judge Dawson exploded in comments that made the front pages, calling the prosecutor's conduct in intercepting the mail of a defendant and his lawyer after an indictment "shocking," "terrible," and "stupid" and saying it "smacks of Russia rather than the United States." He didn't throw out the indictment—we never thought he would—but his anger over this prosecutorial zealotry and illegality brought severe criticism down on Morgenthau from the press, including much of the liberal press. And the ACLU issued a statement:

"According to news reports that have not been denied, an assistant U.S. attorney intimated in a statement to the Court that his office had not ordered a check on mail addressed to Roy Cohn or his attorney, Mr. Bolan. In doing so, he misled the Court and was guilty of an inexcusable evasion and lack of candor. The failure of the U.S. attorney to reprimand his assistant's flagrant violation of the lawyer's ethical duty or to replace him in the prosecution of the case may be construed as condonation.

"We believe an inquiry should be conducted by the Grievance Committee of the Bar Association."

No inquiry was ever made. If a criminal defense lawyer had done a tenth of what Walpin and Morgenthau pulled, the Grievance Committee would have had his license pulled before nightfall. But that passel of yo-yos who strut their piety as they stuff their shirts have never so much as held a hearing on that prosecutorial misconduct.

Similarly, nothing ever happened to the government for engineering a smear job against me in *Life* magazine a month after the indictment came down. This was clearly set up by Bobby Kennedy; we knew it the minute we saw that it was co-authored by William Lambert, one of Bobby's favorite journalistic hatchets. Titled "Roy Cohn: Is He a Liar under Oath?", the piece purported to give the unpublished "inside" story of the case. It was simply a brilliantly packaged libel designed to create irremediable prejudice against me before trial.

So, they said I didn't know Murray Gottesman, I brought him in because he was a Republican who could get to the Republican U.S. attorney's office. "According to the indictment," *Life* said, "it was Morton Robson whom Gottesman contacted," and since Robson was chief assistant he "naturally exercised certain authority in any proceedings which might arise in the United Dye case."

Well, I had known Gottesman for years and we had done a bunch of cases together, details of which *Life* could have easily discovered by a minimum of research or just by asking. The indictment contained nothing about Gottesman contacting Robson; the whole bribe story was out of the indictment. And by calling Hazard Gillespie, the writers and editors would have found out that Robson had no authority and nothing to do with the United Dye case.

But the purpose of the piece was to do a number on me, not to tell the truth. And then they really got rough, by charging that I tried to "put the squeeze on Garfield and Roen" through Moe Dalitz, one of Roen's partners in the Desert Inn. Dalitz was a lot more than just Roen's partner. One of the original leaders of the Cleveland mob during Prohibition, Moe was now a four-star general in the syndicate, only a cut below Meyer Lansky. The *Life* story turned me into a bosom buddy of Dalitz, and said he was my "vise" against Garfield and Roen.

I can say this for sure: if Moe Dalitz *had* been my rabbi there'd have been no indictment. Garfield and Roen and their secondary bums wouldn't have dared to testify against anybody Moey was protecting, even if they were telling the truth and even if it meant saving their own skins. That's how strong Dalitz was and you didn't have to know him to know it, and nobody knew this better than Bobby Kennedy, the real author of the *Life* piece.

The truth was, I knew Moe Dalitz's ex-wife Averill (when she was still living with him) far better than I knew her husband. I naïvely thought that Dalitz didn't mind me spending so much time with Averill, until a prosecution witness in my case quoted Moe as saying that he "would spend five years in jail to put Roy Cohn there for one day." Before that came to my attention, I did indeed speak to Moe about his friends, Garfield and Roen.

He said: "I can't answer for these guys. I am not their fucking conscience. But I can tell you one thing. They are no fucking good. Sure, they are my partners. Sure, we own hotels. Sure, we own gambling casinos. But they are no fucking good. They are yellow, afraid to take the rap for what they did. And I'll tell you one thing, if you are making plans, then count on never seeing me on a witness stand."

We moved to dismiss the indictment based on the *Life* piece but Judge Dawson had to turn us down because we had no actual proof that any government official was involved in trying to poison the case through the press. After the mistrial—after the juror's father died—we subpoenaed *Life*'s files. And hit the jackpot.

Tom Bolan's trade-mark is his dead-pan, even when he smiles. But after studying the "Roy Cohn file" at *Life*'s lawyer's office, he couldn't quite control the enthusiasm lighting his face.

"You won't believe it," he said. "Not only do we have proof that the Justice Department, from Bobby on down, collaborated on the article, but it was actually proofread and changed by Mulligan."

Mulligan was William Mulligan, the lawyer for Roen and Garfield. A memo in the file, written by one of the authors of the *Life* piece, said: "These are the suggested revisions given me by Mulligan, in his own handwriting, clipped to the sheets which he proposes revising."

Tom Bolan then told me he'd saved the biggest news for last. "I don't know how it happened," he said, "but mixed in with the papers in your file was a series of secret memos on the Jimmy Hoffa case. They show that Bobby Kennedy personally engineered a vicious article against Hoffa while he was awaiting trial—and Bobby literally begged *Life* to publish it."

Like Jim Juliana said, "Hoffa's number one, you're number two." Legally, this was crucial because it showed a common course of conduct by the Justice Department to use the press in its efforts to make cases against its enemies.

Now we had the proof Judge Dawson said we hadn't had before the first trial. But now we no longer had Judge Dawson. The retrial was assigned to Judge Dudley Bonsal. And though Tom put all of this proof into a powerhouse affidavit, Bonsal refused to throw the case out.

In the event, it didn't matter, because we were acquitted. But it would be too much to say "all's well that ends well." These trials took a tremendous toll on our lives, Murray's and mine, in time, money, tension and loss of clients. It cost the American taxpayer millions, of course. But the worst result of the Kennedy-Morgenthau vendetta was its denouement.

On August 24, 1964, after we were acquitted, after their perjured testimony had been completely rejected by the jury, Garfield, Roen, Barkley, and Swann came up for sentencing before the late Judge William B. Herlands in Federal Court, Foley Square, New York. If there were a Hall of Fame for hanging judges, Herlands would be Babe Ruth. In all my years at the bar, and before at my father's side, I never knew of a more pro-government hit-man than Bill Herlands. Yet faced with the men whom Walpin had characterized as having swindled "thousands of people out of millions of dollars," men who after an 11-month trial had pleaded guilty, this judicial executioner walked them out without a day in prison. On Morgenthau's recommendation, of course. And, of course, after all of them, at my trials, had sworn that they had no deal with the U.S. attorney, had no idea they would escape jail if they testified against me.

This is invariably the line of informers at trial, and it's virtually impossible to disprove. With Sam Garfield, I got lucky. A friend called me after Garfield gave the usual line and said, "Would a man who expected to go to jail buy thirty suits at $250 a clip and six dozen shirts?" It happened that my pal was at his tailor's, and the tailor mentioned he was rushing this order for Garfield.

We checked the story and subpoenaed the tailor, but we never had to use him. My lawyer, Frank Raichle, took care of it on cross-examination. He first had Garfield repeat that he had "no idea" he'd escape prison in return for his testimony against me. Then Raichle confronted Garfield with his recent order of thirty suits and six dozen shirts. Garfield, in shock, said it was "slightly on the high side."

The leftists can say what they like about the Rosenberg case, but the chief witnesses against Julius and Ethel—David Greenglass and Harry Gold—got 15 and 30 years, respectively. And for telling the truth in the crime of the century.

My phony accusers got the lush life. Roen sold his points in the Desert Inn to Howard Hughes and went on to run (with Garfield) the La Costa Country Club in California. Swann picked up his law practice in Ohio. Guterma resumed his wheeling and dealing in Florida. And Barkley-Beckerman became a movie mogul. Thus did Kennedy and Morgenthau do what they said I paid a bribe for—they gave these creeps a clean bill of health, and more; they gave them more fabulous careers.

I got one last lick in, years later, when Roen and Garfield sued *Penthouse* for an exposé on La Costa, calling the joint a mob enterprise. When they lost the libel suit, I shot off a telegram: "But you can't lose 'em all." I'm told it took them three weeks to figure it out.

Chapter Ten

In the fall of 1966, two years after my acquittal, I was deluged with phone calls from friends, clients, my rabbi, even the charge department at Saks Fifth Avenue. Each had received a questionnaire from the Internal Revenue Service announcing that I was under investigation and requesting details of all financial transactions with me over a period of many years.

Few of these callers, clients excepted, had any money dealings with me, so we couldn't figure out how they got on the IRS list. When we discovered that more than three hundred others were also hit with the questionnaire (maybe two of them had financial transaction with me) we were really stumped. Where did this list come from?

As often it goes, a bureaucratic slip-up gave the game away. A soldier overseas had received one of the questionnaires. He immediately notified a lawyer in our office, who happened to be his college classmate. The last time the lawyer heard from his old pal was two years earlier, when the soldier wrote to him at our office to thank him for a wedding gift. The lawyer's name was Robert Cohen. You didn't have to be Sherlock to deduce that the IRS list was made up from names and addresses they had obtained by intercepting our office mail at the time of my trial and that Robert Cohen's buddy got on the list because of the similarity of our names.

Bobby Kennedy had given Morgenthau a ten-man staff of IRS agents to work on me exclusively. It was actually known as "The Cohn Squad," and it began life in 1962 when it orchestrated the nationwide seizure of the proceeds of the Liston-Patterson fight. When Morgenthau put his mail cover on me and Tom Bolan, the Cohn Squad supplemented it by grabbing the incoming and outgoing mail at the law firm. Now they were using the fruits of that labor to try to make a tax case against me.

The minute we found this out we made it public and the story broke on the front page of *The New York Times*. There was an outcry and a congressional probe that established that mail interception by the Post Office Department was widespread and carried out indiscriminately at the request of other governmental agencies.

But neither editorial outrage nor congressional findings could stop the Cohn Squad from its appointed rounds. In 1967 they formally recommended criminal charges against me and Tom Bolan and several of our associates for five separate offenses, one more incredible than the other. We had, for instance, deducted an embezzlement from our taxes. This, said the Cohn squad, was phony, and the only implication was that there had been no embezzlement. Consider how phony it was. The people who embezzled from us had been sent to jail for it by Frank Hogan, the District Attorney of New York County.

The whole thing sent up such a stench that every agency involved—Treasury, Justice and the IRS itself—dropped each and every charge made by the Cohn Squad. We were out clear, but not for nothing. It cost us forty grand, in LBJ dollars, for lawyers and accountants. And these were just direct costs, forget about our time and loss of clients.

I don't beef about money, I don't even like to talk about it, all I want to do is spend it, and over the years I've managed to make enough to keep my vices alive and well. During the vendetta, however, roughly 1961–71, there were periods of big trouble and I was lucky to have good friends who bailed me out with loans and outright gifts. The best of all was Samuel I. Newhouse, founder of the publishing empire and father of my best friend, Si. I remember going to see him, nervous as a cat, and he asked me what the trouble was. I said, "I'm broke." He said, "Tell me how much you need." Mr. Newhouse smiled. "C'mon, Roy, give me a number." When I told him $250,000 he simply wrote out a check for the amount. I nearly fainted. I said I didn't know when I could pay him back. He said, "You don't ever have to pay me back. You've already paid me with friendship."

I totted it up one day in 1969, what the Kennedy-Morgenthau vendetta had run me, and it was $400,000 out-of-pocket. Add to this the time and loss of business and we're way over a million bucks. Plus, Morgenthau destroyed just about every banking relationship I had. He did this by forcing the banks to furnish copies of checks I issued on a daily basis. To avoid the nuisance, the banks closed my accounts. Once I had a loan at a bank secured by stock certificates collateral. Morgenthau subpoenaed the president of the bank and directed him to produce the collateral. And then impounded it. We had to go to the Justice Department to get it back.

But my costs were peanuts next to what the vendetta ran the American taxpayers. Morgenthau called over a thousand witnesses to testify about me in grand juries, and each had to be paid witness and transportation fees. The records he subpoenaed would fill eleven large rooms. He sent three people to Europe to investigate me. He had seven assistant U.S. attorneys working full-time on my cases, not to mention himself and his top executives. There were FBI agents assigned to me alone, and Security and Exchange staffers, and an accounting staff and of course the omnipresent Cohn Squad. Plus the cost of four trials. How much? I can't add that high.

O.K., I survived it. But what about others who don't have the friends or the wherewithal to fight official vendettas? The answer is clear—they're gone. And no way to be recompensed, even after they're cleared. The law provides no route to sue a prosecutor run amok. You may be acquitted three times—as I was—or once, or five times and you get only the acquittal. Of course, that's great when you consider the alternative, but something ought to be done to restrain these people. Unfortunately, there's no constituency for reform here. You'd think the liberals would go to the front on this, but they never do, even when the victims are poor Blacks. I mean, what did they ever do for George Whitmore? He was the guy accused of killing two white career girls—the famous Wylie-Hoffert case of 1963 out of which the Kojak series was spun. The cops sweated him into a phony confession, they wrecked his life, and when he sued for the frame-up he got nothing. None of the bleeding-heart liberals said a word. I didn't either, and I'm not proud of that.

Well, it wouldn't have done any good, whatever I'd have said or done. No constituency, and I wish I knew why not.

What I do know, for sure, is that the IRS has an unfettered power that is the envy of the most vicious prosecutor. I know what they did and still do to me, and if they could do it to me, with all my clout, what can they do to the average person?

They've audited me for 23 years, and they've never closed an audit. This means that they can ask me anytime—as they have— who I had dinner with on October 20, 1967, or something. I'm supposed to keep records of every lunch, dinner, drink for all time, because they refuse to close an audit. So they decided to disallow every deduction I took over these 20-odd years, which is how they claim I owe them eight million dollars. It's easy to get up that high when you add on penalties and interest.

Five years ago, to get them off my back, I made an offer of $1 million to settle the thing. I didn't have the cash; Si Newhouse was going to put it up, he wanted me freed from all this madness. The IRS prepared the papers, I signed them, the whole deal was set—but it never got done. Not because of Si Newhouse or me. Just that nobody on top at IRS was willing to sign-off on the very papers they had prepared.

I don't cry about it; the truth is it doesn't change my life. But that's because I have no family. I don't have to build an estate. I don't have to send kids to school. If I had a family, I couldn't even protect them with an insurance policy. They'd grab any money I put away, and they did. I tried it once. I took out an IRA for $1,500. The next day, IRS seized it.

Am I a tax dodger? Absolutely not. I pay substantial taxes. What bugs the IRS is that I don't accumulate money, I own nothing, and I live great. I happen to have clients all over the world, and I travel first class. I take them to lunch and dinner, I give parties for them, and everything I do is business, no matter that it's my pleasure. And this is where the argument lives: I say it's perfectly legal to deduct these expenses, they say no. I'm doing fine. But only because I'm single and satisfied to die broke. People shouldn't have to make that choice. And that's why I want to make my statement here about the Internal Revenue Service.

One footnote to the above. I have nothing against the agents in the field. They lived in my office for all these years, they're practically family. Tom Bolan thought one of them was an associate in the firm, he saw him around so often. They help our clients with their tax returns and we help them with their legal problems. A few years ago, one of the agents asked if he could talk to me off-the-record: Could I get him an autographed picture of President Reagan? Sure, I said, but why did it have to be confidential? He said, "Mr. Cohn, my superiors wouldn't like it if I got anything from you."

Forgive the pun, but I was up in the air when Morgenthau came down on me again. It was January 17, 1969, and when I walked off the plane from Europe a customs agent greeted me: "I'll bet you beat that stiff again, Mr. Cohn." I didn't ask him what he meant, I went right to a phone and called my office. I was told that Morgenthau had signed that morning a six-count indictment charging me with bribery, blackmail, extortion and conspiracy in connection with my representation, years earlier, of the Fifth Avenue Coach Lines.

Theoretically, I could have done 45 years for these crimes, but when I read the indictment I laughed, this was surrealistic, a sick joke if there ever was one. I later wrote a book about it, *A*

Fool for a Client, where I discussed the entire case in great detail. Here I'll try and put it in a nutshell, let the puns fall where they may.

The Fifth Avenue Coach Lines was the largest private transit system in the world, with over two thousand buses in Manhattan and the Bronx and revenues exceeding $60 million a year. Yet they were close to bankruptcy when I got into the picture in the early Sixties. How come? New York City politics. It seems quaint today, but 25 years ago the biggest issue in New York was the maintenance of the fifteen-cent fare on subways and buses. The Fifth was a private company, but the fare was set by the city. Mayor Robert F. Wagner, Jr., was not about to raise the fare. Wages he raised every New Year's Eve, like clockwork, but the fare had to stay at fifteen cents.

One would think that the people who ran the Fifth would have beefed about this, but the management was "old money" and they were getting theirs in fees, salaries and expense accounts. Only the stockholders were screwed. The prestigious board members owned virtually no stock, so why worry?

Certainly matters would have gone on this way direct to the bankruptcy court had the Fifth not caught the eye of Harry Weinberg, a self-educated, colorful multimillionaire from Baltimore who had made his bundle on transit systems from Scranton to Honolulu. By 1960, Weinberg had become the largest shareholder in Fifth Avenue, and he hired me to wrest control from the establishment crowd. This was my meat and we won it in the courts.

Weinberg immediately laid off people, effected other economies and demanded a fare hike. In March, 1962, Mike Quill, the transit union czar, responded by calling an illegal strike. With the city paralyzed, Mayor Wagner had the choice of going against Quill or Harry Weinberg. This was no choice at all for Wagner, whose father had authored Labor's Magna Carta in the U.S. Senate, the Wagner Act. He went on television and denounced Weinberg as a greedy, inhuman raider whom he would drive out of New York. But the rhetoric was nothing next to what he did. He seized the Fifth, the city took the buses over. Of course, the company and its stockholders were entitled to just compensation, the amount to be fixed by the courts in a valuation lawsuit.

It was for my alleged conduct during this valuation trial that Morgenthau indicted me years later, in 1969. The first half of the indictment charged that I conspired with one Lawrence Weisman to bribe one Bernard Reicher. Weisman was Harry Weinberg's protégé, and like protégés will, he staged a palace coup and took over the company from Harry. Reicher was New York City's spare parts appraiser. His job was to list and evaluate for the court the worth of the thousands of spare parts the city had taken from Fifth Avenue by the condemnation. Morgenthau's rubber-stamp grand jury said that I got together with Weisman to fix Reicher. That was Part One.

Part Two was that I blackmailed Weisman into selling his Fifth Avenue stock by threatening to blow the whistle on the bribery. In other words, I was supposed to be extorting a guy who was in on the bribery with me!

Weisman had made a deal with Morgenthau and was to be the chief witness against me. The other big witness was Reicher's lawyer, who claimed that I passed him three grand for Reicher during my own trial in United Dye, right outside the courtroom. This was what gave Morgenthau federal jurisdiction—the Federal Courthouse being a "federal reservation"—for what otherwise would have been a state crime of bribery.

With these formidable witnesses set to get me, why was I laughing?

First, I was the guy who turned Reicher in before he could give his bribed testimony, I got him fired by the Corporation Counsel and indicted by District Attorney Hogan. I'd been tipped off that Weisman had sent Reicher on a Caribbean cruise with his girlfriend, and my investigators found the documentation on the manifest of the S.S. *Rotterdam*. When we discovered this, Reicher was about to take the witness stand for the city in the valuation trial. I got together with several directors of the Fifth and we decided that a disclosure to the city was imperative, time was of the essence. If Reicher took the stand before disclosure the judgment would be knocked out because of tainted testimony and then the Fifth would have been finished.

The trial had already taken a year and a half and it was a miracle that the company had survived—the city had the assets but the company still had to pay the bills.

When we took this to the board, Weisman went crazy—he certainly wasn't going to stand still for a disclosure that would end up putting him behind bars. Of course, he didn't say this, he admitted nothing—he simply delayed matters until it became obvious that if I didn't move immediately Reicher would take the stand and all would be lost.

On January 21, 1964, I met with Corporation Counsel Leo Larkin and gave him the facts about the bribery. Reicher was grilled and he took the Fifth—the Amendment, that is. On February 3, 1964—the dates are important—Larkin discharged Reicher and he was not used as a witness.

Why did I laugh?

Because the indictment charged that I paid off Reicher, through his lawyer, months after I had gotten him fired. And after the condemnation trial was over. Morgenthau knew this, he could even have known it by simply reading the papers, since Reicher's firing made page one of *The New York Times*. But as in United Dye, Morgenthau believed what he wanted to believe. Why wouldn't I bribe a guy whom I destroyed, and after he could in no way have done me or my client the slightest bit of good?

Similarly, it made no difference to Morgenthau that Part Two of the indictment—that I blackmailed Weisman into selling his stock by threatening to expose his bribery of Reicher — completely contradicted Part One, which accused me of conspiring with Weisman to fix Reicher. Would anyone threaten to expose his own bribery conspiracy?

Certainly, said Morgenthau. By letting Weisman know that I knew he paid for Reicher's cruise, and that I was about to expose it, I allegedly blackmailed Weisman into selling his stock in Fifth Avenue. If this weird logic didn't collapse because of its internal contradiction, it sure went to hell when we cross-examined Weisman. He admitted that he made $500,000 pure profit on the sale and he allowed as how at the time he sold he was afraid the Fifth couldn't stay solvent long enough for the condemnation award to come through. If ever a man did not need to be blackmailed into selling stock it was Larry Weisman.

Furthermore, Weisman never said a word about this "extortion" until Morgenthau threatened to indict him for bribing Reicher—and that wasn't until 1968, or four years after the alleged blackmail. What happened was that in casting about for a new way to get me after the Cohn Squad's efforts failed, Morgenthau dredged this oldy up out of his newspaper clippings, hit Weisman with a grand jury subpoena and ultimately immunized him from prosecution in return for his testimony against me.

What Morgenthau apparently didn't know was that Weisman had been in constant touch with me, on the friendliest terms, throughout all the years following the big blackmail job. He was always getting jammed up with his various ex-wives and I was there to help him every time; as late as April 1968 I got him out of a Baltimore jail where he spent the night for non-support of one of his kids.

Finally, only weeks before he concocted his tale for Morgenthau, Weisman presented his friendly extortioner with a silver pitcher and twelve cups. It had this inscription:

RMC
To the Second Best Lawyer
In the United States
With Regard and Affection
of
LIW—No. 1

My lawyer, Joseph Brill, concluded his cross-examination of Lawrence I. Weisman by unveiling this package to the jury.

In view of all of the above it should be apparent why I was able to laugh when I read the indictment. But this is not to say I took the case lightly. No lawyer has the right to brush off any criminal case, and when he's the defendant you can bet he'll concentrate. But I had two concerns in this case that went beyond these truisms. The judge was completely hostile to me, and Morgenthau was using the press to poison the atmosphere.

On the eve of trial, to cite the most egregious press example, *Life* published a hatchet job by William Lambert, falsely charging (among other lies) that I took the Fifth Amendment before the grand jury. This was the same William Lambert who did the number on me in *Life* in the United Dye case.

The judge, Inzer B. Wyatt, was a man I never met, much less had any previous run-ins with. But from day one I knew he was sure I was guilty, and every move he made afterwards proved me right. Why would he have a mind-set against me? Here are some facts that might tell you, not necessarily in order of importance.

• Wyatt's law clerk was Morgenthau's cousin, a young man who had worked in Morgenthau's office.

• John Allee, one of the two assistant U.S. attorneys handling the heavy work in the case, had been an associate in Wyatt's former law firm while Wyatt was there.

• Paul Perito, the other major prosecutor, spent about ten days hanging out with Wyatt in Monte Carlo in August of 1969, shortly before my trial opened. I found out about this while I was in Monte Carlo. Judge Wyatt admitted it but said that since he paid for Perito's lunch, rather than vice-versa, there was no impropriety, despite the fact that he had invited him to use his beach tent and saw Perito from time to time over the ten-day holiday.

We thought all of this was serious enough to move to disqualify Wyatt, but the way it works is that the judge you want to remove for prejudice is the judge who decides whether he has been prejudiced. Wyatt said no, he had nothing against me. And then spent the entire trial trying to put me away.

The man he harassed most in this effort was Joe Brill, my lawyer. He tongue-lashed Brill repeatedly and at one point threatened to hold him in contempt. Brill had a wonderful reputation garnered through forty years at the bar and he never was subjected to anything like this kind of judicial tyranny. It bothered him plenty. He'd say to me, "Why must he think he knows everything and ridicule every defense contention? Instead of just ruling on the law, he always has to question the good faith of any position I assert."

On the morning of the last day of the cross-examination of the government's last witness, Wyatt issued his customary blast at Joe Brill. At noon, as we walked to lunch, Joe said, "I don't know why I let him get under my skin. I receive fair and courteous treatment from so many of the judges down here—I guess I keep expecting it and forget that this man appears to be on a crusade against you." After lunch, Joe said he was still upset and wanted to walk back to court alone. When I got there he was slumped down in his chair with severe chest pains. It was a heart attack and he was taken by ambulance to the hospital. Obviously, he couldn't come back to complete the trial; in the event, Joe was out of action for months.

The bad news forced me to radically change my strategy. I had decided to take the witness stand, despite Brill's demolition job on all the state's witnesses. I thought that somebody with my public reputation better get up there or the jury would think I was hiding something.

But with Joe no longer available, I had a dilemma. Who would sum up to the jury? Tom Bolan, the co-counsel, had missed parts of the trial due to successive deaths in his family and anyhow he had his hands full—he now had to take over the preparation and presentation of ten or fifteen witnesses we planned to put on the stand. So really I was the only available choice for the summation. I was quite aware of Clarence Darrow's admonition: "He who is his own lawyer has a fool for a client." But there was no alternative. The only question was, should I also take the stand?

I visited Joe Brill in the hospital, and Joe was adamant. For sure, sum up for yourself but don't take the stand. Why not? Because filling both roles would be too much in so short a time span. The case had already lasted nearly two months and the Christmas holiday was moving in. The jurors, who were told by the prosecution that the case would run only three weeks or so, were becoming impatient. If I were on the stand for days and then summed up, they'd have too much of me, they'd be ready to lynch me. I decided not to take the stand.

So I'd sum up, but it wasn't as easy as all that. I had to figure out a way to get in front of the jury without letting the judge or

Morgenthau know in advance. Not because they could have
stopped me, but because they would have arranged ground-
rules, there'd have been admonitions about what I could and
couldn't say. Plus, of course, there's nothing better at a trial, as
in life, than the element of surprise—when you own the surprise.

When the moment came, Judge Wyatt leaned down towards
Tom Bolan and said, "Would you care to address the jury now?"

As Tom began speaking, it became obvious that he wasn't
summing up, he was making some kind of statement. The prose-
cutors looked bewildered and unsure of what, if anything, to do.
Tom was telling the judge about the deaths in his family, and Joe
Brill's heart attack, and finally prosecutor John Allee broke in.
"Could we have this at side bar, your honor?"

Tom ran right over this interruption, his voice rising like a
Nolan Ryan fastball. "This will take just a minute," he said. "I
told Mr. Cohn that he would have to prepare for the summation.
Mr. Cohn has done that, and Mr. Cohn is now ready to sum up
in his own behalf."

Before any of them knew what was happening, I was standing
in front of the jury. Out of the corner of my eye I saw the reporters dashing for the door. Now I had to make sure that the final
headline would be "Cohn Acquitted."

I talked to the jury for seven hours, which is totally out of
character for me, I like to get to the heart of a case and get out of
there fast. But they hadn't heard me yet, they'd heard all about
me, but not me, and I wanted to make sure I covered the
waterfront. When I finished, I was sure they were with me. I
was even more confident after John Allee read his entire summation to the jury. I hadn't used a note, I never do. This guy
couldn't take his eyes off his papers, and the jury looked grim
and unimpressed.

Wyatt tried his best to save the case for the district attorney.
He reminded the jury only of the testimony the state's witnesses
gave on direct examination—omitting what Brill had done to
them on cross. That's not all he did; he did everything but turn
into a witness for the prosecution. This gave me agita. It's not
hard for a judge to charge a jury into a conviction, what with all

that respect for the robes and the general assumption that he's fair, that the judge has no ax to grind.

The jury got the case just before dinner on a Friday night. And now dinner wasn't so pleasant, thanks to Wyatt. I joked with the newspapermen at the next table—we were at a small Italian restaurant near the courthouse—but I couldn't eat the pasta.

Back at the courthouse the deathwatch was on for fair. At about 9:30 the jury had a question that clearly favored us, so naturally we were on a high. An hour later the bailiff gripped my arm: "It's a verdict."

When the jurors marched into the box, none of them looked at me. Jurors always look at the defendant when the verdict is not guilty, and never when guilty; everybody knows that, it's axiomatic. Tom Bolan turned white and my stomach turned over.

We had to wait for the judge to show up and it seemed endless. Finally, he bustled up to the bench, leaned over and commanded "Mr. Clerk"—the instruction for the bailiff to take the verdict.

Not guilty. On all counts.

Shouts, whoops of joy filled the courtroom, drowning out Wyatt's angry gavel; my friends jumped over the barrier into the well of the court to embrace me. All I could say to the press was "God Bless America." It's always been my favorite song, and if anybody thinks it's corny, go get yourself acquitted some day.

I got myself a bonanza out of the case. An instant myth took hold that I had arranged Joe Brill's heart attack in order to avoid taking the stand and undergoing cross-examination, that Joe wasn't sick at all, the whole thing was staged by Roy Cohn. Of course, this brought me a ton of business. If you can get Machiavelli as a lawyer you're certainly no fool of a client. Joe Brill, who had two successive heart attacks after the one that landed him in hospital, wished the myth were true, I'm sure. Anyway, I can hear him laughing now, with the angels.

Morgenthau had one blank left in his gun, though by the time it was shot he was out of his job. He had, you see, obtained two indictments in connection with Fifth Avenue Bus Lines, one the

Reicher "bribery" case, the other a similar frame involving a couple of sleazebags named Edward Krock and Victor Muscat. In 1971, Morgenthau's heirs took me to trial on this one, another ten-count job charging me with bribery, conspiracy, etc. etc.

Krock and Muscat had bought control of Fifth from Larry Weisman. They were disparate characters who shared a love of money and a penchant for perjury. Indeed, Morgenthau had them pinned on perjury and false swearing charges. They pleaded guilty and got a walk, no jail time. In return—you guessed it—they implicated me.

While I was general counsel to Fifth, there was a stockholder's suit against the company and against Krock and Muscat individually. The suit was settled. The settlement was reviewed by a court-appointed referee. The main charge of the indictment was that I paid the referee a $75,000 bribe to approve the settlement.

This allegation was not only false, it was absurd. A referee in a situation where both sides have agreed to a settlement is little more than a notary public, his job is that routine. Nobody pays off for a thing like that, it's crazy. But true to form, Morgenthau wanted to believe so he believed. If he had checked, he'd have seen that there was indeed a $75,000 payment—to the plaintiff stockholders' law firm. All open and aboveboard. Krock and Muscat simply sold Morgenthau a bill of goods, attempting to convert this proper fee into a bribe to a referee to get off the hook themselves.

I could go on here and delineate the various counts and how we systematically knocked them on their respective tails. But just as I didn't bore the jury with my story—I didn't take the stand, partly for the boredom problem, partly because it might have lent credence to the indictment—I won't take any more of the reader's time. Suffice it that this time the jury didn't bother with dinner. They acquitted me within an hour.

So at long last, it was over. Morgenthau had taken all of his at-bats, once with a pinch hitter, and the result was three acquittals, thirty-six jurors, with not one guilty vote.

Of course I was happy and relieved. And it's not so bad to discover when you're still young just who your friends are *not*. It builds character, like they say.

Interlude

On November 1, 1985, Roy Cohn entered the National Institute of Health Hospital in Bethesda, Maryland. I had very little hope for him. I knew he had AIDS, nobody had to tell me that—and nobody did, including Roy. He said it was liver cancer, as if that were a flu-bug, and of course I let it go. He looked so awful and he was so weak when he went into the hospital, that I didn't think it mattered what was ailing him. When I didn't hear from him for about three weeks, and heard no optimistic reports from mutual friends, I figured I'd never see him again. But a few days before Thanksgiving, he was on the phone, his voice much stronger, summoning me to his home in Greenwich. "I'm going to give you all my time now," he said.

Whatever they did for him in Bethesda, he was like a half-new man. But only half. It was clear that he didn't have the stamina to continue a linear narrative. But I didn't have the heart to tell him. Instead, I suggested we wing it for awhile. I said, "Let's have fun. Let's do inside stories on some of your friends and enemies—Reagan, Bush, Nixon, Ford, Agnew, Koch, Trump.

Then we'll go back and hit your private law practice and more of the power-brokering and the kind of swath you cut around the city and the world."

He liked the idea. We never got back to the other stuff or to a straight-line memoir. I'm convinced he wouldn't have done it even if healthy. I'll explain it in an epilogue, and hopefully much more about this intriguing figure I knew for more than twenty years. In the meantime, here's Roy M., carrying on.

S.Z.

Chapter Eleven

I can't remember when I first met George Bush. Except for his wife, who could remember meeting George Bush? I mean, he's about as memorable a character as Fritz Mondale, and maybe it's no coincidence, because he shares something with Mondale: Both of them stand for the proposition that if you don't like my sentiments they can always be changed. Bush is a conservative now because the conservatives control the Republican party. That doesn't mean that a week ago he wasn't a liberal speaking to the Ripon Society fundraiser. He's not kidding the conservatives, they've developed a tremendous dislike toward him; they think he's a phony and they openly call him the Fritz Mondale of the Republican party. But Bush is a formidable man, nonetheless—owing entirely to that famous quirk in the Constitution that keeps a vice-president within a heartbeat of the White House. If President Reagan should die in office—God forbid!—or be unable to serve out his term, Bush is president and thus an odds-on choice to win the nomination in 1988 and maybe the election itself. Were it not for this possibility, I promise you he wouldn't rate a word here. But since I believe that he'd be an international tragedy, I've got a story that sheds more light on the kind of person he is than any polemic I might otherwise be tempted to indulge in.

In the spring of 1985, Ford's Theater in Washington put on its annual charity gala; it's a variety night. The President goes to it every year. I was invited to it, and to a buffet dinner prior to it at the White House for about fifty people.

I'm notoriously late, but when it comes to the White House I'm early. First, out of respect for the President, and second because you can get very messed up trying to get into the White House; they've got fifty different guard posts, gates and entrances. Once they found Rupert Murdoch walking around the cellar with a suitcase. So I make it a point to get there in plenty of time.

I arrived at the Westchester airport an hour before I had to, that's how carefully I planned this thing. I got on my plane and the pilot said, "We are on hold for an hour and 27 minutes." So I said, why? He said, "Because Vice-President Bush has closed down the airport. He's visiting some friends and relatives."

There was a long line of planes sitting there and now everybody had to wait until Mr. Bush decided to show up. It was outrageous. I told the pilot to deliver a message to the secret service man in charge of Bush's detail. The message was that everybody here is clearly and easily identifiable, the planes are all registered, there isn't a plane here that isn't registered with the CAB and that couldn't be checked out in five minutes. To tell us to sit on the ground for an hour and a half while he's having hot toddies with some old friends is an absolute affront. I added, "It's a type of arrogance for which he has long been suspected, and this is just living proof of it, and the reason why millions of Americans who voted for Ronald Reagan won't vote for him, myself included."

The secret service man was a nice guy; I knew him, I know most of them. When he got the message he came over to me and said, "Well, you see why I love this job so much, don't you?"

But although he delivered the message, we never got an answer. Finally, and it was *over* an hour and a half later, Bush showed up, got into Air Force Two, and we were allowed to fly—once he was airborne.

Now we did manage to get to the White House just about on time, but later than you should be. If you're supposed to be there at 6:45, you get there at 6:30 or 6:20. By the time we got there the reception line was over and so I came in the other end, and the first person I bumped into was Mrs. Reagan. I told her what happened and she said, "Write him a real rough letter, say 'You delayed our dinner,' let him have it." Nancy Reagan doesn't like Bush. She never forgave him for the stunts he pulled on her husband during the primaries in 1980. Remember, Bush is the guy who accused him of "voodoo economics"; Bush is the guy who grabbed the microphone away from him in the debate; Bush had his aide shove Ronald Reagan out of the room when Reagan came to see him in New Hampshire the afternoon of the debate. I don't think the President forgets all this, but Nancy *really* remembers. I mean, if I had told the President what happened at the airport, he'd have said, "Oh George wouldn't do a thing like that." And that would have been the end of it for him. But she said, write that letter. And I did.

I laid it on strong. I started by calling him "Dear Mr. Vice-President." Not George—Mr. Vice-President. If it sounds funny to make a point of this, I have to say that Bush had been romancing me for years; he knew I was in with the conservatives and he wanted my support for '88. So not to call him George was a definite statement on my part. And then I outlined the events that took place at the airport, once again as I had in the message to the secret service. I ended by saying, "You made me late for the dinner at the White House. You could have delayed the performance of this charity opening. And why? Because you wanted to have drinks with some old buddies? We all want to have drinks with old buddies, but we don't close down airports in the United States of America. Maybe in the Soviet Union, if the dictator wants to do something they close down airports."

His letter back came from one of his assistants, a guy with a name so typically George Bush it's almost funny, something like

C. Cordinton Pendleton III. It said, "Dear Mr. Cohn: The Vice-President was obviously disturbed at the discomfort which you feel you sustained." I *felt* it. It didn't really happen, I just felt it. And then this jerk starts with details. Things like so: "We have made an independent check at the Vice-President's request and we find the following: The curtain did not go up until 9:14 p.m., so you would have had plenty of time to go to the White House, have supper, and then be at the theater in time. We also checked with the social secretary's office at the White House and found that the President and Mrs. Reagan had a snack before leaving Camp David to come down for this event. So obviously, there was no magic attached to this dinner," and so on and so forth. "We hope this clarifies the matter. Sincerely."

Pathetic, of course, but scary. I mean, here is a man who could become president in a split second, and not only does he close an airport while he's having toddies—he sends his dopey assistants around checking on what the President had for snacks at Camp David. Well I wrote back to this guy with the Princeton name—I was tempted to sign off as Roy Marcus Cohn XIV—and told him what I thought of him and his boss, and for the record pointed out that he didn't have one fact right, unless Ronald Reagan happened to have a Camp David chicken sandwich unbeknownst to the dinner guests, with whom he and the First Lady sat down and ate.

There are people who think Ronald Reagan will endorse Bush for the nomination in 1988, because Reagan once said that Bush was the best vice-president we ever had. I don't buy it, I think he'll use that statement to excuse himself from backing Bush. He'll say, "George, I've already said more than I ever dared, ever should have said. I said you're the best vice-president in the history of the United States. I can't make an endorsement. It will look like I'm using the power of the presidency to dictate a successor. It would be wrong, it would be unseemly. I can't do it."

This is the sensible position for Reagan to take, but there's more to it. For one thing, Paul Laxalt, who's Reagan's closest friend, is death on Bush, so he's the big wedge there. Then there's Nancy Reagan, who's a tigress, who's the most powerful first lady since Mrs. Wilson. She doesn't forgive people who accuse her husband of voodoo economics. And nobody can tell me that Ronald Reagan loves George Bush, either. I was at several White House parties where this was made very clear.

The Bushes weren't invited to the receptions, they'd come in afterwards. I particularly remember one the Reagans gave for Eureka College, the President's alma mater. I'm the chairman of the Reagan scholarship fund at Eureka, and after the reception there was George Bush standing in one of those double doorways, I think it was the Roosevelt Room, though I can never get those rooms straight. Anyway, the Reagans never looked up at him, he could have been the waitress coming in with a tray of canapes. I'm telling you, there wasn't a person in that room who went over and said, "Hello, Mr. Vice-President." Except me. I brought him in and introduced him to my friends. And this kind of thing happened more than once. And for my money, it tells us more about what the Reagans think of him than any statement about how great a vice-president he is. Don't worry, he won't get an endorsement from Ronald Reagan. And unless the very worst happens—if Reagan should die—I say Bush won't get the Republican nomination. I'm betting on Jack Kemp. Anyway, it won't be Bush.

But Ronald Reagan did pick him, in the first place, and kept him on for a second term, in the second place. So what am I talking about? Well it's not the contradiction it appears to be; it's not a contradiction at all, once the facts are known.

When the Republican convention opened in Detroit in 1980, Ronald Reagan was an odds-on favorite for the nomination. But the pros were getting a little nervous about the election. The Democratic convention had taken place, and as bad as Jimmy Carter was, he looked better now; there was a sympathy vote possibility, he was a sitting president, there was fear about the White House and the fireside chats, and maybe he'd get the hostages out of Iran before election day.

When I got to Detroit, a week before the convention opened, it was pretty well settled that Reagan would pick for vice-president a middle-of-the-roader or a conservative. The conservative would have been Paul Laxalt. There were four or five possible middle-roaders, I don't remember who anymore. Bush was not taken that seriously, though he was one of the names in the middle. The big knock against him was what I said before—the primaries, with "voodoo economics" and the shove, and mike-grabbing. So nobody thought it would be Bush.

Then, when the thing got heated up, and the nervousness set in, Henry Kissinger and Alan Greenspan came up with the idea that Gerald Ford should be vice-president. A lot of people liked it, because it would have ensured Reagan's election. But then the Ford crowd—I don't think Ford was part of it, he didn't know which end was up, he was probably out charging fees for appearing on a golf course—pushed their luck. They had the now-famous (infamous) plan to set up Ford as a kind of co-president with Reagan. It had to be Kissinger's brainchild, this "genius" idea. Kissinger would be Secretary of State in complete charge of foreign policy, and Ford would be chairman of a kind of Board of Governors that would essentially run the country. In effect, Reagan wouldn't be president at all, just a reigning sovereign.

The thing almost went, though I knew Reagan hated the idea. Then the break came. Ford announced he was thinking everything over and would have a formal announcement in the morning. This was while the convention was meeting, it was late at night. Right after Ford made this announcement, Reagan decided to come to the convention.

I was on the squawk box at the convention hall, getting bulletins from Reagan's suite, so I knew he was on his way. Somebody said, "What would he be coming here for?" I said, "Well, it could be to apologize for keeping everybody up so late, and then telling them that there's been a development and we'll have a resolution in the morning." Or (I said) it could be he's going to tell them all to go to hell.

What happened was he went to the phone and called Bush and asked him to run for vice-president. And then he came and announced it to the convention. Why? Because Bush was the lesser evil. The Ford-Kissinger-Greenspan triumverate would spend every living moment trying to get rid of him. So Reagan was smarter than all of them. He moved them the hell out and

got a guy who wouldn't be a threat to him. So that's how George
Bush got to be Vice-President of the United States.

Why did Reagan keep him on the ticket in 1984? That's easy.
There was nothing you could pin on Bush, it wouldn't have been
good politics to dump him. Of course, in the eyes of a conservative like me, there was plenty you could pin on him, but I had to
admit it would have been divisive and bad politics to get rid of
him. We had only one interest, the re-election of Ronald
Reagan. Now our main interest better be to make sure that
George Bush doesn't get to be president.

I like Nancy Reagan very much. The quality I admire most
about her is that her husband is more important to her than anyone or anything in the world. She would give her life in two seconds for him. After the shooting incident, a lot of us developed
major doubts that she'd let him run for a second term. I'll never
forget what happened the night the musical *42nd Street* opened
in Washington. There's a scene where a guy and girl get into a
fight and one of them shoots a cap pistol at the other. It was just
a cap pistol but it made a loud noise. Just at that moment I happened to be looking up at the Reagans' box. I was sitting just
below it and I happened to look up, and as that gun went off,
that cap gun, Nancy Reagan jumped halfway out of her chair. I
never saw anything like it. She turned ash white. She was living
with that assassination attempt morning, noon and night. After
that, I would have taken bets Ronald Reagan would not run for a
second term.

Of course, he almost died from that shot and it's lucky he was
treated by the emergency team at the hospital. Who knows what
might have happened had the White House doctors been there
instead. I mean, those people ought to be treating poodles. Or
maybe I shouldn't say that; I happen to love poodles. Look, because they didn't want to "bother" him with a colostoscope, they
let about nine months go by while the cancer festered and grew.
And then they had to take out more than two feet of his intes-
tines.

Prince Trubetskoy, a good friend of mine, a White Russian, a
wonderful gentleman, everybody loves him—the Prince went

for his annual checkup in New York, and when they found something they didn't like, which turned out to be the same thing Reagan had, they had him on the operating table thirty minutes later. And he was fine.

Now, when they finally operated on the President, the team of doctors walked over to Mrs. Reagan and said, "The President has cancer." Period. Just like that. Not, "We caught it," not "Things look good." Just "The President has cancer. We're now going in to tell the President." Nancy said, "Oh no you're not." She said, "Nobody is telling the President anything until after I talk to him." So she went in and said, "Dear, we're lucky again. There was some kind of malignancy, whatever they call it, but they caught it all, and they've taken it all out and you're fine. As a matter of fact, they said you can put your clothes on and go home." And of course that really lifted his spirits. But those jerks were about to go in there and give him a line like that, cold turkey.

She's his political protector, as well. She has great instincts about people, she's the one who says to him, "Ronnie, don't trust that man." Not that he listens to her that often—it's almost impossible for him to fire anybody. But whenever there is a shakeup you can be damned sure Nancy Reagan had something to do with it. One man who really knows the influence she can have is William Simon, the Secretary of the Treasury under Gerald Ford.

Bill Simon is a helluva good man and is one of the economists responsible, in my opinion, for a lot of the progress made on supply-side economics. He is also a man with a tremendous ego. He went down to the ranch at San Andreas, after Reagan was elected, while he was president-elect, and he sat there and dictated his demands to Reagan.

He would prefer the Defense Secretaryship to Treasury, he said, but he would take Treasury again. However, if he took Treasury, he must pick his own staff, give out his own press releases, clear nothing with the White House, and so on. It was an ultimatum, one through a hundred.

Mrs. Reagan was sitting there reading a magazine, while Bill Simon was listing his requirements. Sure she was; you can imagine how she was reading that magazine. She was drinking it all in, was what she was doing. And let me tell you, Bill Simon walked out of the President's life that day. I mean, he couldn't get a phone call through after that. Nancy put her foot down. She pointed out to the President that you don't hire people who make demands before they have the job. After you're in for six months and have the President's ear and everything is smooth, then maybe you can ask for things. But you don't tell the President that he's got to keep out of your hair—not ever, but surely not before you've been appointed.

Well, Bill Simon never heard from the President about this or anything else, and he kept calling, but like I said, no answer. So he became bitter, no one will ever know just how bitter he and his wife Carol were over this. Then, during the Christmas season of 1980, a few weeks before the inauguration, Simon was in Palm Beach. He called up his friend, William Casey, who had a home in Palm Beach. Bill Casey was of course very close to the President; he was then director-designate of the CIA and had been the campaign manager after Reagan fired John Sears (which you'll see is quite a story in itself).

Anyway, when Simon called, Casey said, "Bill, why don't you take a walk over here around 11:30?" So he goes over to Casey's place, a couple of blocks away, and at about five to twelve he's about to leave. Casey said, "Bill, I'd like you to stay for a particular reason. A friend of yours is calling at noon, 12 o'clock sharp." Simon figures, here it comes. You know, Reagan has thought it over, I've been punished, I've been in the dog house, and now he's going to make me an offer.

The phone rings at noon, sharp. After the usual amenities, Casey says, "A friend of yours is here, Mr. President." And he puts Simon on the phone. Simon says, "Oh, merry Christmas and the best to you and Mrs. Reagan for the holidays, Mr. President, it's wonderful to talk to you." Reagan says, "Well, Bill, that's just why I called up, I wanted to wish you and Carol and the kids a very merry Christmas and a happy New Year and may all of God's blessings come to you. If you're in Washington sometime, drop in and say hello." Boom. Just like that.

How do I know this? Ordinarily, I wouldn't say, you take me

at my word or you don't. But this one looks so much like it came from Bill Casey, or perhaps the President, that I have to source it. I got it from none other than the Simons themselves. Bill and Carol. One night at Barbara Walters' home. I was never that close to the Simons. So I figured they must have told 5,000 people. But it never reached print, it never made the papers. So maybe they didn't spread it around, who knows? But now you know.

I have a John Sears story that's delicious, although until the last minute John Sears wasn't delicious at all; he nearly wrecked Ronald Reagan. Sears was Reagan's presidential campaign manager. He convinced Reagan to stay out of Iowa, out of the Iowa caucus. As a result, Bush won and there he was on magazine covers looking like the reincarnation of the Dewey-Rockefeller wing of the party. Sears had earlier written a god-awful announcement speech for Reagan; he was just the pits, but knowing Reagan, there was anything but a guarantee that he'd get rid of this guy.

After the Iowa debacle, Tom Bolan and I ran a fund raiser at our townhouse (which doubled as our offices) for Reagan. There was a reception later at Regine's restaurant run by the Conservative party, and Tom said to Reagan, "Governor, we almost never get a chance to talk, can I ride with you?" Reagan said, "No, Tom, but I'll ride with you. My car, well the guy was going around the block when I got here and I don't know if he's ever coming back." So Tom and Reagan and a third guy, who Reagan didn't introduce, got into Tom's car.

Tom said, "Governor, seconds are precious. I might not see you again for a month or be able to communicate with you. Get rid of John Sears. To stay out of Iowa was a disaster. It was like one of your home states. Your first job was there. It wasn't a loss, it was a default. And that horrible announcement speech . . . how many times do you have to get hit on the head? Change now, before it's too late."

Well, Reagan was clearing his throat; the best he could do was get out the word, "Tom." But Tom kept talking, time after all was of the essence. Finally, Reagan got his attention. He said,

"Tom, I don't think you've met John Sears." Who happened to be the third man in the car.

O.K. that was funny, however embarrassing to Tom. But what wasn't funny was that Reagan wasn't about to bounce Sears. I mean, he'd rather take on a platoon of Nazis single-handed than fire somebody. David Stockman understood that. After he did that thing in *The Atlantic*, where he made Reagan look like a liar, a knave, a man who wanted to rub the noses of the poor into the dirt, Stockman was dead in the water. But later that week, when Mrs. Reagan was in New York on a shopping trip, he marched into the President's office without an appointment, and started crying. The President said, "Dave, I was going to ask for your resignation. But I can see now that you've been under terrible pressure working for me, so . . ."

Now we knew Reagan would win big in New Hampshire. And we also knew that if we did nothing in advance to hurt Sears, he'd take credit for the victory and would entrench himself. So we entered into a conspiracy before the New Hampshire primary—Bill Casey, Bill Loeb (publisher of the Manchester *Union Leader*), Charles Wick, Tom Bolan, four or five others—to make sure that Reagan would dump Sears regardless. On the day of the primary, I must have made and taken a hundred calls. I took a private room in a restaurant in Greenwich, Connecticut, and conspired, mainly with Bill Loeb, who was really the number one conservative, the most powerful man in New Hampshire.

When the results came in, and it was clear early that Reagan was the winner, Bill Loeb said, "Well, what do you think he'll do about Sears?" I said, "He'll duck out. He won't do it." Loeb said, "You're wrong. He's going to do it. He told me, 'I can be an altruist just so long.'" And of course he did do it, he got rid of Sears. Bill Casey was named campaign manager and from there on in we didn't have a bad minute.

I mentioned that Gerald Ford didn't know which end was up during the Detroit convention, that he was probably out charging fees for appearing on a golf course. Lest anyone think I was simply tossing off a joke or indulging in hyperbole, here's what Ford pulled one day on Don Kendall, the head of Pepsi-Cola. Kendall had been one of Ford's biggest contributors and boosters over the years. Now he was in Palm Springs with a group of his top executives and he got the idea that it would be nice if Ford dropped by and said hello to them. Ford lives in Palm Springs, of course. So Kendall called and said, "Jerry could you come over to the club and just shake hands with the boys?" The club was about 50 yards from Ford's house. Ford said, "Don, for you I'll be glad to do it, but you know what my standard charge for these appearances is." Kendall said he didn't know and didn't know it would apply to him. Ford said, "Yes, it's $10,000." Kendall said O.K.

Well, Ford appeared at the given time, did the round of hand-shakes and left. But before he entered the room, he grabbed Kendall's sleeve—Kendall had greeted him at the door—and said to Kendall, "Isn't there something we have to take care of first?"

Kendall said, "You mean the $10,000?"

"Yes."

"Jerry, I don't carry $10,000 in my pocket, and if after our long relationship and the hundreds of thousands I've given to you, you don't want to trust me for $10,000 until the office opens tomorrow morning, it's just too bad."

He's become a pretty despicable character, our ex-president, and I know of a second incident that's even worse than this Palm Springs story. He took ten grand to make a couple of campaign speeches for Lowell Weicker during Weicker's re-election campaign for the United States Senate. He was paid by the Connecticut Republican party, and I think it's the height of immorality for a former Republican president to take money to make a speech in behalf of a Republican candidate for the Senate.

I'm hardly one of those Boy Scouts who run around promoting phony ethics laws and rules regarding money and politics. Hell, I don't think Agnew did anything wrong. But it's one thing for a poor man to take campaign contributions, and quite another for Ford to trade on the office of the presidency. He's not running for anything, he's just pocketing money because he was an accidental president.

Agnew was a poor man. He wasn't a Rockefeller, he wasn't a Kennedy. If somebody gave him a few suits of clothes or if he got campaign contributions of $10,000 with some regularity, so what? That didn't make him a crook or anything like it. It showed that he was a poor man who all through his public career as County Executive of Baltimore, as Governor of Maryland, had been by and large way above the average in honesty and so ended up with nothing, to the point that he needed help. And I think a very appealing jury argument could have been made for him in a state which had elected him to office on so many occasions. When he pleaded guilty in Baltimore, I wrote an op-ed piece for *The New York Times* blasting him. I remember the opening line. "How can a man who made courage a household word have lost his own?" He never spoke to me after that, maybe because down deep he knew I was right.

I mean, what did Agnew do that about 90 percent of governors don't do? If someone drops into their office and says, "Governor, you're running, here's a campaign contribution," nine out of ten will grab it—barring any illegality in the taking of it, and by that I don't mean some technical laws, I mean a bribe. Barring that, they take it. And again, why not? The fact that Agnew got contributions while he was vice-president, in the Executive Office Building, didn't mean a damn thing. The point was not the situs of the transfer—only that Agnew was a guy from the wrong side of the tracks and he had to scrounge, unlike the Rockefellers and the Kennedys. If we apply the code of ethics we applied to Agnew across the board—the way they tried to do it to Nixon in 1952, with that "slush fund" that led to his famous Checkers speech—we'd have a government of multi-millionaires.

I once gave Nixon an envelope with five thousand dollars in it. It was just before the Al Smith Dinner at the Waldorf, when he was running for president. Red Blake, the old coach of Army, was very tight with Nixon, and I called him in Nixon's suite at the Waldorf. I said, "Coach, I wonder if it would be possible for me to see Mr. Nixon on something highly confidential. It will take 30 seconds." Blake said sure.

I was ushered in immediately and I said to Nixon that I didn't want to take up any of his time, that I knew how busy he was. Then I reached into my coat pocket for the envelope. When Blake saw that, he pointed me towards the bathroom. The bathroom door was open, but I didn't quite know what he was doing. Finally, it registered. I walked into the bathroom. Blake walked in after me. I gave him the envelope. He said, "Thank you very much. I'm sure this will be very helpful, because nobody knows more than you do about international Communism and how it threatens the world today." And that was that.

I didn't see anything wrong with it then, I don't see anything wrong with it now. If anybody tried to prosecute me under the election laws, I would love it. I'd waive the statute of limitations. I mean, the whole thing is flaky. The rich can put all their own money in but a poor guy has to worry about these ridiculous laws. No jury would convict me, I guarantee it. No jury would have convicted Spiro Agnew. Both he and Nixon got the worst kind of legal advice. Lawyers are forever telling people to plead guilty or to quit. I guess it makes their lives easier—they don't have to do the time or otherwise pay the penalty. Watergate was of course more complex and quite different than Agnew's situation—but I think what they had in common was lousy advisers.

People often ask me what I would have told Nixon to do had he asked me. He did call me in, but by then it was just about over, he was all but finished. If I'd been there at the outset, I'd have told him to burn the tapes. Since he was under no obligation to make the tapes of conversations in the Oval Office, he had every right to destroy them—before they were subpoenaed.

Obviously, others have made the same point, I'm not claiming genius here. Indeed, it's so obvious, I've lately rethought it. If Nixon had burned the tapes, he never would have had to resign. So why didn't he do it? I have heard some theories, including that he thought he had so much on the others, like John Dean, that they would never dare testify against him. Also that he wanted the tapes for his book, for posterity. And other ideas as well.

Well, maybe all these theories have some basis in fact, or in Nixon's mind at the time. But they don't seem to explain anything so serious as the loss of the presidency. So the more I thought about it, the more I looked for another reason. And I think maybe I have it. I think Nixon thought—or even knew—that there were other copies of the tapes around. I mean, the guy that blew the whistle about the tapes, Butterfield, was an ex-CIA man. Maybe the CIA had copies. Why did Butterfield break the story in the first place? It makes sense that Nixon would worry about copies. He knew J. Edgar Hoover well. And Mr. Hoover made his career out of keeping copies. Just ask me about Hoover—whom I revered. The point is that anyone who worked those streets in the late Forties and the Fifties—such as Nixon, such as I—would have to think about copies before burning anything. The wonder is that it took me so long to think about it when I thought about Watergate. If Nixon even worried about it, he couldn't burn the tapes. So while I'll never know for sure, it's not a bad bet. Nothing else makes sense.

But even if he couldn't burn the tapes, he did everything wrong, and for this I blame his lawyers and other advisers, who after all are there to help him, not to ruin him. Even after the scandal got out of control he should have gone on television and said: "Let me tell you what happened here. Nobody suggests that I was in on the Watergate break-in. I knew nothing about it. I never heard about it until you did—until the whole thing was all over and blew up. At that point, I had a choice of blowing the whistle on Haldeman and Erlichman, two of my trusted aides. Instead, I stonewalled it, and that was a big mistake. The American people are always responsive to a truthful explanation, and I should have done it. It was misplaced loyalty. My loyalty belonged to the people. And for this, I apologize, for this I was dead wrong."

I believe he'd have won over the public had he done that. Not at the very end, but when there was still a chance for chemotherapy, for interferon. If he did it at the outset, the whole thing would have blown over in a trice.

In a sense, though, Nixon has emerged stronger than ever, has won back large elements of the public which sees the pettiness of the attenuated course followed by the Watergate critics.

His writings have been perceptive and so have his commentaries on the world situation. But the acid test to me is that Nixon is one of the few politicians I've ever seen at a ball game who is applauded rather than booed.

(Roy's views on Mayor Edward I. Koch follow. They come out of an interview I conducted with him on December 9, 1985—a month before the great New York City scandals began to break, with the then mysterious wrist-slashing of Queens Borough President Donald Manes. During the next few months, I tried to get him to talk about the scandals, but no soap. Not because he didn't know what was up; probably just the opposite. All he would say was that he was worried about his partner, Stanley Friedman, the Bronx County leader. In November, 1986, Friedman was convicted on a host of racketeering charges in Federal Court, New Haven. Roy knew what to worry about. I think his comments on Koch are more persuasive, and relevant, for having been made while Koch was viewed as a hero—not only in New York, where he had just won a third term with 75 percent of the vote, but in the nation at large, where his book Mayor: An Autobiography *was the number one best-seller. S.Z.)*

Ed Koch has an incredible knack of telling the great majority of people what they want to hear, by telling a few people what they don't want to hear. I mean, he'll go to a small group and bawl them out about something that he knows the mass of the voters will then jump for joy about. It's a brilliant political ploy. It makes him appear as a man of total candor, of courage, of devotion to truth and principle. When in fact, he's totally duplicitous. He's a man who will ride the coattails of others every chance he gets, a double-dealing hypocrite if I ever saw one—and I have seen plenty.

I know Koch from the early 1960's when he beat my friend Carmine DeSapio for district leader in Greenwich Village. Koch wasn't the first reform Democrat to defeat Carmine—another guy had done it a couple of years before—but he's the one who became famous for it. It wasn't just a district leadership fight. DeSapio was the biggest boss in New York. By losing the district, he lost the county leadership and thus much of his power. Koch in those days was a big liberal, and of course the greatest enemy of bossism. A few years later, when he got to Congress, he began to drift over to the conservative side, but he didn't make much of it; it was not politic to do it then. In 1977, when he ran in the primary for mayor, he ran on a law-and-order platform; he was one hundred percent for the cops and for capital punishment. But still he campaigned against the bosses. He accused Mayor Beame of being a "clubhouse" politician.

The minute he won the primary—actually, he came in first by a point or two over Mario Cuomo, and so he had to go into a runoff against Cuomo—he met with Meade Esposito, the Brooklyn boss, at Meade's mother's house. It was the Sunday after the first primary. And he made a deal with Meade, and ultimately with the other Democratic party leaders. And that's how he won the runoff against Cuomo.

Now I'm hardly a guy who's against the party bosses. They are my friends and my colleagues. My politics are the opposite of what is known as "reform" politics. So it would ill behoove me to complain when a reformer sees the light and comes over to my side. And let's remember, this was and is my side—on the local level, I'm a Democrat, and a party Democrat. When Koch made his arrangements with my pals, I was pleased. I'd never had any run-ins with him, he was always cordial and gracious to me, and vice-versa. It remains that way until this day, and indeed we've been allies in a number of enterprises, public and private. I'll talk about one of them later—when Koch sabotaged Jimmy Carter in the 1980 presidential election, in return for the Republican nomination for mayor. For now, suffice it to say that I don't have to like a politician in order to do business with him.

Perhaps the most duplicitous act in Koch's duplicitous life was his attempt to claim credit for snatching New York City out of financial disaster and making it a self-sustaining enterprise. This was false from beginning to end. What progress was made must be credited to Mayor Beame, who had years of experience as Controller of New York City, and who engineered the programs that kept the city alive. But even Beame would never take the full bow for saving New York from bankruptcy. As in many other

cities in the country during the late 1970's, immediate collapse
was averted largely through federal help and guidance. Plus,
there was an influx of rich foreigners into Manhattan—people
fleeing dictatorships or potential revolutions. Italians, French-
men, hoards of wealthy people from South America bought up
expensive real estate and increased the tax rolls. This made
Koch look good, and I'm sure he'd take credit for all the foreign
upheavals that caused it, if he could get away with it.

Well, he does take credit, in effect. And gets away with it. He
always comes up the hero. Why and how? Because anybody can
get away with anything if he can control the press and can put on
a convincing insincere performance for the public.

But the truth is, New York has not been saved from anything.
The city is in a deplorable state financially. Let Mayor Koch take
a ride around sections of Manhattan, the Bronx, Queens,
Brooklyn, and let him explain the crumbled buildings, the va-
cant multiple dwelling places, all of that.

New York is not Paris. New York is a city with an outward façade of Trump Towers and big hotels—and an inner city of di-
lapidation and destruction and poverty.

Almost half the people who live here don't pay taxes and make
no contribution toward municipal government. We have the
largest rolls of welfare recipients, homeless, and food stamps
users, of any place in the country. We are a city inundated with
Hispanics and Blacks. I don't say that critically, because I feel no
prejudice, or much less prejudice than Ed Koch does, towards
these groups. A lot of them have fled adversity, and have
brought their penchant for adversity, rather than work, to New
York by the weekly boat from Puerto Rico or the buses from the
South. This is a fact of life, and we must deal with it. Koch won't
do it; he ignores it as an economic, social reality. The only thing
he does, regularly, is to scream about crime.

But for all his talk, he has failed to deal with crime in an effective way. For example, he appoints a judicial committee which
clears nominees for criminal court judgeships. These panels are
full of left-wingers whose idea of qualifications for judgeships is
an advance assurance that they will sympathize with the crimi-
nals and forget about the victims. When these judges then sell

out the honest people of the city in favor of the hoods, the first one to attack them is Ed Koch—the man who appointed them. It's as if he had nothing to do with it at all!

The reason he stocks this screening committee with lefties is vanity. Koch cannot exist unless he is loved by everybody and is all things to all people. So this is the sop he throws his old liberal crowd. And then, because he's basically an incompetent as an administrator, he doesn't investigate to see who these judicial candidates are, he just takes what the committee feeds him. Then when they do something outrageous, but quite predictable considering who they are, Koch is the first one to scream bloody murder.

As far as loyalty is concerned, Koch is a one-way street. He takes a certain perverse delight in hurting his own friends. A perfect example is what he did—or rather tried to do—to Donald Trump.

During Koch's first re-election campaign in 1981, Trump raised over $300,000 for the mayor. There came a time when Donald needed Koch, and his need was totally legitimate and proper. Donald had been denied a partial tax exemption for Trump Tower, the fabulous building that has since won worldwide acclaim. Trump had bought the site on 56th Street and Fifth Avenue in Manhattan, where the broken-down Bonwit Teller building sat. When he purchased the site, Donald had every reason to believe, to *know*, that he'd be getting this tax exemption or abatement. That's because there was a law on the books granting this exemption to such projects, and had been for more than ten years. Every building of like nature got the abatement; for example, Aristotle Onassis got it for Olympic Towers.

So Donald goes ahead and begins to construct Trump Tower—when suddenly the building commissioner denies the exemption. Of course, the building commissioner did this at Koch's bidding, which is what every commissioner does under Koch. They don't dare walk across the street without his O.K., although they will be the first to deny publicly that they ever talked to him—and admit privately they were acting under his orders.

Trump had called Koch towards the beginning of his project,

and Koch acted as if he didn't know there was an abatement law, didn't know about Trump Tower. "I will check with the commissioner, Donald, and get back to you." What Donald got back was this shockingly unequal treatment; he was just singled out to get screwed, it was a complete double-cross. I mean, Koch was changing the rules in the middle of the game. And to prove that I'm not just talking as Donald's friend, or that I'm prejudiced because I'm his lawyer—we finally won the tax exemption by a unanimous vote in the New York Court of Appeals. And what better proof is there that the building commissioner wasn't acting on his own against Trump, than that Donald later hired him. Anthony Gleidman, who Koch claimed did all of this on his own authority, is now a top executive at Trump's firm.

As for Koch—in his book, *Mayor*, he brags about how he would do nothing to influence a decision on behalf of a campaign contributor, and he rags Donald for trying to get something out of his support in the election. The truth is, Koch tried to deny him his legal rights, and when the highest court in the state kicked the dickens out of him, Koch responded by attacking the court. "Outrageous," he said. "Unfair," he said. He should have been looking in the mirror.

Koch wanted the Republican nomination for his mayoral re-election campaign. Not that he needed it, the Democratic line assured him victory in New York, of course; but he wanted it. As I say, he needs to be loved by all, to be all things to all people, and now he wanted to be all things to all parties. I was right in the middle of this, because I was very active in the Reagan presidential campaign here. If Koch was going to get the Republican line in 1981, he'd have to do something for Ronald Reagan in 1980. As a Democrat, he couldn't come out for Reagan. But that made it better for Reagan. Koch could say he was supporting Carter and then sabotage him. And that's just what he did. He just killed Jimmy Carter, on the Israel issue, and he did it under the auspices of the Democratic National Committee. They sent him down to the Miami area, where so many Jews live or spend the winter, and Koch said, "If Carter continues to treat Israel the way he's doing it, may his soul rot in hell." I mean, what else could you say to destroy a president? For this reason, Carter was right when he told Koch on the campaign roundup in New York, "You've done me more harm than any living person."

Now, I was delighted by this, and had plenty to do with it. But look what it says about Koch's character—if you consider loyalty to your own party's president part of character. While the public probably thought he was just being honest and sensitive to Carter's lousy position on Israel—which might have been legitimate, to do this as a matter of ideological demands—what they didn't know was that he had struck a deal with the Republicans for the line. And he got the line in '81.

Roy broke this Koch-GOP story on "NewsForum," Gabe Pressman's NBC-TV show, February 16, 1986. He asked me if it was O.K. to do it. If I could have stopped him I would have done so, but I didn't know him all these years for nothing. Put Roy Cohn in front of a camera, or even a reporter from a Kansas City weekly, and he'll say anything he feels like saying. So I said, "Go get him," and it turned out better than I could have imagined. Roy said of Koch, "He slit Carter's throat from ear to ear." And did it, he said, in exchange for Republican support in the 1981 race.

Mayor Koch branded Cohn's allegations as "absolutely untrue," and said that he did not meet with Republican leaders to discuss the possibility of getting the GOP nomination until after Reagan was elected. He was supported by George Clark, who had been the Republican State Chairman at the time. Clark said, "Cohn doesn't have his dates right." The talks with Koch, he said, took place in early 1981, months after Reagan's landslide victory over Carter.

I knew Roy was right. I was in close communication with him during the first Reagan campaign, exclusively on the subject of Israel. I believed President Carter had double-crossed the Jews of America on the Israel question, and though I held no brief for Ronald Reagan, I wanted Carter out of there. I'm sure Koch felt the same way and was entirely sincere when he rapped Carter. But Roy told me then what the deal was with the Republican party.

Still, I was a little upset when George Clark stood with Koch.

Roy never kept records; he didn't take notes about meetings and certainly no tapes. Now he was terribly sick—the word about AIDS was so strong that the press was reporting, "He says he has liver cancer." When Koch responded, "Here is a guy who is very sick, and I'm not going to attack a dying man," the code was clear: Roy Cohn, understandably, had memory problems.

Well. On February 19, 1986—or three days later—The New York Times reported, "Mayor Koch has made a mistake." He, and not Cohn, had had his dates wrong. Koch conceded that he had met to discuss the mayoralty with Republican leaders in January, 1980, ten months before the presidential elections. And that he had dined with Vince Albano, the late Manhattan Republican leader, toward the end of 1979. "I was in error," Koch admitted.

I called Roy to congratulate him. He said, "If Ed Koch says I'm right, I'd better rethink it."

Point of Order

In the Broadway musical *Top Banana*, Phil Silvers is told that to segue into his "Doctor Skit" the stage must be set with oxygen tent, examining table, X-ray machine, stomach pump, medical books, desks, bandages and iodine.

"Nah, nah, nah," Silvers says. "We don't need any of that stuff. I'll just step out there and say, 'Well, here we are in the doctor's office.'"

In that spirit, I turn from Roy Cohn telling the Roy Cohn Story to me telling Roy Cohn stories.

Chapter Twelve

I invited Roy to a party at my apartment in November, 1966. By then, I had known him for more than two years. I had talked to him by phone at least once a week. He had tipped me to scores of stories, some of them page one. More important, he warned me off a few "scoops" that would have gotten me into hot water. Without question, he was the best source I had, the best any reporter could have. I used to say to my wife, that bastard Roy, he knows where the bodies *aren't* buried. But only my wife knew that Roy Cohn was my source.

I liked to think the reason was pragmatic. When I worked for the New York *Post*, it would have been suicide to let anybody on that liberal-left paper know I was *talking* to Cohn, much less getting stories from him. When I switched to *The New York Times*, with the lofty title of Metropolitan Legal Correspondent, it seemed even more urgent to keep Roy Cohn in the closet. "Punch is a good friend," he said to me, meaning Punch Sulzberger, the publisher of the *Times*. Even if I believed this I wasn't going to be caught dead with Roy Cohn. This was the Gray Lady; what would I be doing running Roy Cohn scoops in the Gray Lady, for Chrissake.

I ran them, of course, but said nothing. Until finally I recognized that pragmatism was a fancy word for cowardice. So for this big blast we were having, a party that would be filled with *Times* people, with judges, prosecutors, writers, actors, musicians, we sent an invitation to Roy. And Roy sent a case of Chivas Regal. Which I left out in its gift-wrapping for the guests to inquire over. "Roy Cohn's dropping in later, this is his calling card," I answered.

What? Roy Cohn? You invited Roy Cohn? You're having that sonofabitch in your home, that scumbag? I wouldn't touch him with a ten-foot pole.

He arrived at the shank of the night, a hundred people milling around the living room, sunken in the manner of the old West Side apartment houses. This made a drop-dead entrance possible, since everybody was down here and the door up there. When he walked in, the roar dropped to a low buzz. He walked straight across the room. I went up to greet him. We chatted for a minute, probably less. When I turned around, there was a queue, half the party was lined up waiting for an introduction. The most scandalized were the first in line. "A pleasure to meet you, Roy." It took him a half-hour to get to the bar. Nobody left the place till Roy left.

Over the next twenty years, I witnessed this head-turning and buzz-buzzing hundreds of times—at restaurants, bistros, ringside at the Garden, Broadway openings, the Series, the opera, elegant parties in the Hamptons. The gawkers weren't star-worshipers. They were the stars! Wealthy and powerful men and women of the world, shakers of industry, politics, the judiciary, real estate, the arts, the unions, the mob. People who could buy and sell Roy Cohn before breakfast. Many professed to despise him, or what he stood for. A few said so openly. It made no matter. Most of them kissed his ass and all of them were in need of head-braces when Roy Cohn walked into the room.

Why was this?

Maybe these stories will explain.

I was standing forlornly outside the hall at the Democratic National Convention in Chicago, the summer of 1968. I couldn't get into the joint because the *Times* refused to send me, on the grounds that the editor in charge of convention coverage hated my guts. I signed on with *Ramparts* magazine, but *Ramparts*, the most radical anti-Vietnam war paper in the country, the Bible of the kids, was turned down for floor credentials by the White House. So there I was, looking a little foolish, while my *Times* colleagues walked in and out, their chests emblazoned with visa-like badges.

I felt a tug at the sleeve. It was Roy, tanned-up, looking sleek and happy. I said, "What the fuck are *you* doing here?" I had seen him in unlikely places, sure, but I never figured on this. Chicago was now peace marchers and tear gas, candle-lights and truncheons, a Democratic party civil war like never before. I was well aware of his connections with the New York City Democrats, but that was inside-power stuff. His public reputation was strictly hard-line, right-wing, pro-Nixon Republican, and if he had an ideology that was the ideology. So what the fuck was he doing here, indeed.

"It's dead at '21' tonight," he explained. The "21" club in Manhattan was his favorite hangout.

He could be here for the action, sure, but there had to be something else, he wasn't the spectator kind.

"Let's go in," he said. "We'll take a look at the zoo."

"I have no credentials."

He laughed. "I know Mayor Daley's got big brass ones, but even he can't keep the *Times* out of the hall."

I told him I wasn't here for the paper, I was covering for *Ramparts*, and I gave him a twenty-second explanation, which is all he ever needed.

"C'mon," he said. The next thing I knew we were on the convention floor.

"How'd you pull that?" I said. "What have you got, letters of transit from General de Gaulle?"

"No problem. Let's say hello to a few people and we'll go over to the Stockyards for dinner."

The next half-hour is a blur, it was so fast and furious it was a blur while it was happening. Delegates were shouting at him from all parts of the floor, and not hack delegates—these were governors, senators, union leaders, bosses. There were hugs, backslaps, whispers. We were in Ohio, Florida, Texas, California, and of course the New York delegation, and when I could stop to think I thought only how he must go down with the Republicans if this is happening in enemy country.

"Let's go over to New Jersey," I said to him. I wanted to see for certain if this was as remarkable as it looked. Jersey was my home state, I lived there for 30 years, I was in the party, I was an assistant U.S. attorney, I knew the power levers in Jersey. Now I'd see if Roy knew them.

He breezed right past the governor, past the U.S. senator, and went directly to Johnny Kenny, the most powerful man in the state, the guy who years back had moved out the great Frank Hague. When he and Kenny embraced, I had enough, all I wanted now was a drink.

It wasn't enough for Roy. He was on to me. I wanted "proof," now he'd rub it in. He took me from boss to boss, from congressman to congressman, introducing me to people I knew, watching me squirm as they nodded me off and talked to him. He was savoring this and he waited until the last to put me away for fair. He waved over to Tony Grossi, my old county leader, the man who put me in the U.S. attorney's office.

"You know Sid, don't you, Tony?"

"Sure. How are ya, kid?"

And with that, walked away with Cohn, arm in arm, whisper in ear.

What made this *tour-de-force* all the more extraordinary was that Roy was between decades—no longer the *enfant terrible* of the Fifties and not yet the power broker and legal executioner of the Seventies. Within a few months he'd be indicted again by Morgenthau, indicted twice, and go through a period that would nearly bust him financially and severely reduce his political clout. He knew big trouble was ahead, but he never let on; he worked this convention like he owned it. And there was more to come.

After steaks at the Stockyards Inn, we came back to the hall.

"Let's sit for an hour or so and watch the show," Roy said. Where did we sit? In Eugene McCarthy's box. Just me and Roy Cohn in the box of the leader of the peace movement!

"Now this is absurd," I said. "How the hell did you swing this?"

He shrugged and gave me a wan smile. No pride in this shrug-smile and nothing else either. Years later it dawned on me what may have been going on in his mind that night. Years of watching him ushered to Table One at the best restaurants, the fifty-yard line at the Super Bowl, the owner's box at the Series, fourth row center at Broadway openings. Could it be that while I was knocked out that he managed to get Gene McCarthy's seats, he was a little pissed that someone had relegated him to the loser's box?

I threw it at him one day while we were doing this book. He shrugged and gave me a wan smile.

We finished this convention night with drinks at the Pump Room. Roy said, "Come out on the yacht tomorrow, I've got a good story for you." I wanted a hint, I had a million things to do the next day, but he wouldn't give. "Be there at noon, you won't be sorry."

It was a different yacht, quite smaller than the one I'd cruised on up the Hudson, the big baby with photographs of Cardinal Spellman, Joe McCarthy, Richard Nixon, Everett Dirksen, and other civil libertarians of the era. What's going on here, I said, what's the name of this oversized rowboat, *Poverty Level*? Roy said, "Nelson Rockefeller's using my boat this week, I couldn't say no to him." Just three weeks earlier, in Miami Beach, Rockefeller had failed in his bid to take the Republican nomination from Nixon. Cohn was at that convention, of course, and was all for Nixon, of course, so of course he couldn't say no to Nelson Rockefeller.

William F. Buckley, Jr., and his wife Pat were on board for the trip, and a couple of other people including a blond young man who was introduced by Roy as a member of the crew. He did not seem to have any duties, however, except to drink Bloody Marys. This wasn't the first time I'd seen this beautiful blue-eyed kid thing with Roy, but it was the first time I took serious note. Roy's mother had died about a year before, and he'd lived with her all his life. The rumors about Cohn being gay were as old as the McCarthy hearings. But only after his mother's death did these youths begin popping up, and for some reason it was only on this day that I thought yes, I thought at least maybe.

After lunch, I said to Roy, "It's always charming to be with Bill Buckley and Pat, but didn't you say something about a story?" He said, "The story will come aboard after we drop everybody off."

Sure enough. On board came Patrick Cunningham, the Bronx Democratic under-boss, and State Senator Ivan Warner, one of the city's most prominent Black politicians. Roy quickly turned the conversation on to the up-coming Democratic Judicial Convention, which in New York City amounts to the election of State Supreme Court judges. A few weeks earlier, in an apparent bow to reform, the Democratic bosses of Manhattan and the Bronx had agreed to allow a Citizens' Screening Committee to have veto power over the choices of Supreme Court nominees. Since the committee was headed by Bernard Botein, the highly respected Presiding Justice of the Appellate Division, it looked like New York was, at long last, going to do something about its one-party hack clubhouse judiciary.

Now, cruising on Lake Michigan, Roy Cohn said to Cunningham, "Pat, what do you think of the Botein Committee?" Cunningham answered, "It's always good to have an advisory group." Ivan Warner, who was looking to get a Supreme Court judgeship, nodded approvingly.

"You guys consider the Botein Committee 'advisory'?" I said.

"What else can it be?" Cunningham said. "The State Constitution places the nominating power in the Judicial Convention and ultimately the electorate decides at the polls." Ivan Warner nodded again and so did Roy Cohn.

"Therefore," I said, "any veto power by Botein would be a usurpation of constitutional government."

"Exactly," said Cunningham.

"I couldn't say it better," said Roy.

"Perfect," said Ivan Warner.

"Ivan," I said, "have those elitist bastards turned you down?"

"That's what they did, can you believe it?"

How could anybody believe it. Warner had been a material witness in a big heroin trial, but he wasn't indicted, nobody could say he was indicted.

"Outrageous," I said.

Roy said, "Terrible."

Cunningham shook his head.

"Who else did they reject?" I asked.

The District Attorney of the Bronx and a criminal court judge.

"And you won't stand still for this, right?"

"How can we?" Cunningham said. "They have no warrant to do it."

But the bosses did make a deal with Botein, it was all over page one; they had their arms around him, no?

"There was no deal," Pat Cunningham said. "There couldn't be a deal."

"Unconstitutional," said Roy.

"How could anyone make a deal in violation of the Constitution?" said Ivan Warner.

This was a great scoop, and the moment I got back to New York I ran with it and the *Times* played it on the front page. My editors, unhappy that I had gone to Chicago for *Ramparts*, bought me drinks at Sardi's that night. But in the morning, no.

I showed up whistling, and was greeted by one of the deputy editors as follows: "I'm sure as hell glad my name isn't on your piece today."

What?

"The leaders just issued a statement denying everything, every word, word by word. Call Clay Knowles at the National Democratic Club, he'll read it to you. You poor bastard, I feel for you."

Only me and my laundryman knew how scared I was then. I didn't think for a second that Roy had set me up; I simply assumed that once the bosses read the story they decided to back off. That had been on my mind from the outset, but Roy had told me not to worry. Now I had to worry, Roy didn't have to worry, his name wasn't on the line.

I called Clayton Knowles. He was a veteran political reporter, he went back years at the paper, he'd done everything. He said "I'm sorry, kid, but this is what happens when you get into areas you're not accustomed to. Don't worry, it's happened to all of us, it'll pass, it'll be a good lesson."

Suddenly, I didn't like Clay Knowles anymore. I said, "Just read me the statement." It was a long one, and it seemed to sound my death-knell. The leaders would keep their word to the Botein Committee, they would never violate their sacred trust, the story in the *Times* was hogwash, rumor, hearsay, slander. Any judicial candidate found wanting by the Citizens' Committee would get no support from the leadership.

As Knowles read on and on I was so depressed I almost missed the punch line. But I heard something and I made him repeat it. It said. "The Judicial Convention will make the ultimate decision." I hung up and ran to the desk. "The story stands," I said. "The statement is strictly bullshit. The bosses absolutely control the Judicial Convention, so when they say the convention will decide they endorse our story."

My editor said, "It won't wash here. They'll make you write a correction for tomorrow's paper. Whether you're right about this or not, nobody's going to buy it. The only chance you have is to get the leaders to renounce their attack on the *Times*. They're going to be over at the National Democratic Club on Madison Avenue at noon. You get your ass over there and see what you can do." He shook his head sadly, he knew I was dead in the water.

I called Roy. I read him my notes from the statement. When I got to the last line he laughed. "What else do you need?" I said, "You say that, and I say that, but the paper doesn't say that. You have to understand that my life is on the line here. I want you to check it out, make sure that the story itself didn't kill the story. How the hell can I be sure they haven't changed their minds *because* of what I wrote?"

Roy Cohn said, "I'll call you back in ten minutes."

He called me in five minutes.

"It's a hundred percent. Everything is 'go.' It won't change. Stick with your story. They're going to deny it all week, but it will not change, every man you mentioned will be nominated."

Seated around a big table at the Democratic Club were virtually all the city bosses, their acolytes, and the relevant members of the Fourth Estate. When I walked in they were laughing and when they saw me they jovially waved me over. Stanley Steingut, the Speaker of the State Assembly, said, "Well, my boy, somebody sure fed you a line of horseshit last night." Henry McDonough, the Bronx boss, said, "I don't know where you got that stuff. I wish I'd been around to correct you, I know you tried to reach me, I'd have set you straight." Pat Cunningham, sitting right at his boss McDonough's elbow, looked straight at me and nodded in assent. A hell of an actor, Pat, I thought to myself, and I certainly wasn't going to give him up. Especially since I knew from Roy that the story was gold.

The Gentlemen of the Press were overjoyed, especially Clay Knowles, who didn't like me treading on his turf. Actually it was more my turf; he covered city politics, yes, but I covered the legal scene. Anyway, he thought he owned this kind of story, and in the past he and the rest of the regular beat guys did own it, which is why the papers generally printed what the bosses wanted printed. But Clay said nothing. A guy from the *Post* couldn't hold it in. "What were you looking for, Zion, the Page One Award or the Pulitzer?" Laughter.

I threw a hundred on the table. "Anyone want to fade me?" I looked at Steingut, at the Manhattan leader Frank Rossetti, at McDonough, at the newshawks—and no takers. Just laughs, but this time a little nervous, just a little. Out of the corner of my eye I saw Ivan Warner, standing in a corner, looking terrible.

I walked over and put my arm around him. "Whatsa matter Ivan, you look a little pale." He was in no mood for jokes. "You killed me," he hissed. "How could you do it, what did I ever do to you?"

"Don't worry about a thing," I said.

"Don't worry? Don't *worry*? Are you crazy? They're sitting over there laughing at me, I'm finished. I had it made and now I'm gone, thanks to you."

"Do you mean to say that Roy didn't tell you that our little talk on the boat was going to be in the papers?"

"Of course not, he said it was all off the record, we could trust you with our lives."

I laughed now. It really never had occurred to me that Roy would pull this on Warner, and on Pat Cunningham, who had less to lose, but plenty if he were nabbed talking to the *Times*. All he asked me to do was keep their names out as the source. So wow! Roy Cohn was not just a piece of work, he was the works. But he was my sonofabitch and I realized I shouldn't have let on to Warner that Cohn knew I was going to write the piece.

"Ivan," I said, "it had to be a misunderstanding. Roy may have meant off the record but I took it as not-for-attribution. My fault, really. But still, not to worry."

"How can you keep saying not to worry?" He didn't give a damn about journalistic ethics, let's stick to the point.

I liked Ivan, I like him still. I couldn't torture him a minute more. I said, whispering in his ear, "Ivan, I just talked to Roy. And Roy says you're in."

"How would he know?"

"Doesn't he know everything?"

"What *time* did you talk to him?"

"An hour ago. I asked him to make a call, to find out if the story had changed anything. He made the call, and called me back. He said, 'It's go, it's gold.' "

"You're not kidding me?"

"Ivan, on my grandmother's grave."

He lit up. He hugged me. "God bless you," he said. And practically danced out of the building.

Back at the *Times*, nobody was dancing. I had no bacon to bring, the bosses were sticking to their line. I couldn't tell the editors that they wouldn't fade my bet. And I sure as hell couldn't tell them that Roy Cohn guaranteed the story. Hell, if they had known Roy was my main source the story wouldn't have made the paper to begin with. A few years later, sure; but like I said, Roy Cohn in the late Sixties was not considered your Reliable Source—not by the Gray Lady, probably not by any newspaper.

The heat was on for me to back off the story or get off it altogether, let one of the political reporters take over. There was no way I'd do either, I'd quit first, but push never came to shove. I had a couple of hole cards. One was Arthur Gelb, the Metropolitan Editor. He had brought me up at the *Times*; Artie liked me and respected me. The other ace was my own reputation, which I put directly on the table. I said to Gelb, "Artie, stick with me on this, I've never embarrassed you, the story will hold, I lay my name on it." Arthur Gelb said, "That's all I need to know."

But the next couple of days were rough, the other papers were shooting at me and my own guys were hardly better. Roy assured me—again—that it was wheat in the bin, but I had to worry that the bosses might get cold feet and go Good Government. Talk about irony. All my life I was for judicial reform, now I prayed that the bosses would stand tall, would say fuck you to the Goo-goos.

It finally happened, but only on the morning of the Judicial Convention. The Bronx mahout, McDonough, said of the Botein Committee, "They are men who wear the halo of good government." I broke open a bottle of Dom P, and made my way to the Commodore Hotel, the site of this historic Democratic convention.

As I left the elevator, I walked into Frank Rossetti, the Manhattan leader. He grabbed my lapels. He said, "You sonofabitch, you rat bastard, you fucked us, you think this is some kind of joke? We're fighting for our lives here against these fucking reformers and you fuck around with fucking stories in the fucking New York fucking *Times*."

There were a dozen people standing there when he made these comments, I said nothing, just walked away, into the convention hall.

Fifteen minutes later, a man walked over to me and said, "Mr. Zion, would you please come outside?" I thought he was considering something funny, he looked like a guy you wouldn't go outside with. He said, "Mr. Rossetti wants to see you." I said, "Tell him to come in." "He can't come in." I said, "Why not?" He said, "The leaders aren't allowed to step foot in the convention, it's the law."

He was exactly right, I'd forgotten about that. The bosses, in order to appear to have no power over the Judicial Convention, barred themselves from appearing on the floor.

Of course, they ran the whole game. Just before this emissary

from Rossetti walked in, I had interviewed a bunch of the delegates. They were the kinds of people I knew from Jersey—the
clubhouse crowd, nobody here ever read Justice Holmes. When
I asked them who they were voting for, the answer was: "We're
waiting for them to give us the list."

I told Rossetti's guy to go back and tell Frank I'd be out in due
time. I didn't want to honor him, I wanted him to cool his heels.
A half-hour later, I came out.

He rushed over to me. "Sid, how could I do this stupid thing,
how could I say such terrible remarks to a man like you, please
Sid, I must have lost my mind, forgive me, it was dumb,
stupido."

I shook his hand. I said, "Frank, forget about it. I know you're
a friend. Don't let it bother you."

"No, *you're* the friend, we know you're our friend. So please."

"Frank," I said, "When you go back upstairs, tell Carmine
hello for me."

"Absolutely," Rossetti said. And then thought a second. And
slapped his own face. "Oh, my God, please, don't print it, Sid,
please."

"Hey, Frank, tell Carmine hello from Roy, too."

"Oh, thanks, Sid, thanks," said Rossetti.

He had gone up to the suite, after having berated me, and
bragged about it to Carmine DeSapio. Carmine ordered him
down to apologize. The only trouble was, Carmine was only recently out of jail. He wasn't allowed to be calling the shots at the
Judicial Convention, he wasn't allowed to be anywhere in the
vicinity of the Judicial Convention. So that's how come Frank
Rossetti slapped himself in the face.

How did I divine all this?

Hey, you don't know Roy Cohn for nothing.

Chapter Thirteen

In the spring of 1973, Roy Cohn changed the course of New York City politics. He did it with one turn of the stilletto and he left no fingerprints. You will hear it all in his words. But first the stage needs setting.

It was a watershed year going in, 1973, for it was a certainty that the city would now return to its traditional one-party Democratic rule. John Lindsay had been elected mayor in 1965, the first Republican since LaGuardia and only the third in this century. In 1969, Lindsay lost the Republican primary but won re-election on the Liberal line against a fatally divided Democratic party. Before his second term was up, Lindsay switched to the Democrats but not with a third term in mind. In 1972 he announced his candidacy for President of the United States, and entered the Florida primary in the belief that the Miami Jews, many of them transplanted New Yorkers, would put him across. It turned out that many of the Miami Jews had left the city to get away from Lindsay. He was wiped out and it ended his political career.

The consensus choice of the old-line Democratic leaders for mayor was Abraham Beame, former City Controller and loser to Lindsay in the '65 election. Beame had the frame of an old jockey and the charisma of a bookkeeper. This made him central casting for the bosses, who like charisma like drunks like water. Now, in a year that looked like shooting fish in the barrel, Beame was an even more perfect choice.

But trouble came fast, in the person of Mario Biaggi, an ex-cop who parlayed heroism on the force to a seat in Congress. Biaggi wanted to be mayor and it didn't faze him when his own Bronx organization endorsed Beame. He leapfrogged ahead of the colorless Beame and looked like odds-on to win the primary and thus the election.

Biaggi was certainly no reformer; the bosses never had trouble with him and in the ordinary course of events could live happily with him in City Hall. What made Biaggi a threat to boss rule was the support he had from Matthew Troy, the wise-cracking, big talking Queens leader who had been driving the elder bosses bananas. It was obvious to them that Matty had in mind to wire the city behind Biaggi. Nobody had wired New York since Charley Murphy—and that was before the First World War. What had prevailed since was a Duchy system, wherein power resided in the various county leaders, who basically respected territorial limits. Matty respected nothing, Matty was such a brass-balled bastard he once said to the papers, "I always keep my word—except when I can't." He was a rolling hand grenade, the Bugsy Siegel of New York politics and as such he had to go.

But how to do it? The only way was to stop Biaggi. But how stop the hero cop?

Enter Roy Cohn.

When I was interviewing Roy for this book, the Biaggi story was not on my agenda, because I didn't know he had anything to do with the gutting of Biaggi's mayoral campaign. But I did remember something, a fragment really, a glance, a look. I had asked him at the time who put Biaggi away. And Roy Cohn said nothing, just grimaced. There was, I thought then, a guilty note in that grimace. I had never known him to show a scintilla of guilt. And I had never seen him shut up when I asked him for an inside story.

That's all I had to go on, when I took a shot at him. I said, "Why do you seem to blame yourself for the fact that Mario Biaggi didn't get the nomination for mayor in '73?"

"I love Mario, he's a great friend. I've known him forever. I was his law professor when he was a cop going to New York Law School. He's a wonderful man. I'd do anything for him and he'd do anything for me."

I said, "So I guess I remember it wrong. I thought you maybe hurt him in that campaign."

"I knocked his brains out," Roy Cohn said.

"Tell me how."

"Is it important?"

"How'd you do it, Roy."

Roy said: "He was called before a federal grand jury and he asked us to advise him, Tom Bolan and me. They were going into a whole lot of things, but he was worried about his daughter; they had some bullshit about his daughter being on the payroll of one of his contributors and whether or not she really worked or was it a pad job. There was immigration stuff too, but the daughter thing worried him. We told him to go in and answer every question. He did, about the immigration business, but when they got to the daughter he wavered and said he wanted to see his lawyer. They gave him time, and he met another lawyer. This guy told him to take the Fifth. I told him never to do that, they had nothing on him, but he took the Fifth."

I said, "That's what ruined him, right?"

"Sure. And he denied he took it. Which became the big issue, the whole thing."

"The denial."

"Right."

"Well," I said, "why should you feel badly? You told him not to take the Fifth Amendment."

"Yes. But that was a year before. Now he was running for mayor."

"I don't get it."

"The lawyer who advised him to take the Fifth," Roy said, "assured him that it would never get out, since grand jury testimony is secret. When it became public, that's what destroyed him."

"So?"

"I was the one who broke it on him."

"You leaked it to the press?"

"I gave him fair warning, I told him," Roy Cohn said.

"That you were going to make it public?"

"Not that way, but I warned him."

He leaked it to the party bosses first. They didn't know Biaggi had taken the Fifth. They only knew that *they* were in trouble, not Biaggi. They were stuck with Abe Beame and they couldn't afford to lose with him; it was the Troy thing.

"Beame was an old friend, a fine man," Roy said. "He was up, it was his turn. It shouldn't have been a problem."

What?

"We had it figured out just right. I met for lunch at the Westbury Hotel with Meade Esposito and Pat Cunningham [respectively the Brooklyn and Bronx bosses]. I arranged for Mario to meet me after lunch at the townhouse, our place, just around the corner from the Westbury. If he had listened, he'd have had no trouble."

I said, "Explain."

"That's when I told him," Roy said. "That was the fair warning. I told him to settle for President of the City Council. That if he did that he'd be mayor next time. Abe Beame was not a young man, and he was a thoroughly decent guy. He'd move aside after one term and Mario would have it. Simple as that."

"Did you tell him this was from Meade and Cunningham?"

"Of course."

"Was it a direct threat? That otherwise they'd break the Fifth Amendment story?"

"It was an offer. I said if he did it this way the story would never break."

"What did Biaggi say?"

" 'Fuck 'em.' "

"He really thought this rule about grand jury secrecy would hold, would protect him?"

"His lawyer had assured him."

"And he figured he couldn't lose the election."

"He didn't have the nomination, remember that," Roy said.

"But he was way ahead."

"He was a cinch."

"So he said, 'Fuck 'em.' "

"And he left," Roy said.

"And then he was through."

"It was the front page of *The New York Times*."

I said, "I've seen Biaggi at every one of your parties all these years since."

"I don't know if he knows to this day that I let it out."

"He says nice things about you."

"And I do about him," Cohn said. "I love him."

Chapter Fourteen

"Are you familiar with the term 'killer fruit'? It's a certain kind of queer who has Freon refrigerating his bloodstream. Diaghilev, for example. J. Edgar Hoover, Hadrian."
> —Truman Capote, *Answered Prayers*

A group of gay activists called on Roy Cohn in the late 1970's. Their mission: to get Cohn to represent a teacher who had been fired from his job because he was a homosexual. Roy listened respectfully to the pitch. But he said nothing. When it was over, he still said nothing.

"Are you interested in the case?" the spokesperson asked.

"Sure."

"You think it's winnable?"

"No question."

"Ah," said the spokesperson, "that's marvelous. Of course, we can't pay your usual fee but we don't expect you to do this for nothing."

With a wave of his hand, Cohn said: "I never even take expenses in a public interest case. This is a matter of great concern to the American people."

Everyone smiled. The spokesperson said, "We are very pleased that you see it this way."

"The way I see it," Roy said, "the school system is a hundred percent right."

"Pardon?"

"A hundred ten percent."

"I don't understand."

"Well maybe this will make you understand," Cohn said. "I believe homosexual teachers are a grave threat to our children, they have no business polluting the schools of America. It's tough enough to instill traditional values in kids today, what with drugs, the divorce rate, and liberal 'relativism.' Putting homosexuals in the schools makes a terrible problem just about impossible.

"You've got the wrong lawyer, gentlemen. And I've got the wrong client. If I'm fortunate enough to get a call from the Board of Education, I'll see you in court."

They were lucky that didn't get collective lockjaw after that performance. Gay Liberation was at its apex, and who more likely to defend its rights than Roy Cohn? True, he hadn't officially "come out" but he was all over the place, way beyond the subterranean fag scene, he was showing up everywhere with his young bloods, from Studio 54, which he practically ran, to Steinbrenner's box at the Stadium. The townhouse on East 68th, where he lived and kept his law offices, was festooned with gays of all colors. Roy Cohn was the Babe Ruth of the Gay World—or more accurately, Yogi Berra. Not because he hit bad balls; just that he was maybe the world's greatest catcher.

What the gays didn't get was how he could be out front and closeted at the same time. The straights couldn't figure it out either, but there was a difference. Most of Cohn's straight friends looked the other way; indeed, they told others, if not themselves, that what they were seeing wasn't true. Roy Cohn, they said, was asexual. He just didn't have time for women. He used to fuck them but he was too busy now. One day he'd marry, probably he'd marry Barbara Walters. That's what he always said, and who could deny it?

Roy understood the difference between *de facto* and *de jure*. He could do anything he liked as long as he didn't admit it. A confession had the force of law—*de jure*. The rest was gossip—*de facto*. I watched him play this for twenty years. He never admitted it to me, either. All I got was Barbara Walters. But here's what I saw.

Two stories out of the annual Fourth of July party in Greenwich. These parties were never on the Fourth but a few weekdays before the weekend of the Fourth. The invitations were the same, an American flag on top, just a white card with room for the name of the invitee, and an insert with directions. The directions were fine until a critical point—and then gridlock would set in, with limos backing and pulling and moguls and judges cursing and chauffeurs conferring and car phones ablaze with nothing but busy signals from the point of destination.

It was a good country house deep in the woods. Roy acquired it in the mid-Seventies, after all the trials were over, after Morgenthau failed so often to get him that all he got him was immunity from prosecution. The property wasn't in his name, nothing was in his name (the IRS stuff), but it was all his, a colonial house, waterfall and nicely appointed woodland.

Towards the end of my first night there, Roy was standing around the pool with Carmine DeSapio and Meade Esposito. I ambled over, figuring I might pick up a story or three. But before I could so much as get within earshot there was this big splash. Lo and behold! Four or five of Roy's young studs had slipped into their swim togs and there they were frolicking in the moonlit water.

Now this behavior was a difference in kind from the old days at the townhouse. Then, a couple of them would sidle down the staircase or pop out of the potted plants, but it was all very discreetly done, almost as if they were part of the help.

But we hadn't seen anything yet. Suddenly they were out of the pool, all agiggle, trying to toss Roy in, fully clothed. Roy resisted while trying to laugh it off, but I wasn't paying attention to Roy. I watched Carmine and Meade as if they were potato bugs. And sure enough, this scene was not registering on their retinas, they had willed it away. These two old pols, these veterans of a thousand and one smoked-filled rooms—you don't have to ask what they thought of fairies—they weren't going to see this at all.

I didn't even smile. I thought, wow! I thought, power.

A few years later, and all I could do was laugh. It was 1980, Roy was at the top of his game, the Greenwich joint was mobbed with pols, mobsters, builders, labor skates, judges. Rubbing elbows. And looking a little uncomfortable.

The trip had been unusually long, every year it seemed to get tougher to find the damned country house, and this time there had been an accident on the highway. So after a quick look at the crowd I made my way for the john. And saw a line about a half-mile long, mainly women waiting outside the ground floor facility. So I tried the one upstairs. No line up there. I figured the squares downstairs didn't know about this one. I opened the door—and in the bath was a young man bubbling away, reading a book, totally at peace. When I went back down I asked the queue how long the upstairs john had been taken. They told me forty-five minutes. And no end in sight, this beauty was taking his sweet time.

Meanwhile, on the outside guys were squirming like kindergarten kids. I wish I could have televised this scene. Some of the most powerful men in America looking for trees. Me too. Right next to a judge. "Your honor," I said, "do you know why we're here?"

"It's a goddam disgrace," he said. "Why can't he have arranged for toilets for Chrissakes!"

"He did."

"Where?"

"On the second floor," I said. "Off the bedroom."

"Well why didn't they let us know?"

"It wouldn't have helped."

"What do you mean it wouldn't help?"

"One of Roy's nephews is in there."

"Roy has no nephews."

"You know, one of the blond boys."

"I don't want to hear this," the judge said.

"He's taking a bubble bath, right now, as we pee. You want to see, I'll go up there with you."

"This never happened," His Honor said. And returned to the party.

On the morning of that party, I got a call from a New York *Daily News* editor, Joan Massivera. "You going to Roy Cohn's tonight?" I said sure. She said, "Well, I've got something here you might want to present to the host. I'll messenger it up, you'll have it in an hour." I asked what the hell . . . but she hung up.

There arrived a magazine called *NOW East* with a slick cover depicting a Gay Pride Week parade, a cartoon, that had in the forefront a sign: Roy Cohn's for Gays. The contents, though printed on butcher paper, was expertly laid out, with ads that appeared to be the real stuff: E. F. Hutton, American Express, Smirnoff, New York restaurants, department stores, hotels. There were some bathhouse ads to go with it, but the approach was on its face legit.

The rest of the magazine was hard-porn. And all of it on Roy. The cartoons depicted him in the sleaziest sex scenes; the lead piece was titled "Confession: An Open Letter to the Gay Community," by Roy M. Cohn.

Apart from the fag stuff, every crazed rumor ever whispered about Cohn was there, including murder. And this screed was now in every newsroom in New York. All day I got calls from my pals in the press. "Did you see . . ." They knew it was fake, of course, but everybody loves a hoot, and this was the hoot of the decade.

Well, not everybody thought it was funny. Jerry Finkelstein was driving me up to the party that night. Then, as now, he was the publisher of *The New York Law Journal.* He knew Roy since Roy was a kid; he knew Roy's father; Jerry Finkelstein knew everybody. As a young man he had worked for Tom Dewey during Dewey's crime-busting days and in the late 1940's he was Mayor O'Dwyer's campaign manager and then head of the City Planning Commission. In the early Fifties he had a public relations firm that employed William Safire and Barbara Walters. Safire had inscribed one of his books, "To Jerry, who taught me all I know—but not all he knows."

The one thing I knew Jerry didn't know was that Roy Cohn

was gay. No matter the evidence, no way he would concede it. Unlike the political bosses and mafia leaders who didn't want to see it, Jerry simply couldn't imagine it. "That's impossible," he'd say to me. "I know Roy, that can't be."

When his chauffeur paid the last toll on the Connecticut Turn- pike, I handed Jerry the magazine without a word. "What's this?" he said. I shrugged.

He leafed gingerly through the pages. And then did a freeze. A double take. A second leafing.

"What . . . what . . . this is . . . what . . . terrible, terrible . . . who did . . . what . . . vicious . . . who, what, wha . . ."

I was afraid he was going into cardiac arrest. But not afraid enough to let go.

"You think it'll hurt him?" I said.

"It's . . . it's . . . it's . . . who . . . what . . . how . . . did it . . . who . . ."

"When we get there, Jerry, we'll show it to Roy. I'm sure he can tell us who pulled off this little prank."

"Show it to him? Show . . . this prank?"

"Well, don't worry about it," I said. "You always told me there was nothing to this gay stuff, just crap. Roy'll clear it up, relax."

"What . . . what . . . who . . . show it? To him? What?"

Jerry Finkelstein. Like that. And I'm sure he wasn't the only one to hyperventilate.

"Anybody who knows me or knows anything about me or who knows the way my mind works or knows the way I function in active life, would have an awfully hard time reconciling that with any kind of homosexuality. Every facet of my personality, of my aggressiveness, my toughness and everything along those lines is just totally, I suppose, incompatible with anything like that."
                                                  —Roy M. Cohn, 1978

This quote never appeared in print. It evolved out of a long interview conducted by Ken Auletta for *Esquire.* The piece was terrific, a cover story with the line: "Don't Mess With Roy Cohn—The Legal Executioner." Roy bought 500 copies of the magazine and it made him a fortune. What client doesn't want an executioner? But the gay thing was cut. Ken Auletta gave me the transcripts of his tapes. I'm grateful, because I never did what Ken did. I never asked Roy if he was gay. The answer he gave Auletta is classic Cohn, and it served him well across the years. No major publication ever said he was a fairy, and maybe the persona he floated had something to do with it. We know about leather now and tough-guy fags, but when Roy Cohn was making his mark everybody wasn't Dr. Freud.

Why didn't I ever put it to him? In the years before I began working with him on this book, there was no occasion. And I knew he would have denied it, anyway, and finally I didn't need to ask, there it was before me, before everybody who cared to see. When we began this project, he was dying of AIDS.

In the fall of 1985, *The New York Times* ran a story about why their Book Division had deleted references to Cardinal Spellman's alleged homosexuality in a biography of His Eminence. Of course, this made it all the more public; it was a big goddam piece about how Times Books had killed the thing.

I said to Roy, "What do you think about them saying Cardinal Spellman was a fag?"

"Hey," Roy Cohn said. "They say it about *me*."

Closer to the end, he complained, "They're saying I've got AIDS. Imagine me having AIDS?"

Hey. Do you think Hadrian considered himself a pansy? (At one of the Birthday Parties in Studio 54, a gaggle of Roy's Twinkies—Killer Fruits have stables of youngbloods known as Twinkies—dressed in togas, crowned Roy with golden laurel leaves. This picture made the tabloids, the Twinkies standing around him singing Happy Birthday, Roy looking every bit the modern Emperor Hadrian.)

How, you ask, could he possibly think of himself as straight? Because that's how he wanted it. Because, conversely, he hated the gay stereotype, which he held in his own mind. He totally meant it when he said that homosexuals (he always called them "fags") have no business teaching children in school. And of course, on a strictly pragmatic basis, he knew that if he "came out" he would no longer be welcome where he was always welcome, he would not have the clients he had—can one imagine "Fat Tony" Salerno with a statedly fag lawyer, or Donald Trump—not to mention invitations to the White House and carte blanche in Steinbrenner's box.

But this ability to deny, even on a certain internal level, is hardly unique to Roy Cohn or other closet queens. I've known a bunch of hit-men, but never one who thought himself a murderer. Or a rent-gouger who considered himself a slum-lord. As a criminal lawyer I defended a few alleged drug dealers. All of them thought of themselves as businessmen. Has any president who threw us into wars ever believed he was anything but a man of peace?

Crazy? Of course crazy. But only if you don't share their passion. Which is to do what they want to do when they want to do it.

The party line on Roy Cohn's homosexuality—that is to say, the line delivered by his closest straight friends—was that it all began after his mother died. I suspect they believe this; I don't think it's anything they made up in concert or in the privacy of their own musings. And, of course, until the cause of death was published, they only said this much to each other. The outside world was told that he was asexual.

Roy's mother died in 1967, when he was 40 years old. The notion that a man could change his sexual orientation at that age is possible, but only in the sense that nothing is impossible. The men who told me this over the years are no fools. They come out of an era that was not terribly sophisticated in the ways of homosexuals—like Roy told Ken Auletta, who'd think a tough street-fighter like RMC was gay?—but they're not disconnected from reality. So how come they believed, and still believe, that it all began when the mother died? Her name was Dora, but everyone called her "Muddy."

First, because they saw it with their own eyes. "I was in the same room with him, both of us fucking these broads." I heard this from five different guys, at least five. "He called for girls every town we were in, from Buffalo to Paris." Hookers, to be sure, but so what?

And then, through all the years Muddy lived, Roy Cohn lived

with Muddy. "The child," she called him, and it's doubtful that the boy had any boys sleeping with him in that Park Avenue apartment. So protective was she, that when Richard Nixon called one morning, while he was vice-president, she refused to wake Roy. "Roy has been working very hard," she said. "He'll call when he gets up. I can't disturb him."

So it's understandable. While Muddy lived, he was in a cold-stone closet. Afterwards, and at first gradually, the nephews began to appear. Looking back at it now, that day on the yacht in Chicago, 1968, was a bit of a landmark, with that blue-eyed kid drinking Bloodies. Until then, all I knew were rumors. After that, all I saw with "the child" were boys.

Roy's active homosexual life began in his freshman year at Columbia. He was fifteen years old. I found this out after his death. The source was one of his doctors. He had to be out front with the doctors, who were constantly treating him for the usual gay problems.

"He was promiscuous as hell," the doctor said. "The moment we learned about AIDS I was terribly afraid for him. He was in the highest risk group. He had just come back from Europe, he'd chartered a plane and gone over with a bunch of his lovers. I asked him to tell me what he knew about them. He said, 'I can tell you about the ones in the cabin, but the guys in the cockpit . . .' "

I recognized this as the famous 747 flight, which made the tabloids, though without note of homosexual doings. Roy chartered the plane on credit. Whatever he and his pals did inside the cabin we can only imagine. But the physical condition of the cabin is history. The cabin was trashed, the seats broken, the whole thing wrecked like a victim of gang-rape.

The airline sued and won hands-down. And never collected a dime. What the hell, Roy had no money in his name. In desperation, an executive of the line called Donald Trump. Would Trump help defray the cost, being that Trump was Cohn's client and friend?

Trump told him, "Are you kidding?" And the guy practically broke down crying on the phone.

"I felt for the poor bastard," Donald says, "because Roy just wiped out that plane. But what was I supposed to do? Hey, it was Roy, what's anybody supposed to do? They couldn't get anything from him, and this guy kept telling me, 'We've won in every court, every court!' "

A couple of years before this incident, Roy Cohn wanted to have a baby. What?

"Yes," said the doctor. "By now he couldn't think of having sex with a woman. He had been bi-sexual, but no more, not for many years. He wanted a child, though. And he had a woman picked out for artificial insemination."

"Who was this woman?" I asked.

"I won't tell you her name."

"Fair enough. But what happened?"

"Well, he had it all worked out. He was going to set up a trust fund of a half-million dollars to secure the child's future. And there would be sufficient monies in addition to take care of the woman."

"So why didn't it happen?"

"I stopped it."

"How?"

"I said to him, 'Roy, that's all fine and good. But what about the child? How do you expect a child to grow up sane in an atmosphere like that? Isn't it tough enough for children in the best of all worlds? Please, Roy, consider this.' And he nodded. It was all over, thank God."

A second issue of the magazine *NOW East* made its appearance in time for Roy's 1981 birthday party. The cover had Roy in Roman toga, crowned with laurel leaves, standing atop a monument with this legend:

ROY M. COHN
Attorney
Lecturer
Statesman
Fairy

And this thing was politely handed to the black-ties as they entered the Armory on Park Avenue to toast Roy's 54th birthday. (The Armory? Well, Studio 54 was no more, the owners were doing a little ping-pong time—small and light—for tax evasion.) Anyway, if you didn't look closely you might have thought it was an official program of the birthday boy's big night—and this is exactly what the fiancée of one of New York's most famous politicians thought as she dropped it into her handbag. When she got home and snuggled under her covers, she picked up the "program" with a nice smile on her face. Which turned to stone, the minute she opened it to a brilliantly fake photo of Roy in drag. And that was the least of the porno crap that filled this magazine.

The man behind it was one Richard Dupont, who once owned a gay spa called The Big Gym in Greenwich Village. He had been represented by Roy in a dispute over ownership of the gym and he claimed that Roy had sold him out, had taken money from a rival claimant and thus "stolen" his property. To get even, Dupont created *NOW East*, and with this second issue he was really upping the ante, distributing it everywhere Roy went—"21," Le Cirque, Jim McMullen's—outside these places, of course, but of course only whenever he knew Roy was about to appear.

But what could Cohn do about it? If he raised a stink it would get more publicity, it would make the major media. Of course, any one of his Mafia clients would have been happy to take care of the matter, but this wasn't in his line, despite what some of his friends and most of his enemies believed.

For once he was really in a bind, I thought; there was simply nothing I could imagine he could do to stop this guy. And so he did the one thing nobody every would have figured he'd do. He went to the district attorney. Who now happened to be Robert M. Morgenthau, his oldest living prosecutorial enemy. And Bob Morgenthau indicted, tried, convicted and jailed Richard Dupont—on a range of charges from attempted coercion to aggravated harassment.

When I asked Cohn about it, he said, "Hey, I wasn't going to let this bum run roughshod over me, telling these lies, embarrassing my friends. Sure I knew it would make the papers, and there'd be stuff about this fag bullshit, but I decided the hell with it. Nobody who knows me would ever buy that fag stuff, and the others I didn't care about, they've been saying that stuff about me since the McCarthy days. They said I was in bed with Dave Schine. Dave! Who married Miss Universe and has a bunch of great kids and grandchildren for God's sake. So let them say what they want, I had to do something. And I must tell you, Bob Morgenthau was a gentleman, he did a great job."

So full circle, his oldest enemy jailing his latest enemy. Only Roy Cohn could do it. Imagine Mr. Dupont's mind as he sat in the cooler. You go to the can in this town for calling Roy Cohn a fag?

And Roy Cohn went to his grave fag baiting. I was interviewing him at the Greenwich house. The cardinal's office called. "Sure," Roy said. "I'll get on it immediately. We can't allow these people to take over the city."

"What was that about?" I said.

"The city council is about to pass a Gay Rights Bill. The cardinal wants me to help stop it. So I've got to make some calls."

He called Andrew Stein, the President of the City Council. Andy was the sponsor of the Gay Rights Bill. He is also Jerry Finkelstein's son, and Roy knew him the day he was born.

"Andy," Roy said, "you've gotta get off this fag stuff, it's very harmful to the city and it's going to hurt you. You know how the cardinal feels. And that's how most people feel. These fucking fags are no good, forget about them. Why are you putting your neck on the line for them?"

He said to me, when he hung up, "I don't think our friend Andy would dare to switch on this thing. Well, who could blame him? the press would be all over him. And the fags, I don't care about them, but they're not like you or me, they're hysterical, they'd drive him nuts. But I had to ask him, and I think I'm right to do it. What do you think?"

I didn't answer. I didn't have to answer. Roy Cohn was back on the phone, calling city councilmen.

"Now look, we can't let the fags just . . ."

Chapter Fifteen

Roy Cohn calling.

"C'mon over, I've got a dynamite story on Paul Castellano."

This was a couple of days after the Mafia don was gunned down in front of Sparks Steak House in Manhattan, December, 1985.

How long do you think it took me to c'mon over?

Roy met me in his small office on the ground floor of the townhouse. This was unusual, as we generally talked in the living room, or if he was feeling lousy, in his bedroom. The first thing he did was wave off the tape recorder. We didn't always talk on tape, but he never waved it off before, either. He said, "You don't need that, it's a short story, you'll remember it."

He began by telling me about Rudolph Giuliani, the United States Attorney for the Southern District of New York.

"As soon as Rudy was appointed," Roy said, "the rumors began that his big thing was to ride to governor or the Senate or

247

even higher office by prosecuting top Mafia leaders. I got the word through underworld sources."

I smiled when he said that and he did too. He needed underground sources for this? "O.K.," he said, "it was an open secret. Rudy was going to arrest every single mob leader. And, of course, he's doing it and nobody else has ever done that."

"I hear you went to see Rudy for Castellano."

His eyes flickered. For a second I thought he might ask me how I knew that. But he recovered. Roy Cohn doesn't ask those questions. He tops you by telling you what you don't know.

"Tommy Gambino asked me to do it, and I was glad to do it. Tommy's a good friend and he was right."

Tommy Gambino is the son of the old godfather Carlo Gambino and the nephew of Paul Castellano, who took over the Gambino Family after Carlo died. "Carlo Gambino Dies In Bed," the New York *Daily News* headlined on page one, and of course this is every don's dream headline.

"Rudy," Roy continued, "was about to indict Paul and others for everything from car-stealing to loansharking to murder. Plus drug-dealing. The drug stuff was what bothered Tommy. He said to me, 'My uncle Paul is not in drugs. He's violently anti-drugs, just like my father was; my father kept that shit out, he insisted on that.'

"Tommy was right," Roy said. "I knew for sure he was right about that. So I said I'd certainly see Rudy and try and convince him not to put these drug charges in against Castellano. Without the drug charges there wasn't much sex in the case."

There was only murder and loansharking. But I knew what Roy meant. They only kill each other and they were loansharking gamblers. Drugs means kids. Drugs gets everybody up in arms. No sex without drugs.

"I went to see Giuliani," Roy said. "Present were his top staff. This was two or three weeks before the indictment was to come down. I made my speech. I started by saying that I knew these people, I knew Paul for 20 years, and they knew I had represented Tony Salerno. I said, 'It's a funny thing. The people who kept drugs out of New York City in large quantities all these years are Carlo Gambino, Paul Castellano, Salerno, all of them.

So now you're going after Paul for drugs. I tell you, I think it's crazy, it's wrong.' "

Giuliani, according to Roy, said that there was a witness who would testify that Castellano was always going to a restaurant where drug deals went down.

"I knew who he meant," Roy said. "It was one of Paul's bodyguards."

Cohn told Giuliani, "Rudy, you're here now. There could be a lunch meeting ten blocks away and someone could say that you were there, that drug deals were happening and you were there. How can anybody protect himself against this stuff? It's double hearsay."

What did Rudy say to this?

"He didn't say anything. His people wanted to know if Paul would take a lie detector test and if he'd testify before the grand jury."

And?

"I said I didn't know what he'd do, but I'd recommend it. They said, 'See you later.' "

Roy continued, "I met Castellano in a car. We went over all the propositions. I told him I'd insist on the questions in advance so there'd be no curveballs. He was 50-50."

What happened?

"It fell apart because of my conditions. The idea of the lie detector and grand jury testimony was to exonerate him from the drug charges. But in testifying he'd have to get into relationships with other people, he couldn't just make a denial."

Was there any talk of him cooperating with the government?

"Definitely."

So that's why it didn't happen, right?

Roy Cohn said, "That's not it."

What do you mean?

"Paul Castellano never gave me a flat 'no' on cooperation."

What the hell are you saying?

Roy smiled. He said, "It never got to the point of giving up people."

So then what?

"Just that he never gave a flat 'no.' "

Do you think that got out to the mob?

"Not from me," Roy Cohn said.

I said, "Roy, are you trying to tell me that Castellano was hit because they thought he would talk? I mean, he was on trial when they hit him."

"It wasn't the drug trial."

"So that's what you're saying, right?"

"He just died the other day," Cohn said.

"So?"

"I don't know why he was killed."

"But you seem to be saying . . ."

"I haven't had a chance to check it out."

"Will you let me know?"

Roy Cohn shrugged.

He never said another word about it.

Maybe he thought he'd already said enough.

Maybe he was surprised that I was asking all these questions.

After all, he started by telling me he had a dynamite story on Paul Castellano.

Chapter Sixteen

I paid little attention to the disbarment proceedings against Cohn, though they were swirling around his head throughout the period I worked with him on this book. I talked to him about it, to be sure, but casually, there was no depth to it. The reason: I didn't believe he'd live long enough for them to disbar him. And then I would't have to write about it, so why waste time when time was the only thing we didn't have?

Six weeks before he died, while he was in the hospital for his final innings, the appellate division disbarred him. His father's old court; and not just his father's. Roy once had plenty of juice there; he put people on that court; it was a court traditionally weighted with Bronx judges and everybody knew his clout in the Bronx. His law associate, Stanley Friedman, was the boss of the Bronx. But now Stanley Friedman was under federal indictment. And Roy Cohn was dying of AIDS. Obviously, I should have been more attentive, knowing these two "buts" alone, only it somehow didn't penetrate to me that they'd put it to him right on his deathbed. Anyway, once he went into the hospital he was out of my reach, and I had no choice but to search out the record and see for myself what the beef was all about.

I reviewed the voluminous testimony, the briefs, the opinion of the court, all with my legal face on, dispassionately analyzing the case against my autobiographer. And I got a little dizzy. It was on the one hand this, on the other that, there was a "maybe" here, a "yes" there, a "perhaps" elsewhere, a "no" and a "why" and et and cetera. I asked myself, am I bending over backwards or too easy, have I paid more attention to X than I should to Y? Furthermore, why the hell couldn't he have died six weeks earlier, goddamit, goddam him, goddam them all, and how can I be fair?

I took a few days off with martinis and steaks and then read all the material all over again. And walked away from it for another week. Until finally I saw what I should have seen the first day.

What this thing was about was a perception of Roy Cohn that had nothing to do with the reality of Roy Cohn. He was disbarred because they assumed he was greedy. The charges stemmed from that assumption. If you believed it, you'd probably find him guilty. But if you knew him, you knew that the one vice he didn't have—perhaps the only vice—was greed. He cared nothing about money, he was in it for the game, the power. He often didn't charge clients and almost never charged them enough. Donald Trump told me, "Roy charged less than any lawyer I've had." Cohn died broke, he left nothing but debts and taxes. And he was disbarred for greed. It was hardly the only irony in his rip-roaring career at the bar, but it was surely the most profound.

Irony had nothing to do with the animus that fueled the disciplinary committee, the court-appointed panel that recommended Cohn's disbarment. It figured they wouldn't like him; anybody who could get on one of these committees would have to despise Roy Cohn, it was definitional. Not so much because of the Rosenbergs or McCarthy or his right-wing politics—Herbert Brownell, who practically pulled the switch on Julius and Ethel, is held in high esteem by this quarter, as is Judge Kaufman. What curdled their blood with Cohn was his headline-hunting, his gun-slinger style, his contempt for the niceties, his contempt for *them*. A bunch of "yo-yo's" he called them later, but he didn't have to say it for them to know what he thought. They saw him black, no shadings; it jumps off every other page in the transcript. From such a perspective, everything he did (or didn't do) was the act of a greed-ridden menace, a sinister figure whose license had to be lifted, even on his deathbed, in order to cleanse the profession of his stench.

First they tried to put him away without a hearing. On two old cases, two opinions out of the judicial dustbins. In one, a Florida judge in 1975 threw out a codicil to the will of Lewis Rosensteil, the liquor baron. Rosensteil was Cohn's long-time friend and client; the charge was that Cohn deceived him into changing his will while he was virtually comatose in a hospital. The other case involved an escrow account set up in 1971. In this one, the *Pied Piper* case, a federal judge in New York rapped Cohn for purportedly dissipating the escrow.

On these bearded charges, the disciplinary committee wanted summary execution.

It was asking too much, it was hugger-mugger; the only lawyers automatically disbarred are those convicted of felonies. The appellate division sent it back for hearings. It was like saying, "Give him a trial before you hang him, you dopey bastards."

They gave him the hearing and added two charges into the bargain. One went back twenty years, and it turned out to be the only case involving a litigant, a live complainant, the only one that came in over the transom: a former client named Iva Lee Schlesinger, who had sued Cohn for partial non-payment of a $100,000 loan and to collect it brought the case to the disciplinary committee. The other was the only one that seemed to be of recent vintage. In 1982, Cohn was admitted to the Washington, D.C., bar. The disciplinary committee in New York claimed that he intentionally withheld critical information in his application and thus got admitted fraudulently. What didn't he tell the D.C. bar? He didn't tell them about the Rosensteil will contest and he didn't tell them about the alleged dissipation of the escrow account, and he didn't tell them about Iva Lee Schlesinger.

The disciplinary committee made the D.C. bar business its first formal charge. I find this fortuitous; since I'm talking about animus here, the way the committee treated this one was animus in living color.

The disciplinary committee had sent him letters of inquiry regarding these three cases (Rosensteil, etc.) and yet on the D.C. application, where it asked whether any charges or complaints were "pending" against him, Cohn said no. This answer, claimed the committee, amounted to "willful falsity." Where's the animus, you say?

On two of the three cases he hadn't heard a word from the committee for two years; on the other, for five years. No hearings had been scheduled, there was no action; all the committee did was send him these letters of inquiry. He didn't think that made them "pending" cases. Because he didn't think it, they decided he had committed a disbarrable offense. Why? They hadn't sent him a letter "closing out" the cases. There was no rule that a case was "pending" until a termination letter was received, and Cohn was never informed that he should treat the matters in that fashion. Still, they sought to punish him for violating a "rule" that only they were aware of. And that's only the half of it.

At the hearing, Charles Work, a former president of the D.C. Bar Association, testified that under the rules of that jurisdiction, a case isn't "pending" until a decision is made to prosecute; therefore, he said, Cohn's answer was proper; the D.C. bar couldn't care less about complaint letters or other documents of similar import. Work's testimony was not contradicted. The committee had made no effort to find out what the D.C. bar thought of Cohn's answers in his application for admission. But what an effort they made to discredit Charles Work!

"Read the transcript on Work," Roy had told me. "They treated him as though he was up on charges of first degree murder."

He wasn't exaggerating by much. One after another panel member hammered Work with questions that ranged from his qualifications to testify to his reasons for testifying to how much he was getting paid for his testimony. His qualifications were first-rate, he practically wrote the questions involved on the application, and of course he was president of the bar. As to compensation, he hadn't even discussed it; he assumed it would be his regular legal fee rate. As to why he was testifying, it turned out that he never met Cohn, that he was asked about the issues by Cohn's lawyers, former federal judge Harold Tyler, Jr., and Michael Mukasey (who became a federal judge in January, 1988), that he was sent all the relevant documents and after studying them he concluded that Roy Cohn had properly answered the D.C. bar's questions.

Work had caught them off-guard, it apparently never occurred to them that Cohn's lawyers would turn up an expert in D.C. bar applications and related ethics issues. You would think it would be the first thing that would occur to them; what could be more important than what the bar he applied to thought of his answers? As noted, however, the New York panel didn't even bother to ask anybody in D.C. To begin to understand this, one has to consider the legal mind.

Thomas Reed Powell, the great constitutional scholar and Professor of Law at Harvard, described it best: "If you can think about something that is related to something else, without thinking about the thing to which it is related—then you have the legal mind."

By deciding that the D.C. bar's view of a D.C. bar applicant's answers to the D.C. bar's questions were irrelevant—as the panel and later the appellate division did—New York gave us the quintessential example of the legal mind working its way up its own sphincter.

In their gut they knew better, and the dead giveaway was in the way they jumped all over Charles Work. If he was irrelevant, why ask him anything, much less grill him?

The questioning went far deeper than whether Cohn should have admitted there were charges "pending" against him. The hearing panel used the occasion to delve into the interstices of the Rosensteil case and the *Pied Piper* escrow account. These two cases were separate counts against Cohn, as well, but since the panel raised them with Work, I'll deal with them here—and for the sake of brevity, get done with them.

On the D.C. bar application, Cohn answered "No" to whether he had "ever been adjudged liable in a civil action or proceeding involving a claim of fraud, conversion, breach of fiduciary duty or legal malpractice."

Mr. Work testified that this was the correct answer, for although Cohn had been severely chastised by a Florida judge in *Rosensteil*, and in the *Pied Piper* Company Wall Street embroglio by a federal district judge in New York, he had not been held liable in either case—and that's all the D.C. bar wanted to know; they weren't asking whether he had ever been criticized by a court.

If that sounds simple enough, it made no headway whatever with the panel, or subsequently with the appellate division. Again, who cares what the D.C. bar meant by its question? Cohn should have flagged these judicial critiques and by not doing so he committed a disbarrable offense in New York, to hell with what the D.C. bar thought or even now thinks. (They never made a move to revoke Cohn's license.)

And of course, to hell with the fact that in *Pied Piper* Judge Edward Palmeiri, who warned Cohn he'd be held liable and in contempt if the escrow account in question were not satisfactorily replenished, eventually dismissed the case with prejudice—meaning it was over—when the owner of *Pied Piper* put the money in. Irrelevant, too, was the fact that whatever the court in Florida said about Cohn in *Rosensteil*, and it blasted him plenty, it adjudged him liable for nothing; what it did was to reject the codicil.

Ironically the disciplinary committee exonerated Roy in the Rosensteil matter; but they found him guilty for not revealing it to the D.C. bar. In other words, you didn't do anything wrong, but you should have told them about it anyway. The appellate division, which upheld all the other findings of the disciplinary committee, reversed them on the substantive count in *Rosensteil*, holding that the obtaining of the codicill was a disbarrable offense.

Standing alone, this ought to raise eyebrows. If the panel, with all its obvious venom against Cohn, found him innocent in the Rosensteil case, shouldn't an appellate court give enough substance to the finding to leave it alone, let it go? But it's worse; it doesn't stand alone. The Rosensteil will codicil affair made front-page headlines when the Florida court rejected it and belted Cohn. And that was ten years before this disbarment. In between time, nobody did a thing about it—not the legal establishment, not the judiciary. Now, suddenly, they were scandalized; how could such conduct be countenanced in a civilized society?

The *Pied Piper* case too was well publicized; I doubt if one member of the judiciary didn't know in 1975 that Judge Palmieri had threatened Roy Cohn with contempt. In 1986, this was terrible; we can't permit this conduct by a member of the bar! That he made pennies in *Pied Piper* and stood to make nothing in *Rosensteil*—what difference did that make in 1986? He must have meant to rip everybody off, and we are shocked beyond recall.

At least Claude Rains smiled when he closed Rick's that night in Casablanca. "What right do you have to shut me down?" said Bogart. "I am shocked, sir, shocked," said Rains, "to find that you permit gambling in this place." The croupier then hands him his winnings.

Nobody got any winnings in the Roy Cohn case, of course not. But the one guy they thought was getting the filthy lucre, the guy who was in it for the money, couldn't have cared less about it, and in the event got *bubkes* for all the talk, all the scandal, all the madness.

What about Iva Lee Schlesinger? Didn't Roy Cohn glom a hundred grand off Iva Schlesinger? His client?

This one seemed to bother Cohn's fans; I heard a lot about it, rumblings all over the place. I don't understand, they'd say, why he would take money from a poor woman, a client, a person who trusted him. Even some of his friends were upset about this one; this one seemed like sleaze itself.

And yet this "poor woman"—amazing how many people put it that way to me—was married to one of the richest men in South Africa, John Schlesinger. By the time Cohn got into the case, in 1966—yes, this one was twenty years old—she had been separated from John fourteen years. She was by then a veteran of the courts, she had lawyers everywhere; he wanted a divorce but she wouldn't settle.

"I used to run into her, her sister, her mother, on the Riviera," Roy told me. "They were always pushing me to handle this divorce, but I had seen and heard enough, because it was all around the legal community that she was really bad news. So I made one excuse after another. But finally I made the mistake of saying, 'Well, contact me in New York, not on the beach.' The minute they hit the shores of New York, they were in my office.

"I said, finally, I'd take the case but that there should be a divorce and each one should be entitled to live her and his life and if I thought the figure was right I didn't want to haggle with him and I didn't want to haggle with her. I wanted to have authority to settle.

"I called in Tom Bolan and he asked how much money was she looking for. Her sister, Helen Moose, replied, 'Oh, Mr. Bolan, you don't understand. We don't care about the money. We just want him to die a slow death of cancer, inch by inch.'"

Bolan is not known for his humor, but he wrote this note to Roy after that conference: "With a sister-in-law like that, who needs a mother-in-law?"

Cohn wrote a letter to John Schlesinger, telling him he was representing his wife and he'd like to get the case closed quickly.

"John wrote me back in longhand," Cohn told me. "He said, 'Dear Mr. Cohn, I have checked your references out and I find that you are a man of your word and a very fair person. Therefore, you and I will negotiate this settlement. There is not much to negotiate, however. I am setting forth here what I am willing to do. Don't ask me for more and I won't ask you to take less.'

"So," Roy said, "he made an offer that amounted to about $3.5 million, including fifty thousand to me in legal fees. The fee was grossly inadequate, of course, but this wouldn't stop her from making up the difference, which is quite a common practice in matrimonial cases. The husband pays part and the wife pays part."

Did he get an agreement from her for fees?

"No. You know me, I didn't bother with it, I trusted her. She knew this was no money, fifty thousand, and I figured we'd work it out later. I just wanted to get the thing done, get the divorce, finish it, it had been going on forever."

Cohn went to South Africa to expedite the divorce. Then came the deal that would end up in his disbarment. Here's Roy:

"I met Iva Schlesinger in Paris and she knew, of course, that John had only contributed the $50,000 *towards* my fee, plus a disbursement figure of $10,000 to cover the trips to South Africa. I asked her if she would give me $100,000 and she said she gladly would. We didn't know how to treat it because there was going to be work in the future and so we called it a loan with no due date. We put on it, loan-renewable. So we could see what the future brought."

I asked him why he took it as a loan when he deserved it as a fee, and he said, "It was not handled in the best technical way by us because we trusted her."

John Schlesinger's explanation makes more sense. Mr. Schlesinger became quite friendly with Roy after the divorce and, indeed, became his client. I met him at a small dinner party tossed by Roy's favorite doctor, Fred Dick. The date was June 19, 1986. A couple of days later, Roy went into the hospital for the last time. Four days later he was disbarred.

Anyway, I asked John (after Roy made an early exit) why he thought Cohn wrote the deal down as a loan, and he told me it was because of Roy's pressing problems with the I.R.S.

"Iva knew full well," John said, "that the fifty thousand was just my share of the fee, that she would make up the difference. Nobody could have gotten this done but Roy, we all knew that; God knows, we had been unsuccessful for fourteen years."

The Internal Revenue Service was all over Cohn at this time, so you can see why he'd want it as a loan, and he needed the money as well—they were jamming him pretty good. Regardless, something happened later that turned this whole business into a different world. Iva Schlesinger's mother died. And Iva Schlesinger's sister, Helen Moose, had a problem. Mrs. Moose had claimed a deduction of $180,000 she said she loaned to her mother during the mother's lifetime.

"The fact of the matter," Roy said, "was Mrs. Moose could

have made the homeless list and was never self-supporting and could not have loaned $18 to anyone, no less $180,000. Internal Revenue came into the picture and Iva and her sister were scared silly; they thought they were going to jail. They asked me if I could handle the matter for them.

"By this time, Iva was harassing me with letters about the so-called loan, and it was a pain in the ass. I'd send her some money here and there; she was getting nasty, and I figured the hell with it, I paid. But now, I wanted to know what we'd do about the fee, now that she was asking for more help. Iva said, 'You have the balance of the note, and whatever else it is, it will be.' I relayed this conversation to Tom Bolan and he took over the sister's case. He handled it for seven and a half years. And he achieved a settlement at a very modest sum. And of course, there was no criminal prosecution; nobody went to jail."

When the I.R.S. case was finally settled, Helen Moose wrote to Cohn: "I look forward to having my first peaceful holiday in seven and a half years."

Immediately thereafter, Iva Schlesinger retained counsel to collect the balance of the hundred grand she "loaned" Roy Cohn.

"My son visited me on the Riviera," John Schlesinger told me. "He said they *had* Roy Cohn, they had letters and notes and they were going to get him for the hundred thousand he had borrowed from Iva. I told him I was ashamed of him. I said, 'After all he did for your mother and then for your aunt, keeping her out of trouble with the Internal Revenue people, how can you do this to him?' He said, 'We've got him, we're going to get him disbarred if he won't pay up.'"

They sued him and in his answer he said it had never been a loan. This turned out to be a mistake. There was a paper trail two miles long that it was a loan, whether or not it was truly a loan. He had paid back $42,000. Tom Bolan said to me, "The big thing that went wrong was when Roy swore it was never a loan."

Iva Schlesinger's lawyer brought the case to the disciplinary committee. He later told the press that he did this in order to force Cohn to pay up. Brazen as that, and yet it worked. The disciplinary committee—the entire bar association—has always maintained that it never will allow itself to be turned into a collection agency for complainants in civil law suits. And now Roy Cohn made another mistake, this time against his every instinct. He paid up the balance while the case was pending with the disciplinary committee.

Tom Bolan said to me, "Roy was the only one who didn't want to do this. All of us told him to pay, that it would help him in the end. But he knew better, he knew it would hurt him, only he was pushed by all of us, me most of all, and he gave her the money. And then they turned it against him. It was supposed to mitigate matters, when you pay up it mitigates, but they used it to show that he was guilty. And he knew that, and we didn't."

He could have paid her off anytime, certainly by the time she brought the lawsuit. By then he was the hottest power broker in the country; twenty different guys would have given him the dough to pay her off, and he didn't need any of them. This was peanuts, he could have done it without knowing it was out of his bankroll.

He wouldn't do it because he was Roy Cohn. If you're Roy Cohn you don't pay extortion money.

And you don't worry about those bar association "yo-yo's" who are trying to "smear you up," those "deadbeat guys" who live only to get their betters, to get Roy Cohn who always shoved it to them. You're Roy Cohn and you don't take that crap.

That last night I was with him, at the party at Dr. Dick's apartment, he could hardly lift a glass, but he could say: "Those Wall Street bastards, who cares about them, they're losers. The appellate division won't do this to me, they won't let 'em frame me."

One more movie scene out of the forties. In *City for Conquest*, Elia Kazan is about to rub out the bum who rubbed resin dust into the eyes of his pal James Cagney in the title fight at the Garden. But Kazan is careless, he allows a gun to roll free. The guy he's going to kill, shoots him. On his knees, his last words: "Gee, I never figured on that."

Chapter Seventeen

You know just what they mean when they say it, and they say it all the time now. They say, "It's days like this I really miss Roy." Politicians, judges, lawyers, publishers, reporters, columnists, wiseguys, tycoons, husbands, wives, mistresses. Everybody out there who's trying to get a wire in, wanting something done nobody else could get done, needing to find out what nobody else can find out. Jeez, they say, do I need Roy Cohn today!

This about a man who never held public office, never ran a political party, never published a newspaper, never owned a TV station, never controlled a crime family, never built a building, never even owned one.

All Roy Cohn ever had was Roy Cohn.

And this is his legacy, for better or worse. Not the McCarthy stuff, not the Rosenbergs, not the hot-shot lawyering, not the jet-setting. Just all these people waking up in a cold sweat or hot ambition and saying, "Wow, do I really miss that sonofabitch right now."

Here's a potpourri of stories that should help illustrate these last remarks.

Senator Jesse Helms of North Carolina was the premier target of the Jewish Lobby in his bid for re-election in 1984. It wasn't just because his voting record on Israel was terrible; the big thing was that Helms was in line to head up the Senate Foreign Relations Committee. Jewish money was flowing into the coffers of his opponent, the incumbent Governor James B. Hunt, and the election was attracting nationwide media coverage, particularly in New York. It looked like a toss-up, and Helms was very nervous indeed. What to do? Call Roy Cohn.

Roy held a party for Helms, with a guest list made up of some of the richest Jews in New York plus a few wealthy *goyim*, who were either pro-Isreal out of conviction or out of friendship with Cohn. That anybody in the city would show up at a bash for Helms was an act of friendship for Roy, Helms was being portrayed as practically the reincarnation of the Third Reich.

When I got word about this party, I was appalled. I couldn't believe Roy Cohn would go this far. He was pro-Israel, whatever else his madness, he was consistently pro-Israel. How the hell could he allow his right-wing bullshit to bring him to this?

But I'd never act moralistic with Roy Cohn.

All I said was, "How'd that Jesse Helms fund-raiser go?"

"It wasn't a fund-raiser."

"Roy," I said, "I know you held a fucking fund-raiser for Jesse Helms."

"It wasn't that at all," he said. "It was interferon."

"What?"

"Interferon. To stop the flow of pro-Israeli money to Hunt. That's what it was about. We didn't ask anybody for a dime. We told them we didn't want their money. And we didn't. Jesse didn't need money. He only needed to cut off the other guy's money. Anyway it would have been stupid to ask these people for campaign contributions. Let's face it, they couldn't be caught dead backing Jesse Helms. So the cancer cure. Interferon."

"Did it work?"

"Sure. Jesse will win the election."

"But why do you want that? You've always been for Israel."
"Jesse Helms isn't anti-Israel," Cohn said.
"How'd he manage to fool the world?"
"He voted against some Israeli appropriations. He votes against appropriation bills all the time. He votes against the Arabs. He's an old-line Republican. That's all there is to it. I know him forever, he's not pro-Arab, he's not anti-Israel. He's *for* Israel."

Several months after Helms won re-election, he went to Israel with Roy Cohn. Within a week he was a total Israeli hawk, to the right of General Arik Sharon.

When next I saw Roy, I said, "Well, you're the only guy I know who cashed in markers for Israel."

He didn't even smile. He said, "I told you, Jesse Helms was pro-Israel."

"But Roy, nobody knew it until you took him over there."
"I knew it," Roy said.
"Did he know it?"
"He knows it now." And now Roy Cohn smiled.

Shortly after Roy died a man I never met came over to me at a party in the Hamptons. "I understand you're working on the Roy Cohn autobiography," he said. I nodded. "I've got a great Roy Cohn story for you."

This kind of thing happened all the time, before and after he died. I like this one better than most and it's exemplary to boot.

"We were having trouble with our bank in Philadelphia," the man said. "My company ran a major line of credit at this bank and now they were hassling us. It was a multi-million dollar headache and since I'm the principal, it was my headache. My lawyer was a good corporate lawyer, but in this kind of crunch you don't want Harvard types, I needed a gun-slinger."

"So you called Roy Cohn," I said, as if to tell him this better be special, I've heard this song before.

"No," the man answered, "Not yet."

"Proceed," I said, with a laugh.

"I called my banker. I told him I had fired my lawyer and hired Roy Cohn."

"Did he choke?"

"He stammered, I'll tell you that. 'W-w-w-what d-d-did you do that for?' I told him I wanted a meeting within 48 hours."

"Why so long?" I said.

"I thought I needed even more time."

"You had Roy Cohn, what time did you need?"

"I didn't even know Roy Cohn. I hadn't even spoken to him."

Ah.

"Yes," he said. "So I was slightly frantic. My move looked great, but I didn't have my mover. I finally found somebody who knew Cohn well and was willing to put the word in for me. Cohn took my call immediately. This was on a Tuesday. I said could he be in Philly within 48 hours? 'Thursday, first thing in the morning,' he said. I said terrific. I said, 'I'll drop in today and fill you in on the problem,' Roy said, 'You can do it on the train.' He hung up, no goodbye."

All the years I knew him, he never said goodbye. I said, "Did he talk money?"

"No."

That was as good a guarantee as his no goodbye.

"Over breakfast, on the train, I gave him the details," the man continued. "He said very little, mainly just nodded or grunted. I was afraid I wasn't getting the story across, so I started over again. He waved me off. 'No problem,' he said."

"Well, what I'm about to tell you you're not going to believe," the man said. "It was incredible. We sat down with this banker who had been busting my balls for weeks. And immediately he says, 'Mr. Cohn, we should have no difficulty. We're extending the line of credit for two years.'

"Roy turned to me and said, 'Are you satisfied with the terms?'

"I nodded. I wasn't thinking so fast. Cohn made an opening for better terms, for Chrissakes! Me, I just wanted to get out of there before the guy changed his mind."

What happened next?

"Roy shook the guy's hand and we got the next train out. Roy was ecstatic. But not for the reasons you think, not because he made the deal. We were going to get him to '21' in time for lunch."

"How much did he charge you for this service?"

"He never mentioned a price. All he cared about was getting back in time for lunch at '21.' "

"Do you remember what you paid him?"

"How can I forget?"

"Why?"

"I paid him '21.' I paid him $21,000."

"Did he thank you?"

"Yes. Why do you ask?"

"How much would you have paid him?"

"He could have named it. He saved my ass. But what do you do when a lawyer refuses to bill you? I wrote to him asking for a bill and he didn't answer. I called and for two weeks he didn't take my call. Finally, when I got him, he said, 'Send anything you like, or nothing. It was my pleasure.' I thought, maybe he did it as a favor for the guy who connected me with him. I made it 21 G's as a gesture. And he was pleased, you were right."

"But if he had beefed, what would you have paid him?"

"Ten times as much would have been a bargain."

People in jams were always after me to get them Roy. It didn't matter one whit how much they had railed against him or blasted me for having anything to do with this McCarthyite bum. I never counted, but I'd bet more old lefties came at me to set them up with Roy Cohn than any other species. Roy didn't give a damn who they were, only who sent them. But you had to be careful what you sent him.

Anything he could do with a phone call was perfect, or a quick trip, as in the Philadelphia story, or an oral argument in court. But if paper work, if depositions, if long, drawn-out meetings were involved—forget about Roy Cohn. Those who didn't know this suffered plenty. Because he wouldn't say no, he'd take the case. And they'd wind up with the house staff, God forbid.

There were exceptions. Donald Trump turned to him with his most important case, the Trump Tower tax abatement, and Roy gave it everything. He did the same for the Archdiocese of New York, for the Five Families, for tycoons in messy divorces, for the wives of tycoons in messy divorces, for disgruntled heirs in mammoth estate contests. But watch out! Not too much paper work, no dreary depositions. Give Roy Cohn serious drag time and it made no matter who you were, Roy Cohn was in Acapulco.

Here were the conditions that had to be met before I'd send someone to Roy.

1. The problem had to be one only Roy could handle, which meant it had to be practically desperate.

2. There would be an absolute minimum of paper work, no more than a letter or two. I was not sending him Donald Trump, after all.

3. The person I sent had to be a proven friend, or had to be a friend of a very proven friend. Either that, or I owed the guy. I could owe the friend of the friend too, it didn't matter.

4. If it was a friend of a friend, I would send him only if he convinced me beyond all doubt that he would do what Roy asked and he'd forever keep his mouth shut, or at least never tell the press. I didn't insist he never tell his wife.

Why all this?

Because we are living in a world of markers. It's an old gambling word, signifying an I.O.U. A guy runs out of cash in poker and he says, "Here's my marker." If his credit is good, he stays in the game. In the casinos today it's on computers. "Hey, my marker's good for half-a-mil at Caesars." Don't leave home without it.

The world of markers has nothing to do with money, it disdains money. It allows for no writings, no pledges. It goes without saying, or it doesn't go at all. The pure I.O.U.

Nobody understood it better, nobody played it better, than Roy Cohn. He collected markers like real estate moguls collect parcels. It was his coin of the realm. He didn't give a damn about money, except to spend it—money was for pleasure. Everytime he turned around, people threw money at him, and he threw it away. He'd take it, but never enough, never what he was worth, because he had no reverence for it. Markers he treasured. Markers were his life.

What are markers?

Favors. I do you a favor and you owe me a favor. Simple? Never simple, particularly with Roy Cohn. Particularly because there was no way to price it. You sent him a client, he didn't bill the client. If the client decided to send him some money, it made no difference. How much is it worth to save your life? To save your reputation?

What went without saying was that everytime you sent somebody to Roy Cohn, the marker was on you. The client didn't owe him, *you* owed him.

What was the payoff to you? Roy assumed it was the marker you picked up on the guy you sent to him. And I'm sure it worked that way. Only it didn't work for me. Where I owed somebody, where I was able to even up, in that way it worked for me. But mostly I did it for friends. And I never told a friend that because Roy helped him, I owed Roy. If they couldn't figure this out—and virtually none of them figured it out—it didn't occur to them that they owed me. They owed Roy, that's what they thought. Since Roy usually asked them for nothing, it wasn't difficult to forget they owed him. Of course, he forgot who they were two minutes later.

He never asked me to do anything I wouldn't have done for him anyway. But he could have, and that's the main reason why I made all those conditions. I mean, only a crazy man would allow himself to be subjected to Roy Cohn's markers when he was getting next to nothing out of it. And sometimes less than nothing. If it didn't work out, they'd get mad at you, these "clients," these friends. "He didn't do shit for me!" I didn't hear it often, but I heard it.

Sometimes they didn't forgive him when he saved them.

I got a phone call one morning and I had trouble making out the voice. Street sounds in the background, sirens blaring. Can you hear me? Hello? What?

"I just left Roy Cohn's office," the voice said. "I have to see you immediately. It's terrible, just terrible. When can I see you?"

"Take it easy," I said. "Just relax." I was trying to figure out who the hell this could be.

"He treated me like a criminal. I've never been through such an experience in my life," the voice said.

I knew who it was, at last. And I knew why. I said, "Did you explain everything to him in detail?"

"I tried to explain."

"Did you ask him if he understood the problem?"

"Yes, of course."

"And he told you he understood the first time?"

"Right. That's exactly what he said. It was demeaning, I've never been so insulted."

"Did you ask him not to take incoming phone calls?"

"Yes."

"And then he did what?"

"He said, 'Why?' "

"And did he immediately dial out? He made his own calls?"

"How do you know this? It's just what he did, the bastard."

I said, "Rabbi, it's my fault."

"How could it be your fault?"

"I forgot to warn you. Now just relax and I'll call you tomorrow."

Culture shock. It had happened once before to a good friend of mine and I made it my business to prep everyone I sent over to the townhouse. I didn't forget with the rabbi, I just assumed Roy would treat the clergy differently. He might have done, too, but this rabbi did have a tendency to go on.

I reached Roy late that afternoon.

"How'd it go with the rabbi?"

"It's done, I took care of it."

"Great, because he called me when he left you and he was all upset, he was half crazy."

"Why?"

"I was going to ask you."

"He thinks too much. And he talks too much. I expect that from rabbis."

"How tough was the contract?"

"One call."

"It sounded more complicated than one call when he told me the story."

"Not complicated at all. He stole money from a guy in a business deal."

"And just like that it's done?"

"It's taking me longer to talk to you than it did to get the release. If you want to bullshit, tell me when you can make lunch." And he hung up.

When I called the rabbi to tell him the good news, he grunted. He said, "Your friend Roy Cohn!"

"Rabbi," I said, "don't tell me you're *mad*."

"I've never been so humiliated."

"Hey, Rabbi," I pleaded. "He did it. You're out clear and it won't cost you a dime. Be happy, l'chayim!"

"He treated me like I was a piece of *drek*," the rabbi said.

Roy cashed in these markers by asking my advice on how to handle the press. He could have had this without doing me favors, as I said, but he wouldn't have felt comfortable and probably he wouldn't have believed me. He lived by *quid pro quo* and he didn't trust any other way, or at least he didn't know how to do it any other way.

I am aware that by saying he asked my advice on dealing with the press I will raise eyebrows in the press as well as among those who knew him. For they are aware that few people were more adept at handling the press than Roy Cohn. Fewer still had his clout. In his witch-hunting days the Hearst empire was practically at his disposal. He has related how George Sokolsky got him his job with Joe McCarthy. But Sokolsky could only do that because he had the support of Hearst, specifically through Richard Berlin, the operating head of the empire. Not many people, certainly not many young lawyers, could pick up a phone and get Dick Berlin. Roy Cohn could get Dick Berlin, anytime.

He was even closer to Si Newhouse. They had been best friends since their days at Horace Mann. During Roy's fatal illness, Si didn't let a day go by without calling or seeing him.

Roy used the Newhouse connection in myriad ways to enhance his power and influence. There are Newhouse papers all over the country, and Newhouse television stations and national Newhouse magazines and Sunday supplements. It's not exactly one congressman one paper, but it's not too far from it. So if you were a senator or congressman or party leader or anybody in politics Roy Cohn wanted to reach, you risked something if you didn't take his call.

He didn't always get what he wanted, not from the Newhouse chain and not from the politicians. But he always got attention. Hale Boggs couldn't get President Kennedy to keep Bobby off Roy's back, but Hale Boggs tried. And Hale Boggs wouldn't have gone within a million miles of this one if Newhouse didn't run the New Orleans press. And while the Newhouse newspapers pride themselves for their editorial independence from the family, everybody understood that if Roy really wanted something—an endorsement for a candidate, an attack—he had a major-league shot at getting it. It wasn't simply friendship, either. Roy Cohn represented the family enterprise in various legal situations. Which increased the clout geometrically.

In 1984 he had lunch with Ed Rawlins, the political director of the White House and President Reagan's national campaign manager. Rawlins mentioned that one theme was cropping up in the polls which worried them—Reagan's age and health. What to do?

"I thought about it," Roy told me, "and I said it seemed to me that a well-placed magazine article showing the President's physical prowess would be the best answer. The obvious magazine was *Parade*, the Sunday supplement with a circulation of 50 million. I volunteered to speak to Walter Anderson, the editor of *Parade* and a long-time friend of mine. I spoke to Walter and he thought the idea was tremendous. He engineered an article on the President's outdoor activities with a cover piece showing him diving into a swimming pool, his massive chest and strong body, and then leading into shots of him chopping wood at the California ranch. The article served its purpose. It was widely received and acclaimed."

Roy volunteered this story to me in Palm Beach a few months before his death. He was not even thinking about making the point I'm making here, that he had all this juice with Newhouse. He didn't even bother to mention that *Parade* was a Newhouse publication. The only reason he told me about it was he was pissed at David Gergen for taking credit for the piece. Gergen had been director of communications at the White House.

"Gergen never surfaced for one second in the genesis of the article," Roy said. "So I was more than a little surprised that when he was leaving the White House he told a national news magazine that one of his major achievements was the *Parade* cover story knocking down the idea that the President was unfit for office. I never liked Gergen, but any little respect I had for him went out the window when I saw his cheap grab for power recognition based on other people's work."

I was surprised at all the heat here; Roy usually took stuff like this with a laugh—people were always trying to cop credit for what he did. I assume he was foreseeing death and had let some vanity creep in.

In any event, with all this clout he had—and he had plenty more, he had Winchell and Leonard Lyons and later he was very tight with Rupert Murdoch—what could he possibly need from me?

The New York Times.

He thought I knew how the *Times* worked, what would go and wouldn't go there. And this information, this advice, he wanted.

Much of what he asked was trivial; if you didn't know him it was trivial, that is. He'd call to tell me he thought he should run this or that item on Page Six of the *Post.* I'd say why not? He'd say, "Will Abe be upset?" Translation: The New York *Post*'s gossip page, known as Page Six, was kicking hell out of Abe Rosenthal the Executive Editor of *The New York Times.* So: If Roy is praised on Page Six, will Abe get pissed at Roy. Of course not, I'd say, and Roy would say, "Great." It mattered to him, and he was right, there were things that might have upset Abe Rosenthal. And no item was important enough for Roy to get in dutch with Abe Rosenthal, the most powerful editor in the world.

He never asked me to write a word about him in the *Times* or even put in a good word for him. Just advice, and always it was oblique: often the *Times* wasn't mentioned. My favorite story:

"I'm about to go on the Bill Boggs Show," he said to me one morning. "I'm up against Ramsey Clark, God help us. Clark is going to defend Myron Farber. What do you think?"

M.A. (Myron) Farber is a *New York Times* reporter who at the time (the summer of 1978) was in a New Jersey jail because he refused to turn over to a judge his notes and sources in a murder case. Farber had broken a story accusing a doctor of killing his patients with injections, the then-famous "Dr. X" case. He was held in contempt, as was the *Times*, but the *Times* wasn't in the cooler, Farber was. And now Roy Cohn was about to defend the Jersey judge who sent him there. On the Bill Boggs show, a popular noontime New York TV program.

"What do you think?" said Roy Cohn.

"I think it's brilliant," I said.

"What do you mean?"

"If you never want Abe Rosenthal to speak to you again, it's wonderful, it's a genius idea."

"Abe's that strong on it, huh?"

"Just go in there and kick the shit out of Myron Farber, those Jersey judges will love you."

Roy Cohn said, "Don't they have the slightest respect for the First Amendment? They jail reporters in this country for refusing to reveal their sources? It's Nazi Germany, for God's sake."

I laughed but he didn't. "Judicial tyranny," he said. And hung up.

I watched the show. Bill Boggs was amazed. Ramsey Clark nearly fainted. Roy outdid Hugo Black and Bill Douglas.

He called me from the studio.

"How'd it go?"

"Citizen Paine is how it went."

"Shall I send a transcript to Abe?"

"Certainly."

The next morning, Abe Rosenthal had Citizen Cohn on his desk.

The next week, *New York* Magazine ran an item, extolling Cohn for his defense of the First Amendment.

And I had markers on Citizen Cohn.

Generally, I cashed my markers on fights and ballgames. It was great to go with Roy because there was no ticket too hot; you could call on him the last minute and still get the best seats in the house. And hear the buzz-buzz-buzzing—except for Liz Taylor and Sinatra I never saw anybody create more of a fuss at ringside—and not even feel corrupted (as a reporter) because just as sure as you knew you'd get the top seats, you knew Roy wasn't paying a nickel for them.

Once I needed something dead serious for myself and I knew only Roy could get it for me. Just this one time I went to him. In the summer of 1981 I decided to buy a saloon, the venerable Broadway Joe's Steakhouse on West 46th Street in Manhattan. I didn't put the dough up—I had a few partners, the suckers with the money as they say—but I owned a substantial piece because my job was to bring in the customers. Broadway Joe's had been one of the hottest steak houses in town, but no longer. I'd have to juice it up, but first we needed a transfer of the liquor license. Which if you don't know anybody takes at least six months; if you're connected it takes three months. We had three weeks to get it done.

Roy said, "Absolutely no problem."

I said, "Three weeks, Roy, we must open then or we're dead."

"Done," said Roy Cohn.

My partners didn't believe it, and they were all the time up my ass. We were redoing the place and it was costing a fortune, and all they had to go on was my word that Roy Cohn would deliver. And for nothing. The word on liquor licenses was always that you had to heavily grease palms. Even at that nobody promised three weeks. Hell, the Mafia couldn't get it that quick.

We got it in two and a half weeks.

Roy wouldn't even take a bow. It was as if I was insulting him by offering my thanks.

And on this one, he never called a marker.

In the late Fifties, Roy took a trip arond the world with his old pals Neil Walsh and Bill Fugazy, respectively the insurance mogul and travel impresario. Here are a couple of nuggets, as recalled by Walsh.

"At the Imperial Hotel in Tokyo, Roy took a liking to the bath mat and so swiped it as if it were a towel. It was a great looking bath mat, royal blue, the hotel's signature running across its face. In those days, before jets, there were few tourists in Japan. The Japanese efficiency was in peak form. By the time we got to the check-out desk, the hotel authorities knew all about a missing bath mat and were quite aggressive in discussing their concern with us. After a couple of minutes of this interrogation, Roy—in his usual shy and retiring manner—stepped up and said, 'You've got a lot of fucking nerve talking about a bath mat after you bombed Pearl Harbor.' Quicker than you could say Bataan we were out of there with the bath mat.

"By the time we got to Monte Carlo, Fugazy was back home, he'd had enough. But look what he missed! We were invited to Lord Beaverbrook's place, black tie, dinner at eight. We were an hour late—Roy is always late, he was busy all day working the phones. When we arrived it turned out that Beaverbrook wasn't the main attraction.

"Sitting at the table was Churchill. Sir Winston Churchill! And Michael Foote, who later became head of the Labor Party. Lord Beaverbrook apparently wanted Roy there to rag Foote, and in quick time the pair of them were in a shouting match. Sir Winston occasionally interrupted in defense of his countryman. Roy allowed this for a while. But then, in his holdback manner, he reminded Sir Winston of Bundles for Britain, of President Roosevelt giving them the destroyers, and generally of the U.S.A. 'saving England's ass.'

"Mr. Churchill took it all quite well, and didn't show much

reaction until Roy leaned over and started eating off his plate. The butler almost fainted. He signalled to one of the footmen to replace Sir Winston's plate. Churchill waved him off, he seemed to think that Roy had made a mistake. But Roy kept eating off Sir Winston's plate—his own and Churchill's. Sir Winston, I'm sure, had many shocks in his life, but nothing quite like this. Lord Beaverbrook politely asked Roy if he was still hungry, would he not like another portion. Roy said, 'No, this is just fine.' And he continued talking and eating the balance of Sir Winston's plate."

Many's the time he ate off my plate. But when I say, "It's days like this I really miss Roy," I'm thinking of other things. I'm thinking of newspaper stories. Like when I'm dying for the inside and there's nobody left to call, no way to get the skinny. Days like that. So one more Roy Cohn story to show you how it was when he was riding high.

I happened to be watching TV at home the afternoon the attempt was made on the life of Ronald Reagan. The commentators assured us that the President was fine, wasn't even nicked. But I remembered the early reports out of Dallas. I called Roy.

"The President's been shot," he said.

I called everybody I knew. Everybody said I was crazy. Didn't the TV say he was O.K.? Then I said, "Roy Cohn says he's shot." You could hear the freeze.

By cocktail time the President was on the operating table. And the TV said Jim Brady, his press secretary, was dead. Dan Rather gave a moving eulogy of Jim Brady. I was at Gallagher's, drinking martinis for the first time in fifteen years. Everybody at Gallagher's figured the worst. They lied about Reagan at the outset, they're lying now. He's 70 years old, and he's on the table. They said, once they admitted he was hit, that it was minor, like a skin abrasion. Now the operating table. Where's George Bush?

I called Roy.

"The President's in good shape, he's out of the operation, he's fine. Jim Brady's barely alive, but he'll make it."

I reported that to the crowded bar. "You're nuts," said the bar.

"I got it from Roy."

The gloom lifted. Everybody lifted fresh drinks.

For 20 years people asked me why I talked to Roy Cohn. Now maybe they knew.

Name Index